Brain Informatics and Health

Informatics-enabled studies are transforming brain science. New methodologies enhance human interpretive powers when dealing with big data sets increasingly derived from advanced neuro-imaging technologies, including fMRI, PET, MEG, EEG and fNIRS, as well as from other sources like eye-tracking and from wearable, portable, micro and nano devices. New experimental methods, such as in to imaging, deep tissue imaging, opto-genetics and dense-electrode recording are generating massive amounts of brain data at very fine spatial and temporal resolutions. These technologies allow measuring, modeling, managing and mining of multiple forms of big brain data. Brain informatics & health related techniques for analyzing all the data will help achieve a better understanding of human thought, memory, learning, decision-making, emotion, consciousness and social behaviors. These methods also assist in building brain-inspired, human-level wisdom-computing paradigms and technologies, improving the treatment efficacy of mental health and brain disorders.

The Brain Informatics & Health (BIH) book series addresses the computational, cognitive, physiological, biological, physical, ecological and social perspectives of brain informatics as well as topics relating to brain health, mental health and well-being. It also welcomes emerging information technologies, including but not limited to Internet of Things (IoT), cloud computing, big data analytics and interactive knowledge discovery related to brain research. The BIH book series also encourages submissions that explore how advanced computing technologies are applied to and make a difference in various large-scale brain studies and their applications.

The series serves as a central source of reference for brain informatics and computational brain studies. The series aims to publish thorough and cohesive overviews on specific topics in brain informatics and health, as well as works that are larger in scope than survey articles and that will contain more detailed background information. The series also provides a single point of coverage of advanced and timely topics and a forum for topics that may not have reached a level of maturity to warrant a comprehensive textbook.

Ildar Rakhmatulin · Ganesh R. Naik

EEG Signal Processing with Python

Machine Learning Techniques for Brain-Computer Interface Development

Springer

Ildar Rakhmatulin
School of Engineering
Edinburgh University
Edinburgh, UK

Ganesh R. Naik
Centre for Artificial Intelligence Research and Optimisation (AIRO)
Torrens University
Adelaide, SA, Australia

ISSN 2367-1742 ISSN 2367-1750 (electronic)
Brain Informatics and Health
ISBN 978-981-95-4176-8 ISBN 978-981-95-4177-5 (eBook)
https://doi.org/10.1007/978-981-95-4177-5

This Springer imprint is published by the registered company Springer Nature Singapore Pte Ltd.
The registered company address is: 152 Beach Road, #21-01/04 Gateway East, Singapore 189721, Singapore

Preface

Signal processing and machine learning are the primary components of modern neuroscience research, focusing on feature extraction. They enable us to uncover meaningful patterns hidden in the complex, high-dimensional signals generated by brain recordings. In recent years, Python has emerged as one of the most powerful and accessible tools for analyzing and processing neuroscience data. Its flexibility, large ecosystem of scientific libraries, and active community provide researchers with the means to build robust analysis pipelines and to explore brain data in creative and innovative ways.

This book is designed as a hands-on guide to applying signal processing and machine learning techniques in neuroscience using Python. It is written for researchers and students with a basic understanding of Python who want to learn how to apply practical methods to real EEG and brain signal data. Topics range from fundamental concepts such as filtering and spectral analysis, to advanced approaches including time-frequency analysis and machine learning for feature extraction.

With the increasing availability of affordable EEG devices, neuroscience research has moved beyond the laboratory. Today, brain–computer interface (BCI) applications, neurofeedback systems, and consumer EEG headsets are more accessible than ever. The brain remains one of the greatest scientific mysteries, but this book aims to show how Python can help us begin to unravel its signals and apply them in both research and real-world contexts.

How This Book Is Organized

Each chapter begins with a concise theoretical introduction, followed by fully explained Python scripts that demonstrate the concepts in practice. All examples are available on GitHub, so readers can reproduce, adapt, and extend them. By experimenting with the provided code—modifying parameters, adjusting coefficients, and testing ideas—you will develop both an intuitive and practical understanding of the methods.

Why This Book Is Timely

At the time of writing, few resources teach EEG signal processing and machine learning through Python. Most existing materials rely heavily on MATLAB. However, Python has become the language of choice for many researchers due to its open-source nature, versatility, and ability to handle real-time processing. This book aims to fill that gap by providing a structured yet practical introduction to the subject in Python.

How to Use This Book

While the book does not include traditional problem sets, it is structured to encourage active experimentation. We recommend running the scripts, modifying parameters, and observing how the changes affect outcomes. This trial-and-error approach is one of the best ways to gain a deep understanding of signal processing and machine learning methods.

About the Code

All examples are written in Python 3.10, which was the default in Google Colab at the time of writing. Some unimportant parts of the script have been removed from the code, allowing the focus to remain on the core concepts. For full, runnable versions, readers are encouraged to access the GitHub repository. We will do our best to maintain updates online if changes to Python versions or libraries require adjustments.

Using Code Examples

Readers are encouraged not only to copy code, but to experiment with and expand upon it. Try different filters, test alternate machine learning models, or apply the scripts to your own datasets. The skills you build through this process will be more valuable than simply reproducing results.

Resources

All scripts and datasets referenced in this book are available on GitHub:
https://github.com/Ildaron/EEG-Signal-Processing-with-Python

Final Note

By the end of this book, you will have gained both theoretical grounding and practical coding skills in EEG signal processing and machine learning with Python. We hope that it will serve not only as a guide but also as a springboard for your own explorations in neuroscience research and applications.

Edinburgh, UK
Adelaide, Australia
August 2025

Ildar Rakhmatulin
Ganesh R. Naik

Competing Interests The authors declare the following as potential competing interests: The author Ildar Rakhmatulin is the CEO of PiEEG Ltd, the company that produces the PiEEG brain-computer interface, which is used as an example for collecting a dataset in this book. Apart from this, the author declares no other competing interests.

Contents

Chapter 1
Fundamentals of EEG

1.1 Basic Principles of EEG Signals

The study of the nervous system dates to ancient civilizations, such as the Greeks, who considered the brain to be the center of thought and emotion. However, the modern field of neuroscience as we know it today has its roots in the nineteenth and twentieth centuries. In the early nineteenth century, Italian physiologist Luigi Galvani demonstrated that electrical stimulation could induce muscle contractions, laying the groundwork for the concept of "animal electricity." The beginning of the chemical processes of the brain was laid by Du Bois Reymond in 1849, who showed that the brain, like nerves and muscles, has Blanc's electrogenic properties. Despite this, the first human EEG recording was not obtained until 75 years later in 1924 by German psychiatrist Hans Berger, who then called it Britton's "electroencephalogram." This led to further research into the electrical properties of neurons and the development of the first electroencephalogram (EEG) in 1924, which measures the electrical activity of the brain [1].

Neuroscience made significant advances in the twentieth century, thanks to the development of new techniques, including the use of microelectrodes to record the activity of individual neurons and the advancement of neuroimaging techniques, such as magnetic resonance imaging (MRI) and positron emission tomography (PET). These techniques enabled researchers to study the brain's structure and function in greater detail, leading to the discovery of many fundamental brain mechanisms. [2].

In the mid-twentieth century, the field of computational neuroscience emerged, seeking to utilize mathematical and computational models to study the brain's information-processing capabilities. This led to the development of artificial neural networks, which are computer models that mimic the behavior of neurons and are used in a variety of applications, such as image and speech recognition.

Overall, the history of neuroscience has been characterized by a steady accumulation of knowledge and technological advances that have allowed us to understand

I. Rakhmatulin and G. R. Naik, *EEG Signal Processing with Python*, Brain Informatics and Health, https://doi.org/10.1007/978-981-95-4177-5_1

the brain and its functions better. The field continues to evolve and expand, with discoveries and methods emerging all the time [3].

Neuroscience is the study of the nervous system, including the brain, spinal cord, and peripheral nervous system, and how they interact with the environment to produce behavior and cognition. It spans a wide range of disciplines, including biology, psychology, chemistry, physics, and computer science.

At its core, neuroscience is concerned with understanding the mechanisms underlying brain function and dysfunction, and how these mechanisms influence behavior and physiological processes. This includes studying the structure and function of individual neurons, neural circuits, and entire brain regions, as well as investigating how neural activity mediates the chain of acquisition, emotion, thought, and action.

Neuroscience has numerous applications, including the development of treatments for neurological and mental disorders, enhancement of cognitive and sensory abilities, and improvement of education and learning. It also has implications for areas such as artificial intelligence, robotics, and human–computer interaction [3].

Overall, neuroscience is a rapidly growing interdisciplinary field that seeks to unlock the secrets of the brain and improve our understanding of human behavior and cognition. Neuroscience research employs a range of techniques to study the brain, broadly categorized as invasive and non-invasive techniques. Invasive methods involve direct physical intervention within the brain, such as surgeries to implant electrodes or remove tissue for analysis. While these methods provide high-resolution data and can directly manipulate neural activity, they carry inherent risks, including infection, tissue damage, and ethical concerns regarding the use of animal or human subjects. Non-invasive techniques, on the other hand, operate from outside the body, utilizing methods like EEG, MRI, and transcranial magnetic stimulation (TMS). These methods are generally safer and more accessible but may offer lower spatial or temporal resolution compared to invasive approaches. The choice between invasive and non-invasive techniques depends on the specific research question, desired level of detail, and the ethical considerations associated with the study.

An EEG is a powerful, non-invasive window into the brain's electrical symphony. It captures the collective murmur of millions of neurons, providing invaluable insights into brain function and aiding in the diagnosis of neurological conditions. This is achieved by placing small, metal discs called electrodes on the scalp, which detect and record the faint electrical signals generated by the brain [1, 2].

The electrical signals that an EEG records don't come from a single neuron firing. Instead, they represent the synchronized activity of large populations of neurons, primarily the pyramidal neurons in the cerebral cortex. When thousands or millions of these neurons fire in unison, their combined electrical fields are strong enough to be detected by the electrodes on the scalp. This synchronous firing is not random; it's the basis of the rhythmic patterns known as brainwaves. These waves are crucial for communication between different brain regions and are associated with various mental states [1, 2].

The synchronous firing of thousands or millions of neurons in the brain generates the electrical activity recorded by an EEG. These signals can be detected by electrodes and amplified to produce a visual representation of brain activity.

EEG is commonly used in clinical settings to diagnose and monitor various neurological conditions such as epilepsy, sleep disorders, and brain injuries. It is also used in research to study brain function and investigate cognitive processes such as attention, memory, and perception [3].

Overall, EEG provides valuable insights into the human brain's functioning and has numerous applications in both healthcare and research.

1.2 Understanding Brain Signals: Motivation and Real-World Applications

The study of brain signals, a cornerstone of modern neuroscience, is unlocking the intricate workings of the human mind in ways previously unimaginable. This rapidly advancing field offers profound insights into the neural underpinnings of our thoughts, feelings, and actions, leading to transformative innovations across numerous sectors. By deciphering the brain's electrical and metabolic conversations, we are not only diagnosing and treating debilitating neurological conditions but also enhancing human potential and creating more intuitive technologies.

In the clinical realm, analysing brain signals is crucial for diagnostics and treatment monitoring. Techniques like EEG, magnetoencephalography (MEG), and functional magnetic resonance imaging (fMRI) serve as critical tools for clinicians.

- **Epilepsy**: For individuals with epilepsy, an EEG is the gold standard for diagnosis. It can pinpoint the specific region of the brain where seizures originate (the epileptogenic zone) by detecting characteristic abnormal electrical discharges known as epileptiform spikes. Continuous EEG monitoring in hospitals helps neurologists classify seizure types accurately, which is crucial for prescribing the most effective anti-epileptic medication [4].
- **Sleep Disorders**: Polysomnography, which includes EEG monitoring throughout the night, is essential for diagnosing sleep disorders like sleep apnea, insomnia, and narcolepsy. The distinct stages of sleep (REM, N1, N2, N3) are identified by specific patterns of brainwaves. Disruptions to these patterns can reveal the nature and severity of a sleep disorder, guiding therapeutic interventions that can significantly improve a patient's health and quality of life [5, 6].
- **Cognitive Impairments**: Researchers are increasingly identifying brain signal biomarkers for early-stage neurodegenerative diseases. For instance, quantitative EEG (qEEG) analysis may reveal a slowing of brainwave activity in certain regions, which can be an early indicator of cognitive decline associated with conditions such as Alzheimer's disease. This allows for earlier intervention and planning [7].

Beyond the clinic, brain signal analysis is paving the way for revolutionary technologies that augment human capabilities and improve our interaction with the world.

- **Brain-Computer Interfaces (BCIs)**: This is perhaps one of the most groundbreaking applications. For individuals with severe motor disabilities, such as those resulting from spinal cord injuries or amyotrophic lateral sclerosis (ALS), BCIs offer a renewed sense of independence. By interpreting the brain signals associated with intention, these systems allow users to control prosthetic limbs, pilot wheelchairs, or even communicate by typing on a screen using only their thoughts [8].
- **Neurofeedback**: This therapeutic technique involves providing individuals with real-time feedback on their brain activity, training them to self-regulate it. It is increasingly used for managing conditions like ADHD, where it can help improve focus and attention. Similarly, neurofeedback protocols are being employed for stress management and peak performance training in sports and corporate environments, assisting individuals to learn to enter a state of calm focus on demand [9].

The applications of brain signal analysis have also permeated the commercial world and are influencing the future of technology itself.

- **Neuromarketing**: Companies are moving beyond traditional focus groups and surveys to understand consumer behavior on a deeper, subconscious level. By using EEG to measure emotional engagement and attention in response to advertisements or product designs, brands can gather unfiltered insights into what truly captivates their audience, leading to more effective and resonant marketing campaigns [10].
- **Artificial Intelligence (AI)**: The human brain remains the most efficient and adaptable learning system known. Researchers in AI are studying neural data to inspire new "neuromorphic" computing architectures. The goal is to create AI systems that can learn more efficiently, consume less power, and adapt to new situations with the same flexibility as the human brain, moving beyond the brute-force processing of current models [11].

In essence, the study of brain signals is a journey into the very core of human experience. The knowledge gained is not merely academic; it is being actively translated into practical tools that heal, empower, and innovate, promising a future where the boundary between the human mind and technology becomes increasingly seamless.

1.3 Understanding EEG: What It Is and How It Works

When we discuss an EEG signal, we are measuring the voltage difference between two locations on the scalp, typically between a point on the head and the ear, which serves as a reference point. The difference in voltage across different parts of the head ultimately depends on brain activity. Neurons in the brain maintain electrical charges through the movement of ions across their membranes. When many neurons are activated synchronously, their collective electrical currents generate voltage differences that can propagate through the brain tissue, skull, and scalp—a process known as volume conduction. EEG electrodes placed on the scalp detect these voltage differences.

The task of measuring EEG signals is even more challenging and intriguing [2, 12]. More generally, EEG (electroencephalography) is a non-invasive technique used to record the electrical activity generated by the brain using electrodes placed on the head. The nature of EEG signals is characterized by their frequency, amplitude, and time characteristics. The leading indicators for EEG signals are Frequency and Amplitude:

- EEG signal frequency—measured in hertz (Hz) and ranges from less than 0.5 Hz to more than 100 Hz.
- Signal amplitude is measured in microvolts (μV) and ranges from a few microvolts to several hundred microvolts.

EEG signals are typically classified into distinct frequency ranges, including delta (0.5–4 Hz), theta (4–8 Hz), alpha (8–13 Hz), beta (13–30 Hz), and gamma (30–100 Hz), as shown in Fig. 1.1.

Each frequency band is associated with different cognitive and behavioral states, such as deep sleep (delta), relaxation (theta), alertness (alpha), and cognitive processing (beta and gamma).

In general, the nature of EEG signals is complex and depends on several factors, including the brain's state, the task being performed, and the recording conditions. EEG signals are commonly used in clinical and research settings to study brain function and diagnose neurological conditions.

It is worth noting that there are several ways to measure signals from the brain (Fig. 1.2):

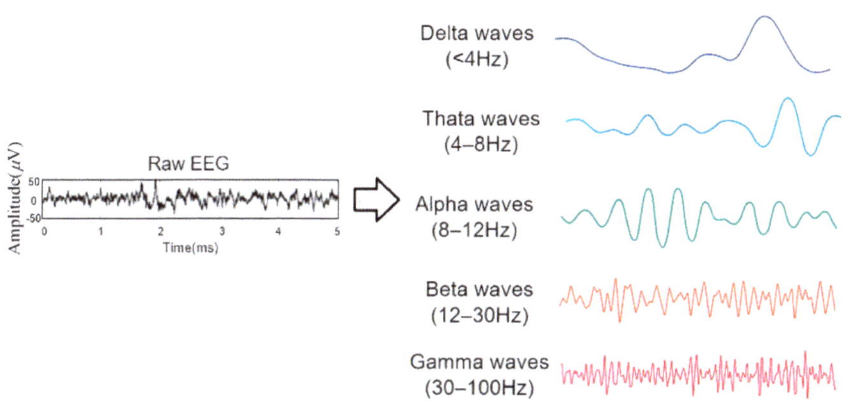

Fig. 1.1 Example of frequency ranges in EEG [13]

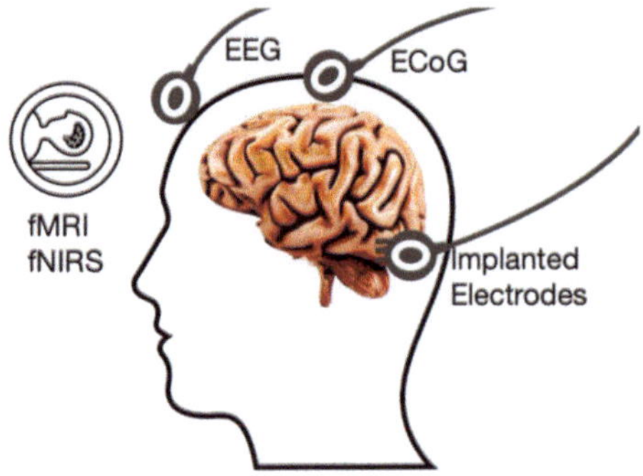

Fig. 1.2 Methods for measuring signals from the brain [14]

- These are invasive, requiring surgical interventions and the installation of electrodes directly into the brain.
- ECoG surgical intervention and placement of electrodes on the surface of the brain.
- FNIRS is a brain imaging technique that uses light to measure brain activity.

Most often, when we hear news about advances in the field of neuroscience and the control of external objects using brain signals or similar technologies, these are invasive methods that have not yet found widespread application outside of the laboratory due to their complexity and the need for surgical implantation. These cutting-edge technologies, while promising, remain limited in their general use owing to the intricate procedures involved in their implementation and the associated risks of invasive techniques.

This book focuses on non-invasive techniques as a more comprehensive and promising method for interpreting brain signals and integrating them into daily life.

1.4 EEG Signal Amplitudes: Are Microvolts Significant?

Microvolts (μV) are a unit of measurement commonly used in EEG studies to quantify brain electrical activity. In the context of EEG signals, microvolts are not considered a large signal amplitude. EEG signals typically range from a few microvolts to several hundred microvolts, depending on the specific frequency range and location on the scalp. However, microvolts can be sensitive enough to detect changes in brain activity associated with various cognitive and emotional states. To put microvolts in perspective, one microvolt is equal to one millionth of a volt ($1\ \mu V = 0.000001\ V$), which is a relatively minimal voltage. For comparison, the voltage of a typical AA battery is about 1.5 V or 1,500,000 microvolts. So, while microvolts may not seem like a huge signal amplitude in the context of everyday electronic devices, they are an essential unit of measurement for studying the brain's electrical activity. This introduces a layer of scientific complexity: how can we accurately measure such tiny voltages on the head? Moreover, we live in an environment filled with electromagnetic noise from various sources such as routers, phones, and other electronic devices. This makes the task of measuring EEG signals even more challenging and intriguing [2, 12].

1.5 Measuring EEG Signals: Methods and Instrumentation

To measure EEG signals, electrodes are strategically placed on the scalp (Fig. 1.3). The paramount concern for accurate signal acquisition is ensuring robust contact between each electrode and the skin. This direct contact has a significant impact on the quality of the recorded signal. The EEG device then reads the voltage differential between a scalp electrode and a reference electrode, commonly positioned on the ear. This analog voltage is subsequently converted into a digital format. Once digitized, the data undergoes processing and feature extraction for analysis.

The electrodes are typically made of metal and are attached to the scalp using a conductive gel, paste, or dry electrodes. Currently, the most prevalent types of EEG electrodes are categorized as active and passive. Among these, Silver/Silver Chloride (Ag/AgCl) electrodes are a ubiquitous choice, as depicted in Fig. 1.4.

As was mentioned, EEG is in the μV range, and generally, we have two ways for data digitization:

- Use an Analog digital converter with high resolution, about 24 bits.

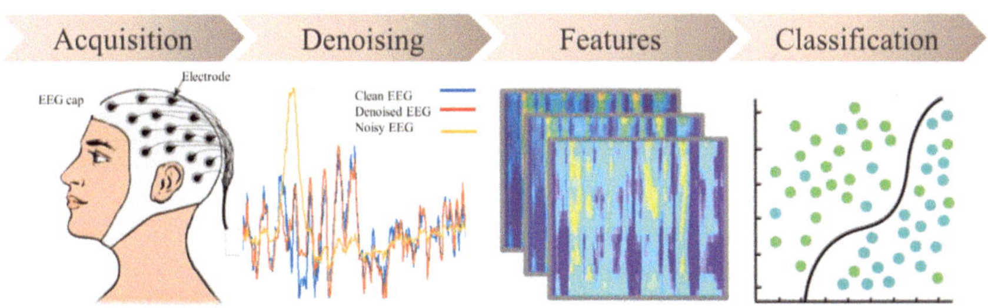

Fig. 1.3 Measure EEG [15]

Fig. 1.4 Different types of EEG electrodes: **a** active and **b** passive [9]

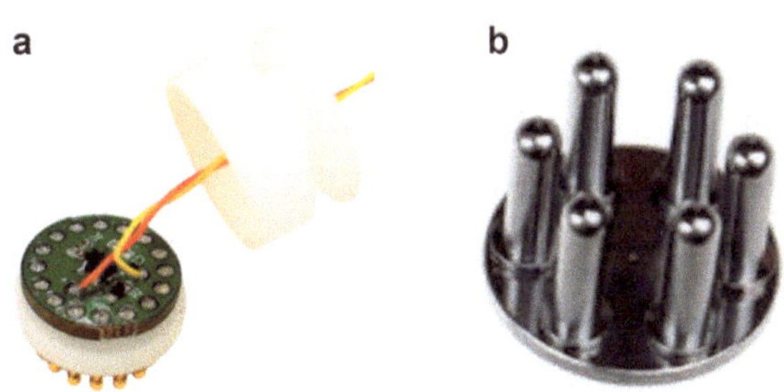

- Use an Amplifier on the analog board that is directly connected to the electrode, and then use ADC with a resolution of about 16 bits.

Active electrodes can provide more accurate signals for EEG systems as they help avoid strong in-phase noise. However, implementing active electrodes in multi-channel EEG systems can be expensive.

The EEG measurement process typically involves the following steps:

- **Preparation**: The subject is asked to sit or lie down in a comfortable position with their eyes closed or open, depending on the experiment or clinical assessment.
- **Electrode placement**: The electrodes are placed on the scalp according to the 10–20 system, which divides the scalp into specific regions and places the electrodes accordingly. The number and location of the electrodes used may vary depending on the study or clinical assessment.
- **Impedance check**: Before recording, the impedance of each electrode is checked to ensure a good connection between the electrode and the scalp.
- **Recording**: Once the electrodes are placed and the impedance is checked, the EEG recording can begin. The recording typically lasts from a few minutes to an hour or more, depending on the nature of the study or clinical assessment.
- **Data analysis**: The recorded EEG data are then analyzed using various signal processing and statistical methods to extract relevant information such as power spectra, event-related potentials, and connectivity measures.

In general, measuring EEG requires specialized equipment, including an EEG amplifier and software to collect and analyze data. Trained clinicians or researchers can perform the process and is generally non-invasive and safe.

1.6 Electrode Placement in EEG: Locations and Systems

The placement of EEG electrodes on the scalp follows a standardized system known as the International 10–20 system. This system divides the scalp into regions and determines the locations for electrode placement based on the distance between specific landmarks on the head (Fig. 1.5).

The international 10–20 system involves measuring the distance between two landmarks, the nasion and the inion, which are located on the forehead and the back of the head, respectively. The distance between these landmarks is divided into increments of 10% and 20%, and electrodes are placed at specific points based on these increments. Electrodes are labeled according to their position relative to these landmarks. For example, the letter F is used to denote frontal electrodes, C is used to indicate central electrodes, P is used to denote parietal electrodes, O is used to denote occipital electrodes, and T is used to represent temporal electrodes. The number following the letter indicates the location of the electrode according to the 10–20 system. For example, F3 and F4 are electrodes located in the left and right

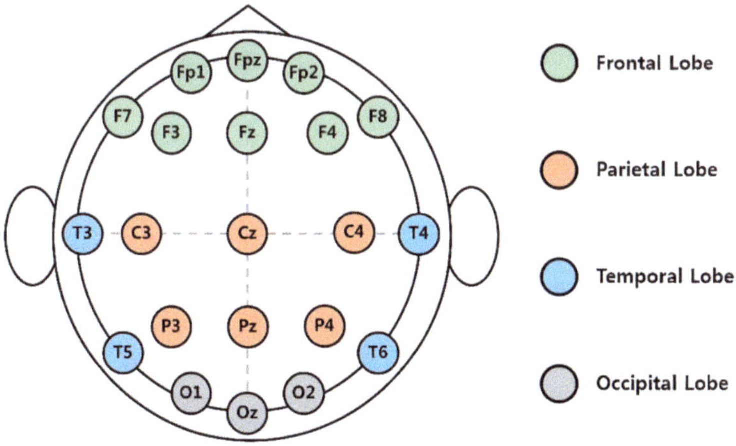

Fig. 1.5 Location of electrodes on the head [16]

frontal areas, respectively, while T5 and T6 are electrodes located in the left and right temporal regions, respectively.

EEG signals may vary depending on the placement of the electrodes on the scalp. This is because different areas of the brain have distinct patterns of electrical activity, and the electrical signals recorded by the electrodes reflect the activity of underlying brain areas.

For example, electrodes placed on the frontal scalp areas (F3, F4, F7, F8) typically record activity in the prefrontal cortex, which is involved in cognitive processes such as attention, working memory, and decision-making. The activity recorded by these electrodes may differ from the activity recorded by electrodes placed on the occipital scalp areas (O1, O2), which typically record visual cortex activity and are sensitive to visual stimuli. Similarly, electrodes placed on the temporal scalp areas (T3, T4, T5, T6) typically record temporal lobe activity, which is involved in auditory processing and memory.

1.7 How Many EEG Channels Are Needed? Factors and Considerations

The number of EEG channels used for signal processing depends on the specific research question and the complexity of the neural processes being investigated.

In clinical and research settings, EEG recordings typically use between 16 and 256 channels, although the number may vary depending on the study design and available resources.

Fewer EEG channels, such as 8 or 32, may be sufficient for basic studies of brain activity or clinical assessments of certain neurological disorders. These systems use electrodes placed at specific locations on the scalp according to standardized international systems such as the 10–20 system or the 10–10 system.

More complex studies, such as those investigating cognitive processes or neural network connectivity, may require a higher number of channels to capture distributed neural activity throughout the brain. In these cases, high-density EEG systems with 128, 256, or even more channels can be used to provide higher spatial resolution and scalp coverage.

However, increasing the number of EEG channels also increases the complexity and cost of the recording and signal processing procedures. Therefore, the choice of the number of channels must be made based on a balance between the desired spatial resolution and the available resources.

1.8 Understanding EEG Noise: Sources and Challenges

As previously established, EEG measures brain activity in microvolts, which means the useful signal from the brain is inherently weak and highly susceptible to extraneous external influences, commonly referred to as noise or artifacts. These unwanted signals can significantly obscure the underlying neural activity, making accurate interpretation challenging. The primary sources of such noise can be broadly categorized as follows:

- **Environmental Interference**: The subtle electrical signals generated by the brain are vulnerable to electromagnetic interference (EMI) originating from various electrical devices and sources within the surrounding environment. Common culprits include fluorescent lights, power lines, and other electrical equipment, which can introduce unwanted frequencies and distortions into the EEG recording.
- **Biological Noise (Physiological Artifacts)**: Beyond the brain's electrical activity, other physiological processes within the body also generate electrical signals that the scalp electrodes can pick up. These biological artifacts often have significantly larger amplitudes than brain signals and can severely contaminate the EEG. Key examples include eye movements (e.g., blinks, saccades), muscle movements (e.g., facial muscle contractions, neck muscle activity), and cardiac activity (as measured by an electrocardiogram or ECG), all of which can distort the true neural signal and complicate its interpretation.
- **Signal Amplification and Filtering Challenges**: Due to their minuscule amplitude, EEG signals necessitate considerable amplification to become detectable. However, this amplification process invariably amplifies any noise present in the signal as well, potentially diminishing the signal-to-noise ratio (SNR). While filtering techniques are employed to remove unwanted noise components, overly aggressive filtering can inadvertently remove parts of the legitimate brain signal, resulting in the loss of valuable information. Striking the right balance between noise reduction and signal preservation is crucial.

- **Incorrect Electrode Placement**: The quality of EEG signals is highly dependent on the precise and consistent placement of electrodes on the scalp. Improperly positioned electrodes can lead to poor electrical contact with the skin, increased impedance, and a degraded signal quality, ultimately resulting in a noisier recording. Consistent application of standardized electrode placement protocols is therefore essential.
- **Individual Variability**: EEG signals exhibit substantial variability among individuals. This can be attributed to a range of physiological differences, including variations in scalp anatomy, skull thickness, cerebrospinal fluid volume, and skin conductivity. These inter-individual differences contribute to variations in signal quality, making the task of reliably separating genuine neural signals from noise more complex across subjects.

1.9 EEG Hardware: An Introduction to Recording Systems

Neuroscience is becoming more accessible to the public as brain-computer interface (BCI) equipment is now available outside of traditional research laboratories. There are numerous BCI devices on the market today, featuring various designs but sharing similar core functions. These devices typically differ in aspects such as the number and type of electrodes, as well as the design of the headset or cap.

These systems typically consist of:

- **Electrodes**: sensors that detect electrical activity in the brain
- **Amplifiers**: devices that boost weak electrical signals
- **ADCs**: components that convert analog signals into digital data
- **Processing unit**: software that analyzes and interprets brain signals

Figure 1.6 illustrates a typical configuration of a modern brain-computer interface system, highlighting its key components and the manner in which they interact to convert brain activity into valid data or commands.

1.10 Conclusion

This chapter has provided a fundamental introduction to Electroencephalography (EEG), laying the groundwork for a comprehensive understanding of this powerful tool for investigating brain function. We began by establishing the compelling reasons for studying brain signals, underscoring the diverse and impactful applications of EEG across various scientific and clinical domains.

Our exploration delved into the core principles of EEG, elucidating its nature as a non-invasive measure of the brain's electrical activity. We then transitioned to the practicalities of EEG acquisition, detailing essential methods such as electrode placement and emphasizing the critical role of standardized systems like the 10–20

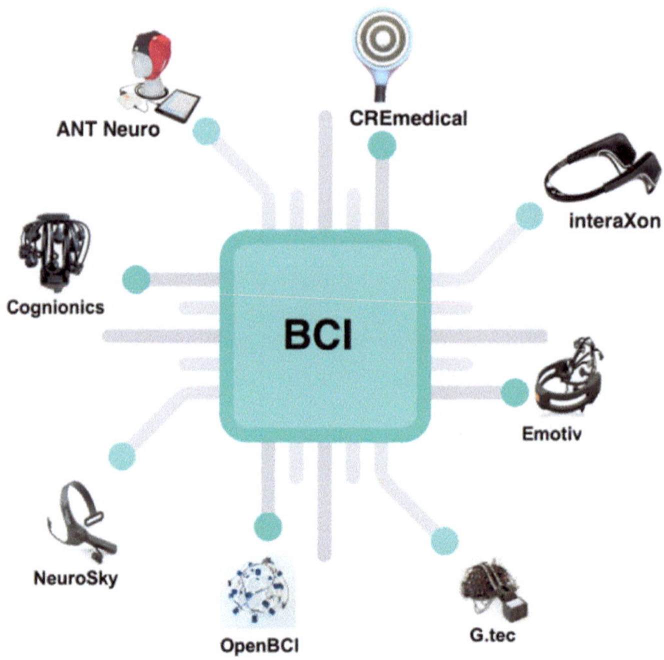

Fig. 1.6 The most popular customer-grade Brain-computer interfaces [7]

system for ensuring consistent and reproducible electrode localization across studies. The discussion on the number of channels highlighted the crucial trade-off between achieving high spatial resolution and managing practical limitations, illustrating how the specific research question directly influences the required channel density for meaningful data.

Furthermore, we candidly addressed the inherent challenges associated with EEG recordings, particularly the pervasive issue of noise and artifacts. This discussion underscored the paramount importance of meticulous experimental design and the application of robust signal processing techniques to mitigate the impact of these unwanted signals effectively. Finally, we offered a brief introduction to the essential hardware components involved in EEG acquisition, setting the stage for a more in-depth exploration of the instrumentation and the intricate signal processing pipelines that transform raw data into interpretable insights in subsequent chapters.

In essence, this introductory chapter has furnished readers with the foundational knowledge required to appreciate the principles and practicalities of EEG. It has showcased EEG's immense potential as a non-invasive window into brain function, while simultaneously acknowledging the inherent challenges that researchers must skillfully navigate to obtain reliable and meaningful data. This groundwork is indispensable for engaging with the more advanced topics and sophisticated applications of EEG that will be presented in the forthcoming sections, fostering a truly comprehensive understanding of this fascinating field.

References

1. Kandel ER, Schwartz JH, Jessell TM, Siegelbaum S, Hudspeth AJ, Mack S (2000) Principles of neural science. McGraw-hill New York
2. Niedermeyer E, da Silva FL (2005) Electroencephalography: basic principles, clinical applications, and related fields. Lippincott Williams & Wilkins
3. Squire L, Berg D, Bloom FE, Du Lac S, Ghosh A, Spitzer NC (2012) Fundamental neuroscience. Academic
4. Noachtar S, Rémi J (2009) The role of EEG in epilepsy: a critical review. Epilepsy Behav 15(1):22–33
5. Petit D, Gagnon J-F, Fantini ML, Ferini-Strambi L, Montplaisir J (2004) Sleep and quantitative EEG in neurodegenerative disorders. J Psychosom Res 56(5):487–496
6. Matheson JK, Singh R, Packard A (2007) Polysomnography and sleep disorders. In: The clinical neurophysiology primer. Springer, pp 393–445
7. Cassani R, Estarellas M, San-Martin R, Fraga FJ, Falk TH (2018) Systematic review on resting-state EEG for Alzheimer's disease diagnosis and progression assessment. Dis Markers 2018(1):5174815
8. Chaudhary U, Birbaumer N, Curado MR (2015) Brain-machine interface (BMI) in paralysis. Ann Phys Rehabil Med 58(1):9–13
9. Arns M, De Ridder S, Strehl U, Breteler M, Coenen A (2009) Efficacy of neurofeedback treatment in ADHD: the effects on inattention, impulsivity and hyperactivity: a meta-analysis. Clin EEG Neurosci 40(3):180–189
10. Plassmann H, Venkatraman V, Huettel S, Yoon C (2015) Consumer neuroscience: applications, challenges, and possible solutions. J Mark Res 52(4):427–435
11. Rathi N, Chakraborty I, Kosta A, Sengupta A, Ankit A, Panda P, Roy K (2023) Exploring neuromorphic computing based on spiking neural networks: algorithms to hardware. ACM Comput Surv 55(12):1–49
12. Makeig S, Gramann K, Jung T-P, Sejnowski TJ, Poizner H (2009) Linking brain, mind and behavior. Int J Psychophysiol 73(2):95–100
13. Delis A, Tsavdaridis G, Tsanakas P (2024) A novel battery-supplied AFE EEG circuit capable of muscle movement artifact suppression. Appl Sci 14(16):6886
14. Kawala-Sterniuk A, Browarska N, Al-Bakri A, Pelc M, Zygarlicki J, Sidikova M et al (2021) Summary of over fifty years with brain-computer interfaces—a review. Brain Sci 11(1):43
15. Alrasheedi AA, Alrabeah AZ, Almuhareb FJ, Alras NM, Alduaij SN, Karar AS et al (2024) Utilizing dry electrode electroencephalography and AI robotics for cognitive stress monitoring in video gaming. Appl Syst Innov 7(4):68
16. Fiedler P, Graichen U, Zimmer E, Haueisen J (2023) Simultaneous dry and gel-based high-density electroencephalography recordings. Sensors 23(24):9745

Chapter 2
Getting Started with Signal Processing in Python

2.1 Introduction to Signal Processing

Signal processing is a branch of electrical engineering and applied mathematics that deals with the analysis, modification, and synthesis of signals. Signals are all around us—any physical quantity that changes in time, space, or any other independent variable. Examples of signals include sound waves, electromagnetic waves, and sensor data [1].

Real-time signal processing refers to the analysis of signals in real-time, which means that the processing must be performed in a timely manner so that the output data is available as soon as possible. Real-time signal processing is crucial in various applications, including audio and video processing, control systems, and signal analysis.

Real-time signal processing is a complex and challenging field that requires a solid understanding of both theoretical concepts and practical techniques. It plays a crucial role in the development of brain-computer interfaces (BCIs), where rapid and accurate signal interpretation is essential. Key techniques used in real-time signal processing for BCIs include:

- **Signal acquisition**: the process of receiving signals using sensors or other transducers and converting them from digital format to microvolts, a more readable and understandable format for researchers.
- **Sampling**: the process of converting a continuous-time signal into a discrete-time signal by taking samples at regular intervals.
- **Digital signal processing**: processing digital signals using algorithms and software.
- **Filtering**: The process of removing unwanted noise or frequencies from a signal using filters.
- **Transformations**: the process of converting a signal from one domain to another, such as from the time domain to the frequency domain, using the Fourier transform.

I. Rakhmatulin and G. R. Naik, *EEG Signal Processing with Python*, Brain Informatics and Health, https://doi.org/10.1007/978-981-95-4177-5_2

- **Compression**: The process of reducing the size of a signal while preserving its important characteristics.
- **Analysis**: The process of analyzing the properties of a signal, such as its frequency content, amplitude, and phase [2, 3].

2.2 Why Is Python Good for EEG?

Python is a high-level interpreted programming language known for its simplicity and readability. It is particularly well-suited for EEG data analysis due to its extensive libraries and tools specifically designed for scientific computing and neuroimaging. Python's ease of use, combined with powerful libraries, allows researchers to build complex EEG data analysis pipelines efficiently. Compared to other languages, Python's simple syntax and dynamic typing enable faster prototyping and easier debugging, which is crucial when working with complex EEG datasets. Additionally, Python's large and active community contributes to a rich ecosystem of neuroimaging tools, making it an excellent choice for EEG research and analysis [4, 5].

Although Python is becoming increasingly popular in the field of EEG analysis, both positives and negatives should be considered when using Python for EEG analysis. Here are some advantages and disadvantages of using Python for EEG analysis:

Positive:

- **Open Source**: Python is an open source programming language, meaning it is freely available and can be used by anyone without any licensing fees. This makes it ideal for academic research, as well as for small companies or startups with a limited budget.
- **Wide range of libraries**: There are many open-source libraries available for EEG analysis in Python, such as MNE-Python, PyEEG, and EEGlib, which provide a wide range of tools for processing, filtering, and visualizing EEG data.
- **Integration with other languages**: Python can be easily integrated with different programming languages such as C, C++, and Fortran, allowing you to process large amounts of data efficiently.
- **Ease of learning**: Python is a relatively easy programming language to learn, with a syntax that is easy to read and understand. This makes it accessible to researchers with limited programming experience [6, 7].

Negative:

- **Limited real-time processing**: Python is not optimized for real-time processing of EEG data, which may limit its use for some applications such as neurofeedback or brain-computer interfaces (BCI).
- **Speed limitations**: Python is an interpreted language, meaning it can run slower than compiled languages like C or C++. This can limit its use for processing large amounts of data in real time.

- **Memory Management**: Python relies on automatic memory management, which can lead to memory leaks or inefficient use of memory. This can be a problem when working with large data sets, as it can slow down processing time or even cause the program to crash.
- **Limited hardware interface support**: Python does not have built-in support for many EEG hardware interfaces, which may limit its use for some applications that require real-time data collection [6, 7].

Indeed, while the Python ecosystem offers unparalleled flexibility and a rich array of tools for scientific computing, researchers and developers working with EEG data must judiciously weigh their specific analytical needs against the inherent trade-offs. Factors such as the desired level of control over low-level operations, the complexity of signal processing pipelines, the need for specialized visualization, and the community support for libraries all play a role in this decision. However, for a vast and growing number of applications, Python has firmly established itself as an excellent and increasingly popular choice, driven by its readability, extensive libraries, and the vibrant open-source community that constantly contributes to its evolution.

Building upon the foundational understanding of EEG principles and practical considerations discussed in the previous sections, the following discussions will explore the most popular and powerful Python libraries essential for working with EEG data. First, we will begin by exploring NumPy library, the basis of scientific computing, offers important tools for numerical operations, array manipulation, and efficient data handling, which are crucial for the multi-dimensional (multi-channel) nature of EEG signals. Next, we will introduce SciPy, which provides important methods for filtering, transforming and analyzing EEG data. Finally, we explain MNE-Python library, an open-source library specifically designed for the analysis of EEG, providing high-level functions for data loading, preprocessing, advanced source localization and statistical analysis. These libraries help researchers to explore the vital information confined within EEG recordings.

2.2.1 NumPy: Numerical Computation

NumPy is Python's essential library for numerical operations, particularly with large datasets such as EEG. It provides a powerful N-dimensional array (ndarray) object, which efficiently stores and manipulates numerical data.

NumPy is crucial for EEG for the following reasons:

- **Data Representation**: EEG data (channels x time points, or trials x channels x time points) fits perfectly into NumPy's multi-dimensional arrays.
- **Speed**: NumPy's core is written in C, making operations on entire arrays much faster than standard Python loops. This is vital for processing large EEG files.
- **Vectorization**: It allows performing mathematical operations on whole arrays at once (e.g., subtracting baseline from all channels) without slow loops, simplifying code and boosting performance.

- **Foundation**: Many other scientific Python libraries, including those specialized for EEG, like SciPy and MNE-Python, build upon and use NumPy arrays as their primary data structure, ensuring seamless integration.

In conclusion, SciPy saves researchers a significant amount of time by providing ready-to-use, high-performance implementations of complex scientific algorithms that operate seamlessly on NumPy arrays. Some essential NumPy functions include:

- np.array(): Create arrays for storing EEG data.
- np.mean(): Compute the mean of EEG signals to analyze average brain activity.
- np.fft.fft(): Perform Fourier transforms, useful for frequency analysis of EEG data [8].

2.2.2 SciPy: Signal Processing Library

SciPy is a powerful Python library that extends the numerical capabilities of NumPy by providing a vast collection of specialized algorithms for scientific and technical computing. While NumPy offers the fundamental tools to manage and perform basic operations on multi-dimensional arrays (like raw EEG data), SciPy offers the sophisticated "machinery" to perform complex signal processing, statistical analysis, and other numerical tasks essential for EEG research.

For EEG analysis, SciPy is particularly valuable due to its robust signal processing capabilities, primarily provided by the scipy.signal module. Filtering is one of the core applications, allowing for the removal of unwanted noise—such as power line interference at 50/60 Hz—and the isolation of specific brainwave frequencies. SciPy supports the design and application of various digital filters, including Butterworth, Chebyshev, FIR, and IIR filters, enabling high-pass, low-pass, band-pass, and band-stop operations on EEG signals.

In addition to filtering, SciPy enhances frequency analysis by offering advanced spectral estimation methods such as Welch's method for computing Power Spectral Density (PSD). This is essential for quantifying the power distribution across brainwave bands like delta, theta, alpha, beta, and gamma. While NumPy provides basic FFT functionality, SciPy extends this with tools better suited for real-world EEG applications. Additionally, time–frequency analysis is facilitated through continuous wavelet transforms (scipy.signal.cwt), which provide insights into how EEG spectral characteristics evolve over time.

In essence, if EEG data is a **ndarray** created and managed by NumPy, SciPy delivers the powerful, pre-built functions to clean, transform, analyze, and extract meaningful insights from that data, saving researchers from implementing complex algorithms from scratch. Some key functions for EEG signal processing include:

- scipy.signal.firwin(): Design FIR (Finite Impulse Response) filters to remove noise.
- scipy.signal.butter(): Design IIR (Infinite Impulse Response) filters to separate specific frequency bands in EEG.

- scipy.signal.welch(): Estimate the power spectral density of EEG signals.
- scipy.signal.csd(): Compute the cross-spectral density between different EEG channels to analyze the relationship between brain regions [8, 9].

2.2.3 MNE-Python: A Specialized Library for EEG

MNE-Python is a highly specialized and comprehensive open-source Python library specifically designed for the analysis of MEG and EEG data, as well as other neurophysiological signals such as Electrocorticography (ECoG) and Near-Infrared Spectroscopy (NIRS).

Unlike NumPy and SciPy, which are general-purpose scientific computing libraries, MNE-Python provides a high-level, neurophysiology-specific framework that handles the entire pipeline of M/EEG data analysis. It builds upon NumPy and SciPy, leveraging their efficiency, but offers user-friendly functions tailored to the unique challenges and requirements of brain signal processing.

Key features and what it does for EEG in brief:

- **Comprehensive Workflow**: MNE-Python supports every major step in the M/EEG analysis workflow, from raw data import to advanced statistical analysis and visualization.
- **Data Handling**: It efficiently handles various neurophysiology data formats (e.g., EDF, BDF, FIF) and provides dedicated data structures (Raw, Epochs, Evoked) to represent continuous, segmented, and averaged brain signals.

Preprocessing offers robust tools for common preprocessing steps like:

- **Filtering**: EEG data often contains noise from sources such as eye movements, muscle contractions, or electrical interference. Filtering removes unwanted frequency components, such as low-frequency drifts and high-frequency noise. Common filters applied to EEG data include:
  - **Bandpass filters**: To isolate specific frequency ranges like Delta (1–4 Hz), Theta (4–8 Hz), Alpha (8–12 Hz), Beta (12–30 Hz), and Gamma (30–100 Hz).
  - **Notch filters**: To remove power line interference (typically at 50 Hz or 60 Hz, depending on the region).
- **Artifact Removal**: EEG signals are often contaminated by artifacts like eye blinks or muscle movements. Techniques to deal with eye blinks (EOG), muscle activity (EMG), and heartbeats (ECG) using methods like Independent Component Analysis (ICA) or Signal Space Projection (SSP).
- **Segmentation**: Raw EEG signals are continuous, but for many analyses, it is helpful to segment the data into smaller windows or epochs. This is especially useful for event-related potentials (ERPs), where you analyze brain activity in response to specific stimuli or events [4, 10].

MNE-Python is also helpful for EEG Analysis and Feature Extraction:

- **Time–Frequency Analysis**: Computing power spectral density (PSD), time–frequency representations (e.g., using wavelets) to study brain oscillations and their changes over time.
- **Source Localization**: Advanced algorithms to estimate where in the brain the electrical activity originates (e.g., Minimum Norm Estimation, Beamformers), often requiring anatomical MRI data.
- **Connectivity Analysis**: Investigating how different brain regions communicate.
- Machine Learning/Decoding: Applying classification and regression techniques to brain data.
- **Visualization**: Powerful and flexible plotting capabilities tailored for neurophysiological data, including scalp topography, time-series plots, sensor layouts, and 3D brain source activations [7].

MNE-Python is the go-to specialized toolkit for neuroscientists and researchers who need to perform in-depth, rigorous studies of EEG data, providing high-level functionality that streamlines complex workflows from raw signal to scientific insight. Common functions for EEG data include:

- mne.io.read_raw_fif(): Load EEG data from various formats.
- mne.filter.filter_data(): Apply filters to EEG signals to remove noise or isolate specific frequencies.
- mne.epochs(): Segment continuous EEG signals into epochs for event-related analysis.
- mne.time_frequency.tfr_multitaper(): : Compute time–frequency representations for analyzing EEG dynamics [7].

2.3 Connect to Python Environment

In this section, you will learn how to access, run, and modify scripts from the repository in GitHub. We will cover how to run them directly in Google Colab and how to set them up on your laptop using Google Colab. This will help you practice the theory with real code.

We recommend using Google Colab for running the provided scripts. Google Colab is a free, browser-based Python environment that does not require any software installation. All you need is a Google (Gmail) account to get started. All scripts in this book are available in **ipynb** (Jupyter Notebook) format and are fully compatible with Google Colab.

2.3.1 Getting Started with Google Colab

Go to the official GitHub page: https://github.com/Ildaron/EEG-Signal-Processing-with-Python

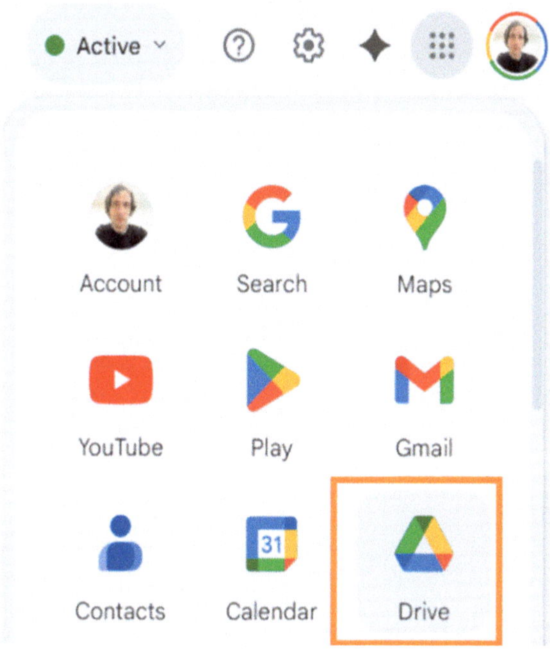

Fig. 2.1 Access to google drive

- Find the .ipynb file for the chapter you want to run (e.g., 1-EEG-Basics.ipynb). These notebooks contain all the code and explanations for that section.
- If the notebook requires any datasets, download them from the same GitHub repository.

2.3.2 Organize the Files

Open Google Drive with your Gmail account (Fig. 2.1).

- Create a new folder (e.g., PythonEEG).
- Upload the selected ipynb file(s) and any necessary datasets into this folder.

2.3.3 Launch in Google Colab

- Right-click on the uploaded notebook in **Google Drive**.
- Select "**Open with**" → "**Google Colab**" (Fig. 2.2).

If you're using Google Colab for the first time, you may need to install or enable it in your Google Drive account. To do this:

- **Right-click** on the .ipynb file in your Google Drive.

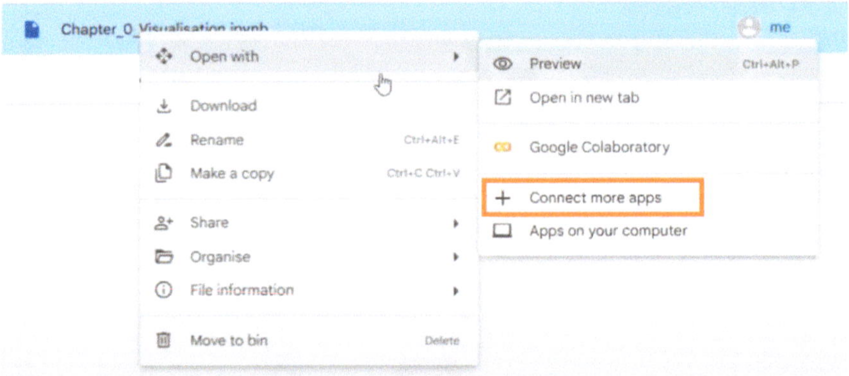

Fig. 2.2 Access to script in google drive

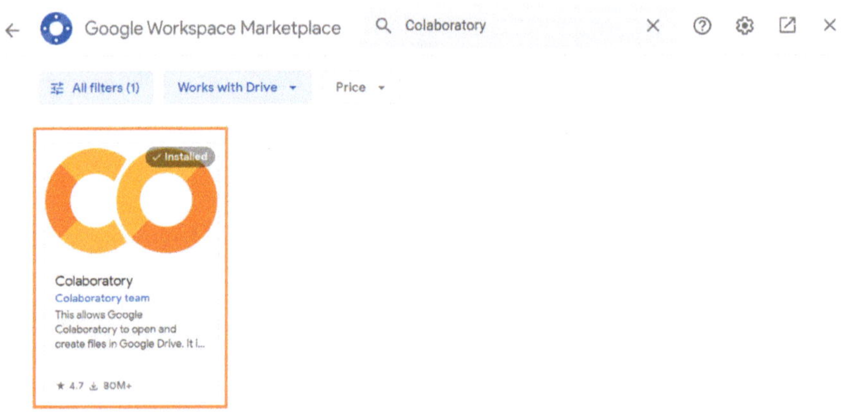

Fig. 2.3 Install Google Collaboratory

- Click "**Open with**" → "**Connect more apps**".

  Search for **Google Colaboratory** and click **Install** or **Connect** (Fig. 2.3). Once it's installed, you'll be able to open any **.ipynb** file directly in Google Colab.

2.3.4 *Launch in Google Colab*

Some libraries are already pre-installed in Google Colab. In most cases, you won't need to install common libraries like NumPy, Pandas, or Matplotlib—they are available by default. However, if you need to install additional libraries, you can do so using a simple command in a code cell. For example:

!pip install numpy (Fig. 2.4).

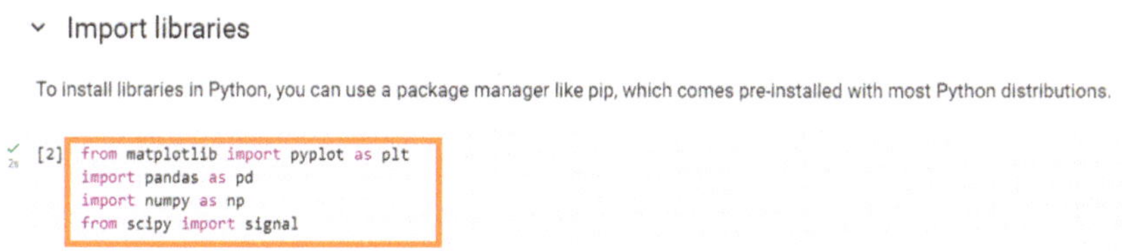

Fig. 2.4 Examples of using libraries

Fig. 2.5 Dataset location

2.3.5 Connect the Dataset

To run the script, only one modification is needed: specifying the correct path to the dataset (Fig. 2.5).

Google Drive is mounted at:**/content/drive/MyDrive/**

Access a file like this: file_path =

'/content/drive/MyDrive/folder_name/your_dataset.csv'

2.3.6 Conclusion

This chapter introduced fundamental signal processing concepts and highlighted the pivotal role of Python in EEG analysis. We established Python's suitability for this domain, emphasizing its rich ecosystem of libraries tailored for scientific computing and signal processing. Furthermore, this chapter provided practical pathways to connect to the Python environment, demonstrating the ease of setup using Google Colab, outlining the structure of a starting script, illustrating the essential import of relevant libraries, and guiding the connection to EEG datasets. NumPy provided the foundation for numerical operations, enabling efficient manipulation of EEG data, while SciPy offered a comprehensive suite of signal processing tools essential for analyzing and filtering brainwave signals.

Furthermore, we explored MNE-Python, a dedicated library that streamlines EEG data handling, visualization, and analysis. This library's specialized functions are crucial for researchers working with EEG, providing a powerful and intuitive interface for complex tasks. Finally, we touched upon the critical stage of EEG signal preprocessing, underscoring its importance in mitigating artifacts and enhancing signal quality. The techniques and tools discussed in this chapter form the bedrock for subsequent analyses, ensuring the reliability and validity of derived insights. In essence, this chapter has equipped the reader with the necessary knowledge to navigate the signal-processing aspects of EEG data using Python. It has demonstrated how combining general-purpose libraries like NumPy and SciPy, alongside specialized tools like MNE-Python, creates a robust and flexible environment for EEG research. This foundation lays the groundwork for in-depth explorations of advanced signal processing techniques and the extraction of meaningful information from EEG data.

References

1. Zhang X-D (2022) Modern signal processing. Walter de Gruyter GmbH & Co KG
2. Apolinário IF, Diniz PS (2014) Introduction to signal processing theory. Academic press library in signal processing. Elsevier; pp 3–28
3. Karl JH (2012) An introduction to digital signal processing. Elsevier
4. Bao FS, Liu X, Zhang C (2011) PyEEG: an open source python module for EEG/MEG feature extraction. Comput Intell Neurosci 2011(1):406391
5. Anderson EW, Preston GA, Silva CT (2010) Using python for signal processing and visualization. Comput Sci Eng 12(4):90–95
6. Lu Z, Li W, Nie L, Zhao K (2024) An easy-to-follow handbook for electroencephalogram data analysis with python. Brain-X 2(2):e64
7. Gramfort A, Luessi M, Larson E, Engemann DA, Strohmeier D, Brodbeck C et al (2013) MEG and EEG data analysis with MNE-python. Front Neuroinform 7:267
8. Rayhan A, Kinzler R (2023) Advancing scientific computing with python's SciPy library
9. Nunez-Iglesias J, Van der Walt S, Dashnow H (2017) Elegant SciPy: the art of scientific python. O'Reilly Media, Inc.
10. Maitin AM, Nogales A, Chazarra P, García-Tejedor ÁJ (2023) EEGraph: an open-source python library for modeling electroencephalograms using graphs. Neurocomputing 519:127–134

Chapter 3
EEG and Visualization

3.1 Introduction to Sources

The analysis of electroencephalography (EEG) data is important for neuroscience and biomedical engineering, requiring a systematic approach to extract meaningful insights from neural activity. This introduction provides an insight into the process of reading and visualizing EEG data using Python.

The typical process begins with the acquisition of EEG data, typically from specialized medical devices designed to capture neural activity with high temporal resolution. The data, whether in its raw or preprocessed form, constitutes the fundamental dataset for subsequent analysis. The crucial role of automation in this process is addressed using programming, wherein code—primarily developed in Python—automates and executes complex analysis procedures with efficiency and reproducibility.

Before proceeding with the analysis, it is essential to establish the correct computational environment. This often involves setting up a Python environment with scientific computing libraries like NumPy and SciPy, or specialized tools such as MNE-Python. Finally, we address the critical initial step: how to import EEG datasets into the Python environment, making them accessible for subsequent processing, visualization, and interpretation. Python's rich ecosystem, with libraries tailored for signal processing and neuroscience, enables researchers to extract meaningful insights from EEG data efficiently. Understanding these foundational aspects—data origin, scripting, the data itself, the Python analysis workspace, and data import—is important for effectively exploring the information within EEG signals [1, 2].

I. Rakhmatulin and G. R. Naik, *EEG Signal Processing with Python*, Brain Informatics and Health, https://doi.org/10.1007/978-981-95-4177-5_3

3.1.1 Scripts

In this book, we explore various practical applications of EEG signal processing using Python. To support your learning and experimentation, **all scripts, code examples, and Python notebooks** presented throughout the chapters are made openly available on GitHub. You can access them at: https://github.com/Ildaron/EEG-Signal-Processing-with-Python.

This GitHub repository is organized by chapters and topics, making it easy to follow along with the book. All Python scripts are named and structured according to the corresponding chapters, allowing you to locate the relevant code for each section quickly. The repository also includes a detailed README file that explains the required Python version and library dependencies, provides step-by-step instructions for installing the necessary packages, and guides you through running and modifying the scripts. You'll also find useful tips for troubleshooting and setting up your development environment, ensuring a smooth experience as you work through the examples.

3.1.2 Dataset

For the signal processing of EEG data obtained at home, discrepancies may arise compared to clinical EEGs due to limitations in both the quality and quantity of indicators.

For signal processing, we specifically used data containing artifacts and noise to demonstrate how signal processing techniques can enhance clarity. In contrast, for machine learning, we used a pre-cleaned dataset with a larger number of channels.

The dataset used for signal processing and visualization is available at the following link: https://github.com/Ildaron/EEG-Signal-Processing-with-Python/tree/main/Dataset.

3.1.3 Environment

As was mentioned in the last chapter of this book, we have chosen to use Google Colab (Interactive Python Notebook) files to present scripts and code examples. This decision was made to enhance your learning experience and provide you with a powerful, accessible platform for exploring and executing the code.

3.1.4 Import Dataset

Data was collected using an 8-channel PiEEG device, which enables EEG acquisition through a Raspberry Pi single-board computer and dry Ag/AgCl electrodes, as shown in Fig. 3.1. The PiEEG system is built around the ADS1299, a 24-bit analog-to-digital converter (ADC) from Texas Instruments. The ADS1299 is a low-noise, simultaneous-sampling analog-to-digital converter (ADC) designed explicitly for biopotential applications, including electroencephalography (EEG). The main advantage of this converter is that the ADS1299 offers extensive reconfigurability through its registers, allowing you to adjust various settings for optimal EEG measurement, such as Gain settings, Lead-off detection settings, Data rate, and operating mode.

Channels are labelled as per the international 10–20 system [3]. EEG electrode placements for the PiEEG are given below:

- Ch1–Fp1
- Ch2–Fp2
- Ch3–T3
- Ch4–C3
- Ch5–Cz
- Ch6–C4
- Ch7–O1
- Ch8–O2 and
- 2 clips electrodes (references and bias electrode)
- A1
- A2.

Electrodes Ch1–Ch8 measure the EEG signal by detecting differences in potential between each channel and the reference electrode A1 (Fig. 3.2).

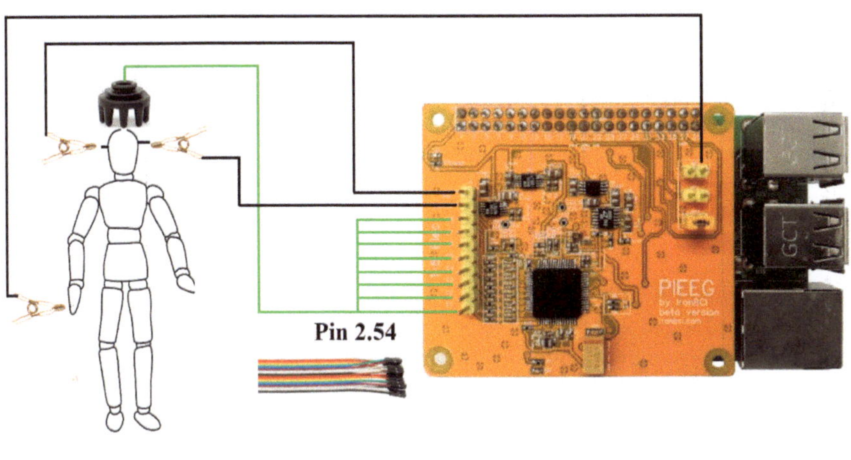

Fig. 3.1 General view of PiEEG device and connections

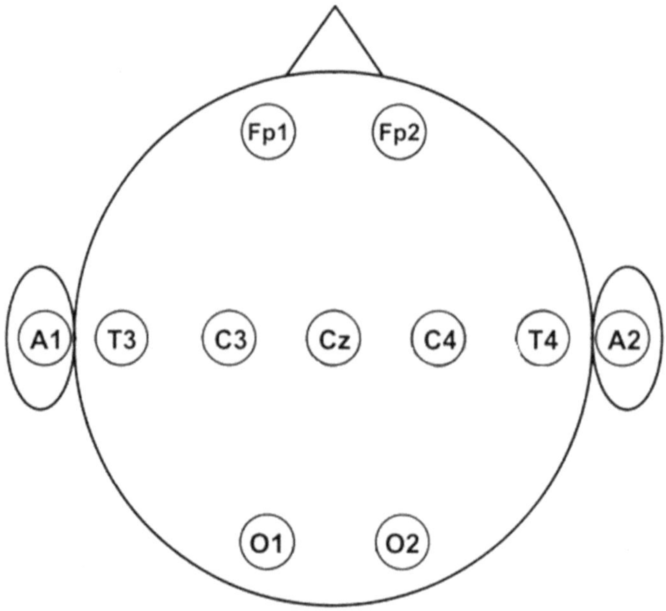

Fig. 3.2 Position of location electrodes from the dataset

The bias electrode (A2) is necessary for common-mode rejection; it helps establish a common reference point for the EEG measurement. This enables improved common-mode rejection, which is required to eliminate unwanted noise that affects all electrodes equally.

The recorded EEG data are then analyzed using various signal processing and statistical methods to extract relevant information such as power spectra, event-related potentials, and connectivity measures.

In general, measuring EEG requires specialized equipment, including an EEG amplifier and software to collect and analyze data. Trained clinicians or researchers can perform the process and is generally non-invasive and safe.

3.1.5 Dataset Details

For the chapters on signal processing, we used a dataset of chewing and blinking artifacts recorded using dry electrodes (Cz) at a sampling rate of 250 samples per second. Chewing occurred in the following sequence: 4 times, 3 times, 2 times, and 1 time, and the same sequence was observed for the blinking process. As a rule, for the visualization traces, we use the following format: Y-axis—processed EEG signal in microvolts, X-axis—samples (250 EEG data readings per second).

3.2 Start Work with the Dataset

To use a dataset in Google Colab, you need to upload it to your Google Drive and access it using the correct file path within the notebook.

```
from google.colab import drive
drive.mount('/content/drive')
# load the Excel file as a DataFrame and specify the correct path for the dataset
eeg_data = pd.read_excel("/content/drive/MyDrive/dataset.xlsx")
```

3.2.1 Convert Data from Digital Format to EEG

PiEEG measures (like other EEG devices) the voltage between electrodes and reference electrodes in absolute format, as the difference in potential, and converts this data into a digital format. After that, it converts raw EEG data from a 24-bit ADC (ranging from 0 to 16,777,215) into microvolts by normalizing the data, scaling it to a 4.5 V reference voltage, and converting it to microvolts, then rounding it to two decimal places. This transformation is necessary for accurately interpreting EEG signals, which are typically measured in microvolts.

```
eeg_data = round(1000000*Vref*(eeg_data/2^24),2)
```

The voltage reference (Vref)—it is a reference voltage in PiEEG, which in an analog-to-digital converter (ADC) sets the maximum voltage range for analog input signals that can be converted to digital values. In other words, if the reference voltage is 4.5 V and we supply 4.5 V to the input, the ADC will represent this signal at its maximum digital value. In our case, with a 24-bit ADC, this corresponds to the highest possible digital output, which is 2^24 − 1.

Data visualization of Raw data available via the following script.

```
display(eeg_data.head())
```

On the Y axis are the channel names, and on the X axis are the digital values represented in microvolts. As we can see, the values are large. On each channel in different digital ranges, which is a standard situation since Even with the same reference, raw EEG amplitudes can vary between channels due to differences in electrode contact quality, varying brain activity beneath each electrode, uneven artifacts like muscle movements or electrical interference, and minor cable lengths inconsistencies (Fig. 3.3).

	ch1	ch2	ch3	ch4	ch5	ch6	ch7	ch8
0	6410.24	791.55	9774.56	10304.67	3329.94	1008.38	8315.22	14155.44
1	6415.23	817.54	9780.35	10284.74	3338.84	999.47	8323.54	14007.41
2	6433.25	844.41	9796.80	10461.31	3358.23	965.94	8342.53	14262.67
3	6441.81	853.83	9803.88	10622.30	3365.77	931.53	8350.57	14621.96
4	6426.65	821.02	9788.67	10529.52	3346.22	952.10	8331.45	14570.11

Fig. 3.3 Dataset visualization via Python scripts

3.2.2 Data Visualization

The simplest libraries for data visualization are Matplotlib and Seaborn. These general-purpose Python libraries are also frequently used for creating custom visualizations of EEG data due to their flexibility and ease of use.

For the most part, we will use the open-source Matplotlib library, which has the advantage of working in real-time. In cases where this is not possible, we provide instructions directly in the script on how to install the required library, as shown in Fig. 3.4.

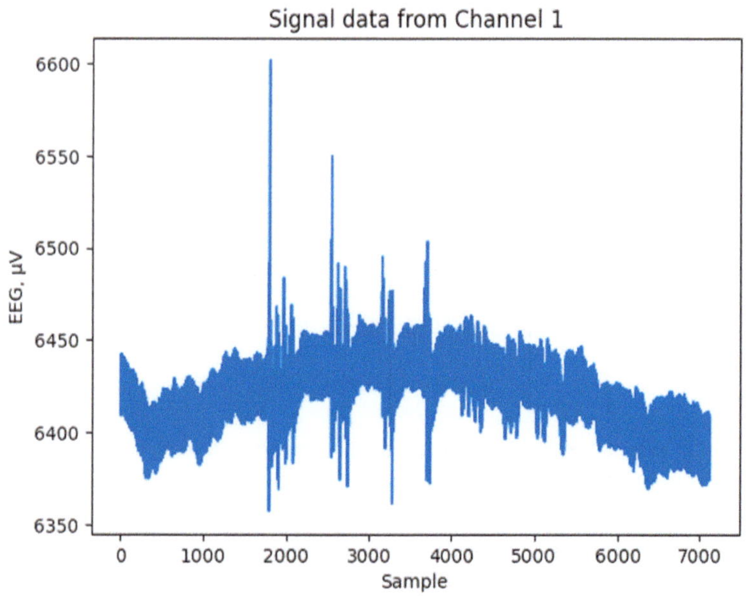

Fig. 3.4 Example of raw EEG data from PiEEG

```
# select the data from the first channel for demo
channel = 0
channel_data = eeg_data.iloc[:, channel]
# Plot the EEG data
plt.plot(channel_data)
plt.title("Signal data from Channel 1")
plt.ylabel('EEG, µV')
plt.xlabel('Sample')
plt.show()
```

As shown in the figure, chewing artifacts are most visually apparent between samples 2000 and 4000, while blinking artifacts are less noticeable between samples 4000 and 5000. The raw data ranges within ± 50 microvolts, which indicates good channel stability for dry electrodes. This shows that although the data contains some noise from electromagnetic fields, it does not significantly degrade the EEG signal. The x-axis represents sample numbers; to convert these into seconds, divide the sample values by 250, since the sampling rate is 250 samples per second.

3.2.3 What Is Raw Data

The availability of raw EEG data is important to researchers because it provides the basis for accurate and reliable analysis of brain activity. It enables data processing algorithms to be applied within the context of the researcher's task. In addition, clean, raw EEG recordings are necessary because:

- They preserve the original integrity of the signal, allowing researchers to capture subtle patterns of brain activity that may be lost or distorted in pre-processed data.
- Raw data allows researchers to apply customized pre-processing methods tailored to their specific research questions, providing optimal noise reduction and artifact removal.
- They allow the extraction of different features in different domains (time, frequency, and time-frequency), providing a comprehensive understanding of brain function [4, 5].

3.2.4 Heatmap of EEG

Spatial and Temporal Context: It provides a comprehensive view of how signals from different channels vary over time, enhancing the understanding of the spatial and temporal dynamics of brain activity. Inter-channel Relationships: Visualizing data in 3D can highlight correlations and interactions between different EEG channels, which might not be as apparent in 2D plots [5]. Detailed Analysis: For datasets with multiple channels, 3D plots can help identify patterns, trends, and anomalies across all channels simultaneously, providing a more thorough analysis.

```
# Create the heatmap
heatmap = plt.imshow(eeg_data    , cmap='viridis', aspect='auto')
plt.colorbar(heatmap, label='EEG Amplitude')
plt.xlabel('Time')
plt.ylabel('Number of Channel')
plt.title('EEG Heatmap')
plt.show()
```

The graphs clearly show moments with chewing and blinking artifacts (Fig. 3.5). As expected, the blinking artifact on channels Fp1 and Fp2 has much stronger power than the chewing artifact because these electrodes are located near the forehead. Heat maps are used to visualize EEG data to quantify brain connectivity effectively. They use an adjacency matrix to illustrate the overall connectivity between different brain regions, enabling researchers to investigate variations in connectivity within those regions. Heat maps are especially useful for EEG data because they can:

- Provide a clear visual representation of complex brain connectivity patterns
- Allow for easy comparison of connectivity strengths between different brain regions
- Help identify patterns or anomalies in brain activity that might not be apparent in raw EEG data.

3.2.5 3D Graph for Data

3D visualization of EEG data is a powerful technique that maps the electrical activity measured on the scalp onto a three-dimensional model of the brain. This process is often referred to as “EEG source imaging” or “EEG source localization” [6]. 3D visualization of EEG data has become an important tool in neuroscience, helping researchers and clinicians identify the neural sources responsible for the signals detected by the EEG electrodes [7]. By representing brain activity in three dimensions, this approach offers significant advantages over traditional 2D methods.

3D visualization of EEG data is essential for several reasons:

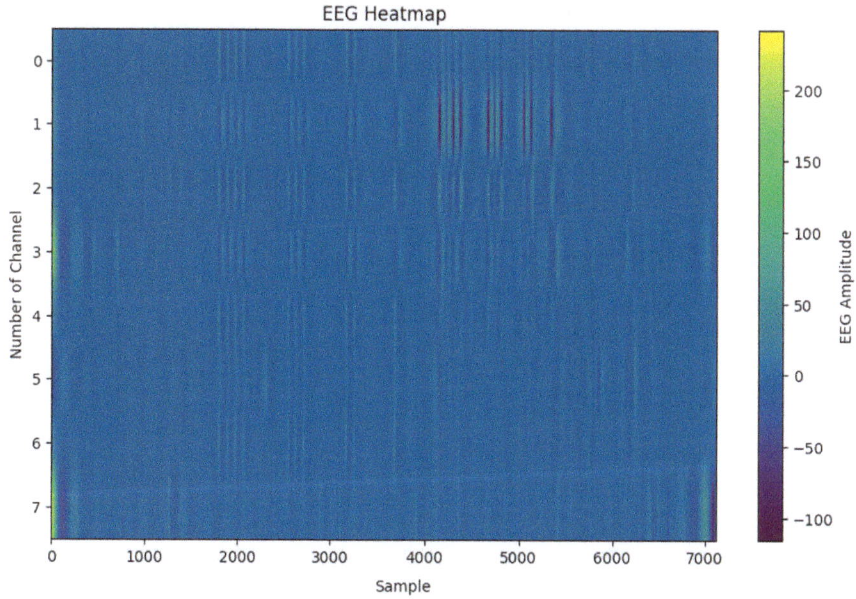

Fig. 3.5 Example of heatmap from PiEEG

- Enhanced Data Comprehension: It allows researchers better understand complex spatial and temporal relationships within the data, providing a more straightforward overview of how different channels interact over time.
- Pattern Recognition: It aids in identifying patterns and anomalies across multiple channels that might be missed in 2D representations, improving diagnostic accuracy and insight.
- Interactive Exploration: It facilitates interactive exploration, enabling users to rotate and zoom into specific regions of interest, enhancing data analysis and interpretation [5, 8].

```
# Define channel names (for 8 EEG channels)
channel_names = ["ch1", "ch2", "ch3", "ch4", "ch5", "ch6", "ch7", "ch8"]
fig = plt.figure() # Create a new figure for plotting
ax = fig.add_subplot(111, projection='3d') # Add a 3D subplot
# Create a meshgrid for x (time/data point indices) and y (channel indices)
# x -> rows represent time/sample indices
# y -> columns represent channel indices
x, y = np.meshgrid(np.arange(channel_data_bp_filtered.shape[0]),
np.arange(len(channel_names)))
# Flatten the EEG data values into a 1D array for plotting in 3D
z = eeg_data_filtered.values.flatten()
# Plot EEG data as a 3D scatter plot
ax.scatter(x, y, z, c=z, cmap='viridis', marker='o')
ax.set_xlabel('Data Point Index')  # x-axis: time or sample index
ax.set_ylabel('Channels')           # y-axis: EEG channel
ax.set_zlabel('EEG, µV')            # z-axis: EEG amplitude (microvolts)
ax.set_yticks(np.arange(len(channel_names)))
ax.set_yticklabels(channel_names)
plt.show()
```

Anomalies in EEG data refer to unusual or abnormal patterns of electrical activity in the brain that deviate from expected normal background activity. Such anomalies may include:

- High frequency oscillations (HFOS) that differ from background activity
- Epileptiform discharges or seizure-related patterns
- Abnormal waveforms that differ from typical EEG rhythms
- Unusual changes in frequency or amplitude in specific areas of the brain.

For example, on channel 1 in the presented dataset, an abnormal increase in amplitude is visible; in this case, we would venture to suggest that this is a consequence of the loss of contact between the electrode and the head (Fig. 3.6).

3.2.6 Correlation Matrix

Correlation matrices help reveal functional connectivity patterns between different brain regions as measured by EEG electrodes. This allows researchers to understand how different parts of the brain interact and communicate during various cognitive tasks or states [5, 9].

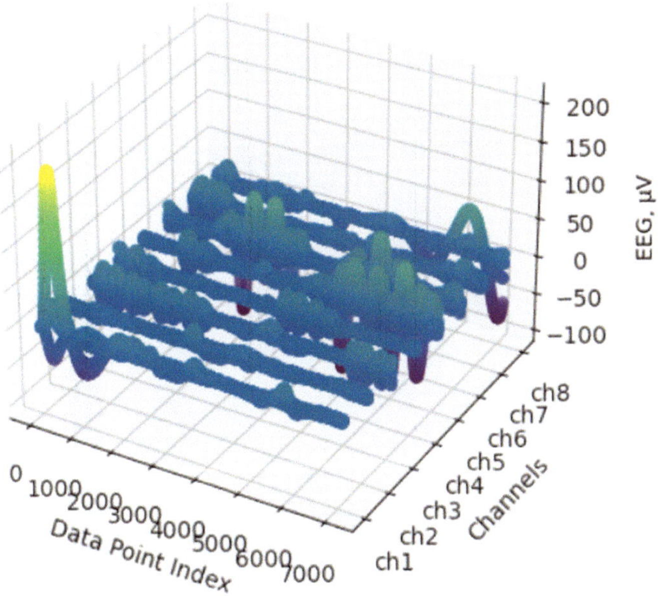

Fig. 3.6 Example of 3d visualization of EEG data

EEG data typically involves many channels, resulting in high-dimensional datasets. Correlation matrices can be used as input for techniques like Principal Component Analysis (PCA) or Independent Component Analysis (ICA) to reduce dimensionality while retaining important information.

The colors in the matrix represent the strength and direction of correlations between each pair of EEG channels. Typically, warmer colors (reds) indicate strong positive correlations, cooler colors (blues) indicate strong negative correlations, and neutral colors (whites or greens) indicate weak or no correlation, Fig. 3.7.

```
# Plot a matrix of correlation coefficients between EEG channels
# 'matshow' displays the correlation matrix as a color-coded heatmap
plt.matshow(eeg_data_filtered.corr())
# Add a color bar to indicate the scale of correlation values (-1 to 1)
plt.colorbar()
plt.show()
```

A correlation matrix for EEG data allows researchers to identify and quantify the relationships between different EEG channels. This matrix provides an overview of how electrical activity in other brain regions correlates, offering valuable insights into functional connectivity patterns. By visualizing these correlations, scientists can detect synchronous neural activity and potential communication pathways between

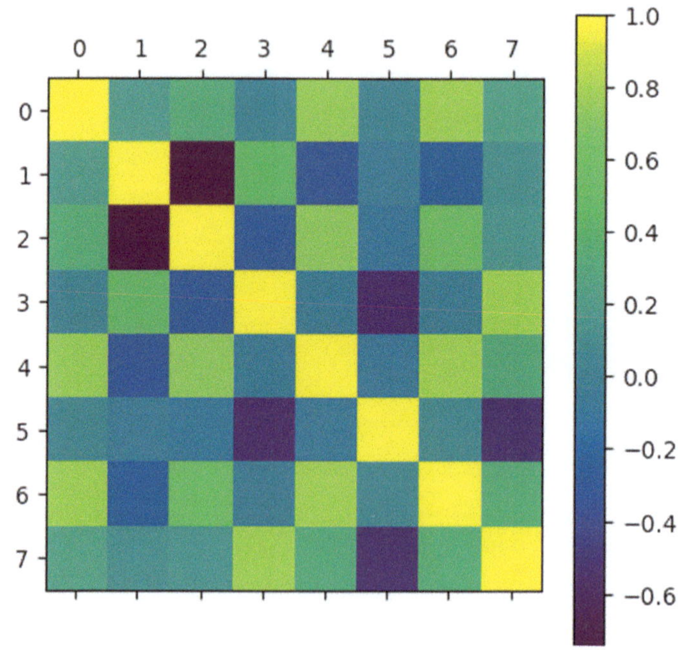

Fig. 3.7 Example of correlation matrix data

brain regions. If there is a limited number of channels, this method may enable you to identify the necessary electrode locations for future feature extraction from EEG data.

3.2.7 Popular Libraries for EEG

MNE library is a comprehensive open-source toolkit designed for processing, analyzing, and visualizing electrophysiological data such as EEG and MEG. It provides robust tools for data preprocessing, artifact removal, and advanced statistical analysis. Its capabilities include 2D and 3D visualizations, facilitating a deeper understanding of complex brain dynamics.

When working with the MNE library, the first step is to convert the existing EEG data format to the MNE library format.

```
# Load a standard EEG electrode montage (electrode placement system)
# 'standard_alphabetic' is one of MNE's predefined electrode layouts
mne.channels.make_standard_montage('standard_alphabetic')
n_channels = 8
# Create EEG metadata (info structure) with channel names, sampling frequency,
and channel type
fake_info = mne.create_info(
    ch_names=["Fp1", "Fz", "Cz", "Pz", "T3", "C3", "C4", "T4"], # labels
    sfreq=250.,       # sampling frequency (Hz)
    ch_types='eeg')  # all channels are EEG type
# Create an Evoked object using filtered EEG data and the channel info
# EvokedArray is typically used to store averaged EEG/ERP data
fake_evoked = mne.EvokedArray(data_after_band_pass_filter, fake_info)
# Assign the standard electrode montage to the Evoked object
# 'on_missing="ignore"' ensures that if some electrodes are not found in the
montage, it won't raise an error
fake_evoked.set_montage(standard_montage, on_missing='ignore')
```

3.2.8 Spatial Distribution of Brain Activity Over the Scalp

The EEG script using times_to_plotand fake_evoked.plot_topomapis essential for visualizing the spatial distribution of brain activity over the scalp at specific time points. The times_to_plot array defines the time intervals (0, 7, 14, 21, 28 ms) at which the topographical maps will be plotted. By using fake_evoked.plot_topomapwith these parameters, you can observe how the EEG signal changes across different scalp locations and time intervals, providing insights into the temporal dynamics of neural activity. This is particularly useful for identifying patterns and understanding the progression of brain responses over time, Fig. 3.8.

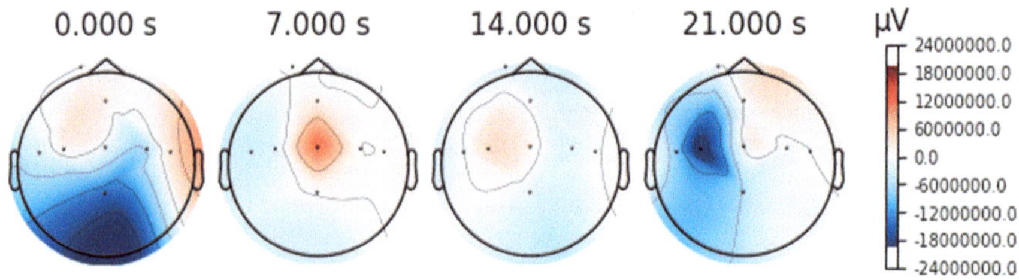

Fig. 3.8 Example of spatial distribution

```
# Create an array of time points (in seconds) at which topographic maps will be plotted
# np.arange(0, 28., 7) → [0, 7, 14, 21]
times_to_plot = np.arange(0, 28., 7)
# Plot EEG topographic maps (scalp maps) at the specified time points
# ch_type="eeg" → use EEG channels
# ncols=len(times_to_plot) → arrange subplots in a row with one column per time point
# nrows="auto" → let MNE automatically determine number of rows
fake_evoked.plot_topomap(times_to_plot,ch_type="eeg",
ncols=len(times_to_plot), nrows="auto");
```

Spatial distribution is crucial for EEG because it provides valuable insights into the localization and propagation of brain activity. It enables researchers and clinicians to map electrical activity across various brain regions, thereby enhancing our understanding of neural processes and their interactions. By analyzing the spatial distribution of EEG signals, we can identify specific brain areas involved in various cognitive functions and detect abnormal activity patterns associated with neurological disorders. Moreover, spatial distribution analysis helps overcome the limitations of EEG's poor spatial resolution by employing techniques like Surface Laplacian transformation, which reduces volume conduction effects and improves both spatial and temporal resolution of EEG recordings [10]. This improved spatial resolution enables more accurate source localization, better discrimination between different brain states, and enhanced performance in brain-computer interface applications [11–13].

3.3 Conclusion

This chapter has introduced fundamental concepts and techniques for analyzing and visualizing EEG data using the Python programming language. We began by outlining the accessibility of EEG datasets and highlighted the utility of platforms like GitHub for sharing and managing source code.

Next, we demonstrated practical data handling procedures, including importing and processing EEG datasets directly within Google Colab, with a specific focus on the dataset.

We then explored key visualization methods for understanding raw EEG data. These included:

- **Heatmaps**: To visualize signal amplitudes across time and channels.
- **Correlation matrices**: To assess relationships between EEG signals recorded from different brain regions.
- **3D graphs**: To represent EEG signals in a more intuitive and spatially informative manner.

Finally, we briefly discussed popular Python libraries dedicated to EEG analysis, such as MNE-Python. We emphasized the importance of visualizing the spatial distribution of brain activity over the scalp to gain deeper insights into cognitive and neurological processes.

This chapter serves as a foundational steppingstone for further exploration into the field of EEG analysis using Python. By mastering these fundamental concepts and techniques, researchers and practitioners can effectively analyze and interpret EEG data, driving advancements in neuroscience, clinical neurophysiology, and related fields.

References

1. Bao FS, Liu X, Zhang C (2011) PyEEG: an open source python module for EEG/MEG feature extraction. Comput Intell Neurosci 2011(1):406391
2. Maitin AM, Nogales A, Chazarra P, García-Tejedor ÁJ (2023) EEGraph: an open-source Python library for modeling electroencephalograms using graphs. Neurocomputing 519:127–134
3. Morley A, Hill L, Kaditis A (2016) 10–20 system EEG placement. European Respiratory Society
4. Sanei S, Chambers JA (2013) EEG signal processing. Wiley
5. Naik G, dos Santos WP, Gargiulo G (2024) Advanced electroencephalography analytical methods: fundamentals, acquisition, and applications
6. Taberna GA, Marino M, Ganzetti M, Mantini D (2019) Spatial localization of EEG electrodes using 3D scanning. J Neural Eng 16(2):026020
7. Koessler L, Maillard L, Benhadid A, Vignal J-P, Braun M, Vespignani H (2007) Spatial localization of EEG electrodes. Neurophysiol Clin/Clin Neurophysiol 37(2):97–102
8. Thakor NV, Sherman DL (2012) EEG signal processing: theory and applications. Neural engineering. Springer, pp 259–303
9. Naik GR, dos Santos WP (2023) Biomedical signal processing: a modern approach. CRC Press

10. Vidal F, Burle B, Spieser L, Carbonnell L, Meckler C, Casini L, Hasbroucq T (2015) Linking EEG signals, brain functions and mental operations: advantages of the Laplacian transformation. Int J Psychophysiol 97(3):221–232
11. Chiarion G, Sparacino L, Antonacci Y, Faes L, Mesin L (2023) Connectivity analysis in EEG data: a tutorial review of the state of the art and emerging trends. Bioengineering 10(3):372
12. Iivanainen J, Mäkinen AJ, Zetter R, Stenroos M, Ilmoniemi RJ, Parkkonen L (2021) Spatial sampling of MEG and EEG based on generalized spatial-frequency analysis and optimal design. Neuroimage 245:118747
13. Zang B, Lin Y, Liu Z, Gao X (2021) A deep learning method for single-trial EEG classification in RSVP task based on spatiotemporal features of ERPs. J Neural Eng 18(4):0460c8

Chapter 4
Bandpass Filter

Bandpass filters are essential for signal processing, as they isolate specific frequency ranges within a signal by attenuating all other frequencies. This is highly useful for applications such as EEG analysis, where distinct frequency bands correspond to different brain states. Python, with libraries such as SciPy, offers robust functions for designing and implementing these filters, enabling precise control over frequency responses. By selectively allowing specific frequencies to pass, bandpass filters facilitate focused analysis and extract meaningful information from complex signals, making them essential for various scientific and engineering applications [1, 2].

4.1 How Much Data and Channels Do We Need

To efficiently process the EEG signal, the optimal configuration typically includes a 32-channel system that records the brain's electrical activity with high spatial and temporal resolution. At the same time, many scientific publications report positive results even when using a single electrode. More commonly, however, studies employ 4, 8, or 16 electrodes—particularly in applied, non-medical tasks such as detecting emotions or stress. For applications involving event-related potential, such as the P300, the number of channels is usually more standardized, and it is advisable to begin with at least 16 channels.

The choice of channel count depends not only on feature extraction methods, but also on data processing requirements. Many algorithms—especially those that operate on signal components—benefit from a higher number of channels, as this improves the accuracy of feature extraction. However, this also introduces a practical challenge: maintaining good electrode–skin contact and low impedance across all channels. With more electrodes, there is a greater chance of encountering noisy channels with high impedance. Fortunately, having a larger set of channels makes it

I. Rakhmatulin and G. R. Naik, *EEG Signal Processing with Python*, Brain Informatics and Health, https://doi.org/10.1007/978-981-95-4177-5_4

possible to discard the problematic ones while still preserving enough high-quality data for analysis [3].

The number of samples required to process an EEG signal depends on several factors, including the sampling rate, recording duration, number of channels, frequency range of interest, and specific research goals [4]. Typical EEG sampling rates range from 250 to 1000 Hz, with 400 Hz being a common choice in many studies. The total number of samples is directly proportional to the recording duration and sampling rate; for example, a 10-min recording at 400 Hz would yield 240,000 samples per channel. Standard EEG setups often use 16 to 32 channels, each contributing its own set of samples. A minimum sampling rate of 180 Hz is necessary to capture the full spectrum of brain activity, including high-frequency gamma waves up to 90 Hz. However, higher sampling rates provide more detailed temporal resolution, which can be critical for specific analyses. While a few minutes of clean, pre-processed data from a 32-channel system with sampling rates ranging from 250 to 1000 Hz is often sufficient for many EEG studies, the optimal number of samples ultimately depends on the specific research question, the analysis methods, and the level of detail required in the study [5, 6].

4.2 Typical Data Length Required for Algorithms

The first question is what length of data to use when starting with algorithms. Epoch is a common technique used to segment continuous EEG data into smaller discrete time windows, or epochs. Each epoch typically contains a fixed number of samples, and the duration of each epoch is determined by the sampling rate of the EEG data [7].

Epochs are helpful for several reasons:

- To separate EEG activity across experimental conditions, EEG data is often collected while participants perform different tasks or are exposed to various stimuli. Epochs can be used to separate EEG activity for each experimental condition, making it easier to analyze and compare EEG signals across conditions.
- To remove unwanted parts of EEG data: EEG data may contain unwanted parts, such as baseline periods before stimulus onset or periods with excessive noise or artifacts. Epoching can be used to remove these unwanted parts of the EEG data by selecting only the epochs of interest.
- To reduce the computational load for analysis: EEG data is often recorded at a high sampling rate, resulting in a large amount of data that needs to be analyzed, which is especially important for brain-computer interface systems that operate in real time. Since epoching can be used to reduce the computational load for analysis by breaking the data into smaller, more manageable chunks, it can be beneficial.

Epochs are typically accomplished by selecting a fixed time window or epoch duration and moving this window across the continuous EEG signal at a fixed interval or overlap. The resulting epochs are then stored as separate data segments for further analysis [8, 9].

The choice of epoch length and overlap may depend on the specific research question and the characteristics of the EEG data. Shorter epochs and larger overlaps may be more suitable for analyzing transient EEG activity, while longer epochs and smaller overlaps may be better for analyzing more stable activity. When selecting these parameters, it is crucial to consider the trade-off between epoch length and overlap, as shorter epochs may yield more epochs with lower signal-to-noise ratios. In comparison, longer epochs may lead to greater temporal smearing of EEG activity [8, 9].

4.3 Band-Pass Filter Implementation

A band-pass filter is indeed a fundamental tool for processing EEG signals. This type of filter allows frequencies within a specific range to pass through while attenuating frequencies outside that range. For EEG analysis, a common band-pass filter configuration is 1 Hz to 40 Hz. This range is chosen because:

- Frequencies below 1 Hz are typically removed to eliminate slow drift, DC offset, and low-frequency artifacts such as pulse and building vibrations.
- Frequencies above 40 Hz are often filtered out to remove high-frequency noise, including power line interference (50/60 Hz) and muscle artifacts.

The band-pass filter helps to isolate the relevant brain activity frequencies, which generally fall within the 1–40 Hz range, including delta (1–4 Hz), theta (4–8 Hz), alpha (8–13 Hz), and beta (13–30 Hz) waves [2]. This filtering approach enhances the signal-to-noise ratio, facilitating the analysis of EEG data for various applications. The general implementation of the band-pass filter is provided in Fig. 4.1.

A bandpass filter for EEG data typically consists of a high-pass filter and a low-pass filter that are combined to pass only frequencies in a specific frequency band. For example, a bandpass filter with a low cutoff of 1 Hz and a high cutoff of 40 Hz will only pass frequencies between 1 and 40 Hz.

EEG signals typically have a frequency range of 0.5 to 100 Hz, with most of the useful signal power concentrated in the 1–40 Hz range. To isolate specific frequency bands of interest, bandpass filters are often used to attenuate unwanted frequencies while maintaining the desired frequency range. For example, a researcher may want to focus on the alpha (8–13 Hz) or beta (13–30 Hz) frequency ranges, and a bandpass filter can be used to isolate these specific frequencies.

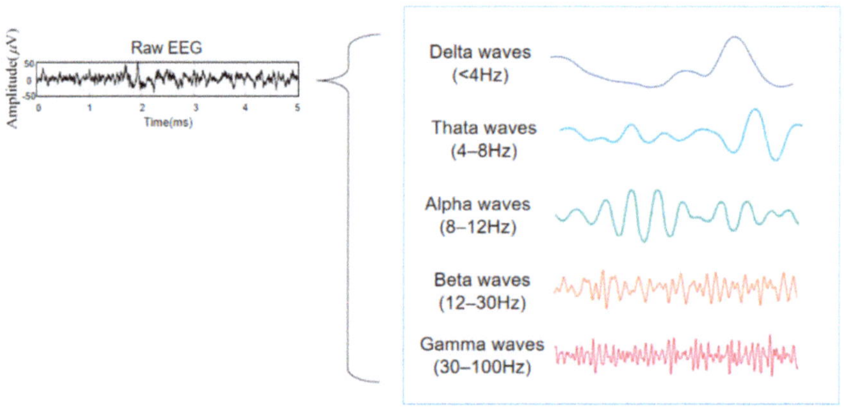

Fig. 4.1 Example of using a band-pass filter for frequency decomposition of the EEG signal [10]

Here we use Butterworth filters via SciPy library. signal.butter is a function provided by the scipy.signal module in Python. It is used to design digital Butterworth filters, which are a type of infinite impulse response (IIR) filter commonly used for signal processing tasks, including filtering EEG signals.

4.3.1 High-Pass Filter

A high-pass filter in EEG processing removes slow frequency components (usually below 0.1–1 Hz) from neural signals, allowing data to be observed without y-axis jumps, in microvolts, effectively eliminating direct current (DC) offsets, baseline drifts, and slow fluctuations caused by artifacts such as sweat. By rejecting frequencies below a certain threshold, the filter attenuates slow frequencies containing DC components and negative excursions, which helps improve the signal-to-noise ratio and prepares the EEG data for more accurate analysis (Fig. 4.2).

As we can see from the graph, our data has become flatter; however, it is still noisy due to high-frequency noise. Since the high-frequency components are not fully removed, the graph appears noisy despite its flatter appearance. To address this, we need to apply a low-pass filter to the data, specifically targeting and removing the remaining high-frequency noise, which results in a much smoother and more useful signal.

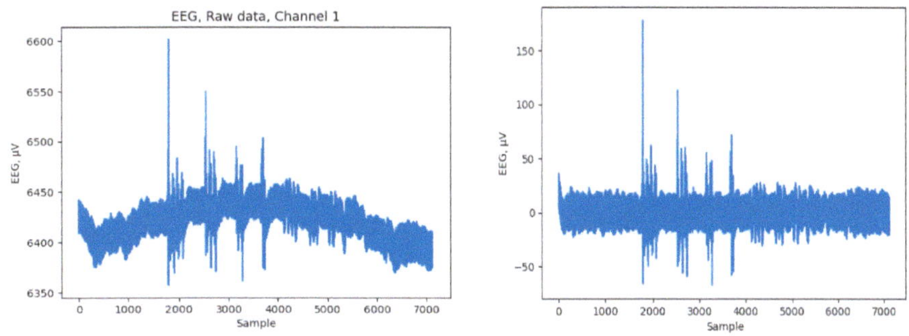

a b

Fig. 4.2 Example of a high-pass filter 1 Hz: **a**—before, **b**—after

4.3.2 Low-Pass Filter

A low-pass filter in EEG processing removes high-frequency components (usually above 40 Hz) from neural signals, effectively attenuating noise from electrical interference, muscle artifacts, and other high-frequency interference. By rejecting frequencies above a specific cutoff, the filter helps reduce unwanted signal variations while preserving the most significant neural oscillations in the 1–40 Hz range. Researchers typically recommend using a cutoff of around 40–45 Hz to minimize noise without significantly distorting the EEG signal, thereby providing cleaner data for analysis by eliminating high-frequency oscillations that do not contribute meaningful neurological information (Fig. 4.3).

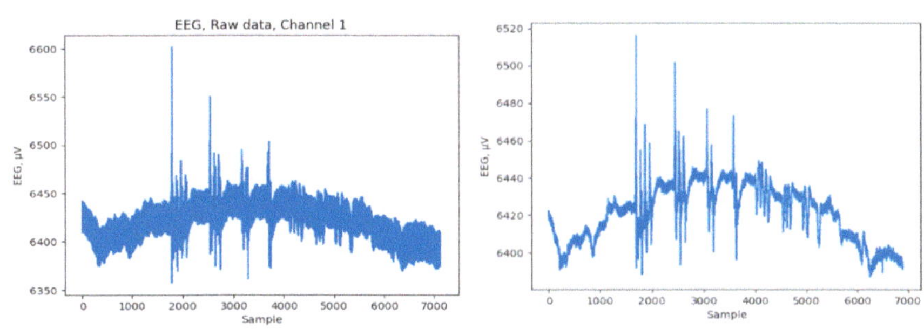

a b

Fig. 4.3 An example of a low-pass filter at 40 Hz: **a**—before, **b**—after

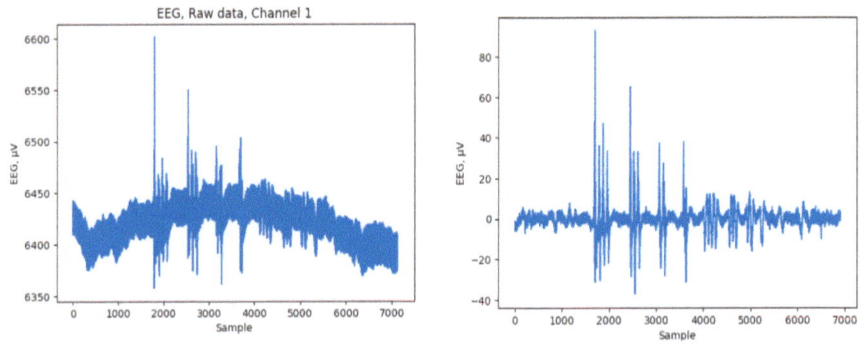

a b

Fig. 4.4 An example of a band-pass filter, 1–40: **a**—before, **b**—after

If we use only a low-pass filter on the graph, we see that our data has become clearer, but the constants on the Y axis, the microvolts, have not disappeared. A constant value, such as a DC offset, can be considered as a signal with zero frequency. Since a low-pass filter's primary purpose is to let low frequencies pass, it will not remove the DC offset. A low-pass filter is used for smoothing and noise reduction, while a high-pass filter is used for baseline correction and trend removal. Hence, to remove both noise and the constant offset, a combination of a high-pass and a low-pass filter (a band-pass filter) is needed.

4.3.3 Band-Pass Filter

Band-pass filter has a High-pass filter and a Low-pass filter together, Fig. 4.4.

EEG data is becoming clearer, and artifacts such as chewing and blinking are becoming more noticeable. This is the first step toward working with the data. Below is a Python script that implements a bandpass filter using the SciPy library and a Butterworth filter.

```
def butter_highpass_filter(data, cutoff, nyq, order=5):
    """Butterworth low-pass filter.
    Args:
        data - EEG data
        cutoff (float): cutoff frequency.
        order (int): order of the filter.
    Returns:
        array: filtered data."""
    normal_cutoff = cutoff / nyq  # normalized cutoff frequency
    b, a = signal.butter(order, normal_cutoff, btype='high', analog=False)
    filtered_data = signal.filtfilt(b, a, data)
    return filtered_data

def butter_lowpass_filter(data, cutoff, nyq, order=5):
    """Butterworth low-pass filter.
    Args:
        data - EEG data
        cutoff (float): cutoff frequency
        order (int): order of the filter
    Returns:
        array: filtered data."""
    normal_cutoff = cutoff / nyq  # normalized cutoff frequency
    b, a = signal.butter(order, normal_cutoff, btype='low', analog=False)
    filtered_data = signal.lfilter(b, a, data)
    return filtered_data

channel_data_bp_filtered = channel_data.copy()  # copy the data\
fps = 250                # sampling frequency
cutoff_high = 1          # cutoff frequency of the high-pass filter
cutoff_low = 50          # cutoff frequency of the low-pass filter
nyq = 0.5 * fps  # Nyquist frequency (half of the sampling frequency). It represents the highest frequency that can be accurately represented in a discrete-time signal.

# Apply the band-pass filter
```

```
channel_data_bp_filtered = butter_highpass_filter(
    data=channel_data_bp_filtered,
    cutoff=cutoff_high,
    nyq=nyq,
     order=5)
channel_data_bp_filtered = butter_lowpass_filter(
    data=channel_data_bp_filtered,
    cutoff=cutoff_low,
    nyq=nyq,
    order=4)
```

The Butterworth filter has the following customizable parameters:

- FPS: how many samples were read per second for channels, in our case, 250 EEG data.
- Lower Cutoff Frequency: The lower bound of the passband.
- Upper Cutoff Frequency: The upper bound of the passband.
- Nyquist Frequency: In this case, half the sampling frequency is 125 Hz. The Nyquist frequency indicates the maximum frequency at which an analog signal can be sampled without losing important information.

Additionally, Order of the Filter: This determines the steepness of the filter's response and its attenuation outside the passband (Fig. 4.5).

The typical recommended filter order for EEG signals ranges from 3rd to 4th order. This order provides a good balance between signal preservation and noise reduction. For most EEG applications, a 4th-order Butterworth bandpass filter is considered standard.

Potential Risks of Inappropriate Order. Too high an order can cause:

- Signal distortion
- Potential loss of original signal information
- Potential filter instability.

Despite its obvious usefulness, the bandpass filter can have both positive and negative effects on the EEG signal.

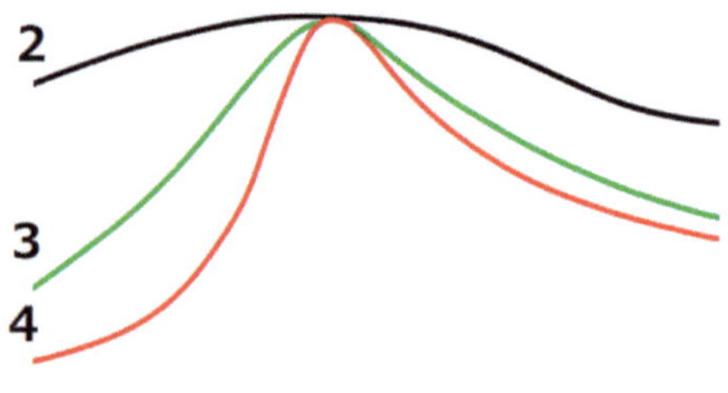

Fig. 4.5 Examples of different types of orders for Butterworth filter

Positive

- Band-pass filtering is a crucial tool in EEG signal analysis, enabling the isolation of key frequency components such as alpha, beta, delta, and theta waves, each linked to distinct cognitive processes. It enhances the study of event-related potentials (ERPs) by focusing on stimulus-relevant frequencies while effectively reducing artifacts such as baseline drifts and high-frequency noise. The consistent application of band-pass filters across channels also improves functional connectivity analysis by eliminating unrelated frequency interference, thereby clarifying neural network activity and ensuring more accurate EEG interpretations.

Negative

- While band-pass filters can be valuable for EEG data analysis, they can also be problematic when used inappropriately or excessively. Here are some scenarios where a band-pass filter might not be suitable for EEG processing.
- Over-filtering. Applying overly narrow band-pass filters can lead to signal distortion and the removal of genuine neural activity. Aggressive filtering might result in the loss of important frequency components.
- Misaligned Cutoff Frequencies. Setting incorrect low-pass and high-pass cutoff frequencies can result in unintended filtering of important neural oscillations or event-related potentials.
- Baseline Drift Removal. Relying solely on a band-pass filter to remove baseline drift can inadvertently remove relevant low-frequency neural signals along with the drift.
- Lack of Understanding. Suppose you lack a clear understanding of the frequency characteristics of EEG signals and the implications of filtering. In that case, you might misuse band-pass filters and draw incorrect conclusions from your analysis.
- Data Artifacts. Band-pass filtering might not effectively remove certain types of artifacts, such as muscle artifacts or eye blinks, requiring additional preprocessing steps.
- Uneven Spectral Distribution. EEG signals often have uneven spectral distributions, and applying a uniform band-pass filter might not accurately capture the underlying neural activity.
- Inconsistent Filtering. If you apply different band-pass filters to different data segments or channels without justification, it can lead to inconsistencies in your analysis.

4.4 Conclusion

In this chapter, we explored the fundamental concepts and Python implementations of band-pass filters, crucial tools for analyzing neural data. We began by understanding the data size and channel (EEG data) requirements for filters, the principles of low-pass and high-pass filters, which selectively allow frequencies below and above a certain cutoff, respectively. Building upon these, we delved into the implementation of band-pass filters, which effectively isolate signals within a specific frequency range.

We demonstrated how to design and apply these filters using Python libraries such as SciPy, showcasing their practical utility in analyzing neural signals. By effectively filtering neural data, we can:

- Enhance the signal-to-noise ratio: Remove unwanted noise and artifacts, to improve the clarity of neural signals.
- Isolate specific frequency bands: Analyze neural oscillations within specific frequency ranges, such as alpha, beta, and gamma bands.
- Extract relevant features: Extract meaningful features from neural data for further analysis and classification.

References

1. Cohen MX (2014) Analyzing neural time series data: theory and practice. MIT Press
2. Mitra SK (2001) Digital signal processing: a computer-based approach. McGraw-Hill Higher Education
3. Niedermeyer E, da Silva FL (2005) Electroencephalography: basic principles, clinical applications, and related fields. Lippincott Williams & Wilkins
4. Lau TM, Gwin JT, Ferris DP (2012) How many electrodes are really needed for EEG-based mobile brain imaging? J Behav Brain Sci 2(3):387–393
5. Alotaiby T, El-Samie FEA, Alshebeili SA, Ahmad I (2015) A review of channel selection algorithms for EEG signal processing. EURASIP J Adv Signal Process 2015:1–21
6. Cohen MX (2017) Where does EEG come from and what does it mean? Trends Neurosci 40(4):208–218
7. Miskin C, Carvalho KS, Valencia I, Legido A, Khurana DS (2015) EEG duration: the long and the short of it. J Child Neurol 30(13):1767–1769
8. Fraschini M, Demuru M, Crobe A, Marrosu F, Stam CJ, Hillebrand A (2016) The effect of epoch length on estimated EEG functional connectivity and brain network organisation. J Neural Eng 13(3):036015
9. Möcks J, Gasser T (1984) How to select epochs of the EEG at rest for quantitative analysis. Electroencephalogr Clin Neurophysiol 58(1):89–92
10. Li H, Zhu P, Shao Q (2024) Rapid mental workload detection of air traffic controllers with three EEG sensors. Sensors 24(14):4577

Chapter 5
Smoothing Filters

Smoothing filters are essential tools in Electroencephalography (EEG) signal processing, used to reduce noise and highlight underlying patterns. These filters work by averaging or weighting neighboring data points to create a smoother representation of the signal [1]. The average filter computes the mean of nearby samples, reducing high-frequency noise. In this chapter we consider popular algorithms for smoothing filters.

5.1 Average Filter

In signal processing of EEG data, calculating the average is a common technique used to improve the signal-to-noise ratio and highlight underlying brain activity. The EEG signal is often contaminated with noise and artifacts (ocular and muscle artifacts), and averaging can help reduce these unwanted components while preserving brain-related activity.

An average filter for EEG works by smoothing out the signal by replacing each data point with the average value of neighboring data points within a defined window. It is necessary to select a proper window size that balances noise reduction with the preservation of important signal features [2, 3].

Like all algorithms, the averaging filter has both positive and negative moments for processing the EEG signal.

Positive

- An average filter can effectively smooth out the EEG signal by removing high-frequency noise and minor fluctuations.
- Easy to implement.

I. Rakhmatulin and G. R. Naik, *EEG Signal Processing with Python*, Brain Informatics and Health, https://doi.org/10.1007/978-981-95-4177-5_5

- EEG signals often exhibit slow oscillatory patterns, such as alpha, beta, and delta waves. Applying an average filter with a longer time window can help visualize these slower frequency components by attenuating faster fluctuations [4, 5].

Negative

- Temporal Resolution. Applying an average filter with a large window can smooth out fine temporal details and fast changes in the EEG signal. Depending on your analysis goals, this may or may not be desirable.
- Signal Distortion. Over-smoothing can lead to the loss of important signal features, including transient responses or rapid changes that might be critical for your analysis.
- Baseline Fluctuations. If analysis involves comparing EEG activity before and after specific events, excessive smoothing can reduce the detectable differences in baseline fluctuations [4, 5].

Below, we provide a Python implementation of a simple moving average filter via the Pandas library.

```
# Function to apply a simple moving average (rolling mean) filter
def average_filter(data, average_length):
   data = pd.DataFrame(data) # Convert data to Pandas format
   avereged_data = data.rolling(window=average_length).mean()  # Apply rolling
mean with the specified window size (average_length)
   return avereged_data


#    --- Parameters controlling the "smoothness" of the signal ---
# Larger window = smoother data, but more lag (less responsiveness)


average_length_window_1 = 40 # Window size for first smoothing pass
average_length_window_2 = 70 # Window size for second smoothing pass
# Apply moving average filter with different window sizes
# Smooth data with a 40-sample window
channel_data_avg_window_1 = average_filter(data=channel_data_bp_filtered,
average_length=average_length_window_1)
# Smooth data with a 70-sample window
channel_data_avg_window_2 = average_filter(data=channel_data_bp_filtered,
average_length=average_length_window_2)
```

```
plt.title("Average filter, Channel " + str(channel+1))
plt.plot(channel_data_bp_filtered, label='Data before average filter')
plt.plot(channel_data_avg_window_1, label='Data after average filter
(window='+str(average_length_window_1)+")")
plt.plot(channel_data_avg_window_2, label='Data after average filter
(window='+str(average_length_window_2)+")")
```

Python implementation of the average filter via the Matplotlib library is shown in Fig. 5.1.

As shown in Fig. 5.1, the average filter smooths out the peaks in EEG data, making the data appear better. If with a step of 40 steps (that is, 40 samples are taken before the current value, summarize and take an average of them) visually one can assume that the data has lost some of the noise but at the same time retained the frequency component, then with a step of 70 it is already evident that there is a shift in the phase components of the EEG signal, which has a highly negative effect on the subsequent extraction of characteristics from EEG data.

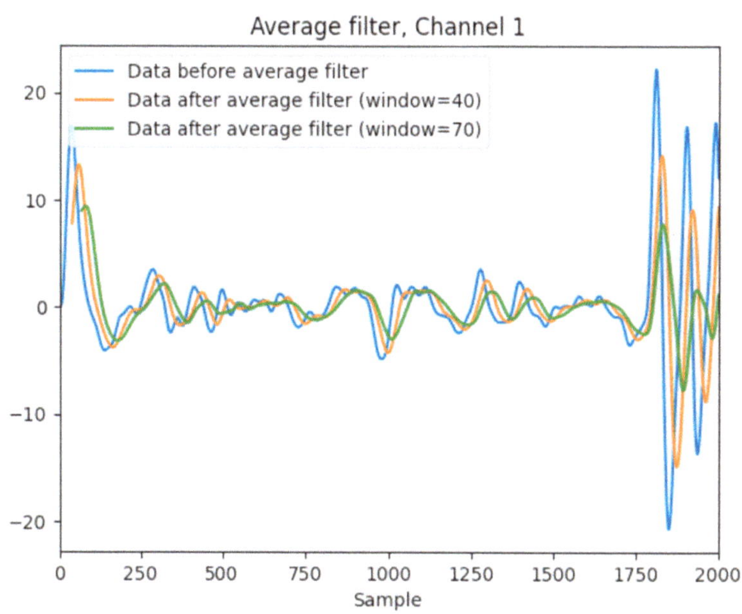

Fig. 5.1 Example of an average filter

5.2 Gaussian Filter

Applying a Gaussian filter to EEG data is a signal processing technique commonly used to smooth or denoise the signals. Gaussian filtering is a linear smoothing filter that uses a Gaussian kernel to convolve with the EEG signal, effectively reducing noise and emphasizing underlying trends or features [6, 7].

Positive

- Noise Smoothing. Gaussian filters smooth out noise in the EEG signal, thereby reducing random fluctuations caused by artifacts and environmental interference.
- Preserving Temporal Details. Unlike simple moving average filters, Gaussian filters preserve finer temporal features by attenuating noise while maintaining sharp signal transitions.
- Event-Related Potentials (ERPs). Gaussian filters are well-suited for enhancing ERP components, such as P300 responses, by reducing noise without distorting the underlying event-related activity.
- Spatial Smoothing. For EEG recordings with multiple electrodes (scalp channels), Gaussian filters can be applied across neighboring channels to improve signal-to-noise ratio and reveal broader neural patterns.
- Frequency-Selective Smoothing. By adjusting the width of the Gaussian kernel, it is possible to selectively smooth specific frequency ranges in the EEG signal, making it useful for targeting noise reduction in certain frequency bands [6, 7].

Negative

- Kernel Size. The width of the Gaussian kernel (often determined by the standard deviation) impacts the amount of smoothing. Smaller standard deviations preserve more detail, while larger values provide more smoothing.
- Signal Distortion. Excessive smoothing can blur rapid changes and transient responses, potentially masking essential features in the EEG data.
- Artifact Handling. While Gaussian filters can reduce random noise, they may not be as effective at removing structured artifacts such as muscle artifacts. Additional preprocessing steps might be needed.
- Parameter Selection. The choice of kernel size (standard deviation) depends on your specific analysis goals and the characteristics of your EEG data. Experimentation and validation are crucial [6, 7].

A Gaussian filter for EEG works by convolving the EEG signal with a Gaussian-shaped curve. This curve assigns more weight to nearby data points and gradually decreases the weight as the distance from the center increases. The width of the Gaussian curve, controlled by its standard deviation, determines the level of smoothing: smaller standard deviations maintain fine details, while larger values yield more smoothing. This makes Gaussian filters suitable for enhancing event-related potentials while reducing noise, thereby retaining temporal precision [8].

Below we provide a Python implementation via the Scipy library. The main parameter is the value for the standard deviation of the Gaussian kernel, which determines the amount of smoothing or blurring applied to the data.

```
from scipy.ndimage import gaussian_filter1d
# --- Parameters controlling the "smoothness" of the signal —
# The sigma value is the standard deviation of the Gaussian kernel.
# Larger sigma = smoother data, but more lag and loss of fine details.

sigma_value_1 = 45 #     Strong smoothing (very smooth signal, slower response)
sigma_value_2 = 15 # Moderate smoothing (less smooth, more responsive)

# Apply Gaussian smoothing with different sigma values
# Smooth data with a large sigma (strong smoothing effect)
channel_data_gauss_window_1 = gaussian_filter1d(channel_data_bp_filtered,
sigma=sigma_value_1)
# Smooth data with a smaller sigma (milder smoothing effect)
channel_data_gauss_window_2 = gaussian_filter1d(channel_data_bp_filtered,
sigma=sigma_value_2)

plt.title("Gaussian filter, Channel " + str(channel+1))
plt.plot(channel_data_bp_filtered, label='Data before Gaussian filter')
plt.plot(channel_data_gauss_window_1, label='Data after Gaussian filter
(sigma='+str(sigma_value_1)+")")
plt.plot(channel_data_gauss_window_2, label='Data after Gaussian filter
(sigma='+str(sigma_value_2)+")")
```

Implementation result of the Gaussian filter via Matplotlib library is shown in Fig. 5.2.

The plot demonstrates the effect of Gaussian smoothing with two different sigma values on EEG data. A larger sigma value ($\sigma = 45$) produces a strongly smoothed signal, effectively reducing high-frequency noise but also attenuating signal peaks and fine details. A smaller sigma value ($\sigma = 15$) provides moderate smoothing, retaining more of the original signal's rapid fluctuations while still reducing noise. This highlights the trade-off between noise suppression and signal detail preservation when selecting the Gaussian filter's sigma parameter.

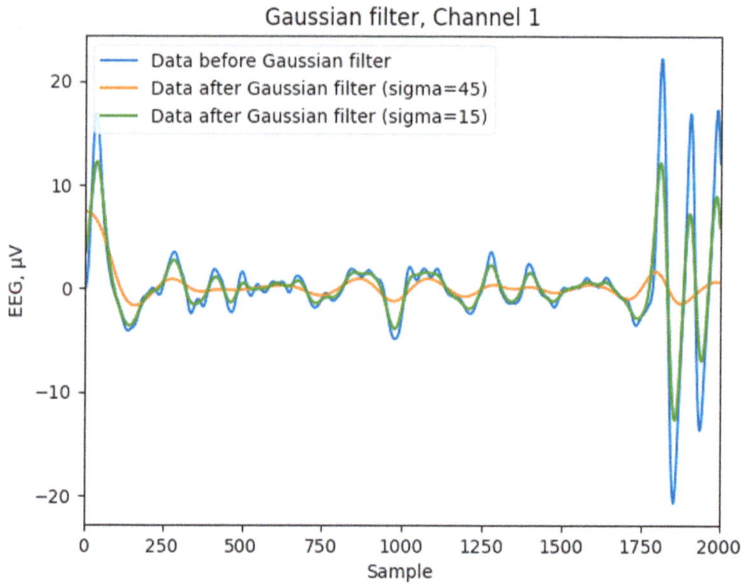

Fig. 5.2 Example of Gaussian filter

5.3 Median Filter

Using the median filter for EEG data is another signal processing technique that can be useful for denoising and removing outliers. The median filter replaces each data point with the median value within its neighboring window, which is effective in reducing random noise while preserving sharp edges or features in the signal [8, 9].

Positive

- Artifact Removal: Median filters are effective in removing transient artifacts, such as spikes and sharp fluctuations, caused by muscle activity or electrode movement. They're particularly adept at preserving the integrity of the original signal during artifact removal.
- Impulsive Noise: EEG recordings can be affected by impulsive noise that causes isolated extreme values. Median filters are excellent at suppressing these isolated outliers without altering the rest of the signal.
- Preserving Features: Unlike some smoothing filters, median filters do not excessively blur or distort sharp features such as event-related potentials (ERPs) or transient neural responses.
- Baseline Correction: Median filters can be used for baseline correction, especially in cases where the baseline exhibits sudden variations [9, 10].

Negative

- Smoothing: Median filters are not well-suited for smoothing continuous, gradual changes in EEG signals. They are designed to remove isolated outliers and sharp transients, so they may not effectively address slowly varying noise or baseline drift.
- Frequency-Specific Analysis: Median filters are not frequency-selective like band-pass filters. If you are specifically interested in analyzing frequency components of the EEG signal, using a median filter could distort these components.
- Event-Related Potentials (ERPs): While median filters can preserve sharp features, they might not be suitable for enhancing ERPs, as ERPs often require specialized preprocessing methods that maintain the temporal integrity of the responses.
- Signal Distortion: Median filters can cause signal distortion, especially if the filter's window size is too large. This distortion can impact the shape and timing of certain EEG components.
- Edge Effects: Median filters can introduce artifacts at the edges of the data, affecting the beginning and end of the filtered signal. Proper handling of these edge effects is essential.
- Baseline Drift: Median filters might not effectively remove slow baseline drifts, which require different techniques such as polynomial fitting or high-pass filtering.
- Non-Impulsive Noise: Median filters are most effective against impulsive noise. If the noise in your EEG signal is not primarily impulsive, other filtering methods might be more appropriate [9, 10].

A median filter for EEG works by replacing each data point in the signal with the median value of neighboring data points within a defined window. This process effectively reduces isolated spikes, impulsive noise, and sharp transients in the signal while preserving the integrity of sharp features.

- Window Selection: The filter defines a neighborhood (window) around each pixel or data point.
- Value Collection: It collects all values within this window.
- Sorting: The collected values are arranged in numerical order [10].

Belong provides a Python implementation via the same SciPy library. In the given script, size_window_1 = 100 defines the size of the window for the median filter operation applied to channel_data_bp_filtered. This value is used as the size parameter in the ndimage.median_filter() function. The median filter with a window size of 100 will:

- Consider a window of 100 adjacent elements in the input array.
- Calculate the median value of those 100 elements.
- Replace the central element with the calculated median.
- Slide the window over the entire array, repeating steps 1 through 3.

A larger window size (100 in this case) results in more smoothing of the data compared to the smaller window size (10) used for size_window. This allows for control over the "smoothness" of the filtered data, with larger windows producing a more heavily smoothed output.

```
from scipy import ndimage
# --- Parameters controlling the "smoothness" of the signal —
# The 'size' parameter defines the size of the sliding window for the median filter.
# Larger size = stronger smoothing (more noise removal), but more distortion of
sharp features.
size_window_1 = 100  # Strong smoothing (large median filter window)
size_window_2 = 10   # Moderate smoothing (smaller median filter window)
# --- Apply median filtering with different window sizes —
# Median filtering is useful for removing impulsive noise (spikes) while
preserving edges.
channel_data_median_window_1 =
ndimage.median_filter(channel_data_bp_filtered, size=size_window_1)  # size It
defines the size of the window for the median filter operation
Channel_data_median_window_2 =
ndimage.median_filter(channel_data_bp_filtered, size=size_window_2)
# plot the data
plt.title("Median filter, Channel " +  str(channel+1))
plt.xlabel("Sample")
plt.ylabel('EEG, μV')
plt.plot(channel_data_bp_filtered, label='Data before median filter')
# After median filter with large window size
plt.plot(channel_data_median_window_1, label='Data after median filter
(size='+str(size_window_1)+")")
# After median filter with small window size
plt.plot(channel_data_median_window_2, label='Data after median filter
(size='+str(size_window_2)+")")
plt.legend(loc='upper left')
plt.xlim([0, 2000])  # zoom in the data
plt.show()
```

Implementation of the Median filter via the Matplotlib library is shown in Fig. 5.3.

A larger window size (size = 100) produces a significantly stronger smoothing effect, effectively removing high-frequency fluctuations and transient spikes, but also flattening sections of the signal, which may reduce important details. A smaller

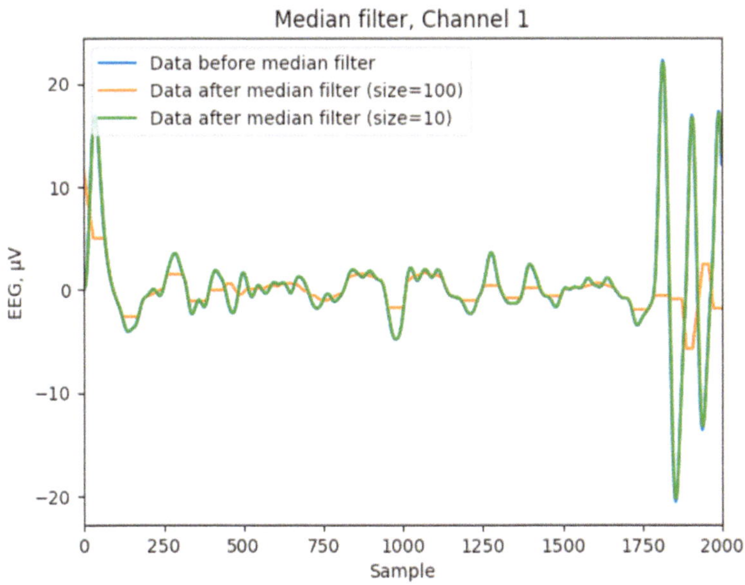

Fig. 5.3 Example of Median filter

window size (size = 10) applies milder smoothing, retaining more of the original waveform dynamics while still reducing short-duration noise. Median filtering is especially effective in suppressing impulsive artifacts without overly distorting signal edges; however, selecting the window size requires balancing noise removal with signal preservation.

5.4 Conclusion

This chapter has explored the fundamental concepts of noise reduction in EEG signals using three standard filtering techniques: (i) average, (ii) Gaussian, and (iii) median filters. We have demonstrated how to implement these filters in Python using simple examples and explained their strengths and weaknesses in handling different types of noise.

The average filter, while simple and computationally efficient, can introduce significant signal distortion, particularly for high-frequency components. The Gaussian filter, on the other hand, provides a smoother filtering effect by weighing neighboring data points based on a Gaussian distribution. This approach effectively reduces noise while preserving signal features. However, the Gaussian filter can still blur sharp transients in the EEG signal. The median filter, a non-linear technique, excels at removing impulsive noise, such as spikes and artifacts, while preserving signal edges. This makes it particularly valuable for cleaning EEG data contaminated by sudden disturbances.

In conclusion, the choice of filter depends heavily on the specific characteristics of the EEG data and the type of noise present. By understanding the principles and practical implementation of these filtering techniques, researchers and practitioners can effectively preprocess EEG signals, improving the accuracy and reliability of subsequent analyses, such as ERPs, BCIs, and clinical diagnostics.

References

1. Einicke G (2012) Smoothing, filtering and prediction: estimating the past, present and future. BoD–Books on Demand
2. Youlian Z, Cheng H (2011) An improved median filtering algorithm combined with average filtering. In: 2011 Third international conference on measuring technology and mechatronics automation. IEEE, pp 420–423
3. Zaini H, Alqadi Z (2023) Improving average and median filters. Int J Comput Sci Mob Comput 12(2):1–13
4. Boudet S, Peyrodie L, Forzy G, Pinti A, Toumi H, Gallois P (2012) Improvements of adaptive filtering by optimal projection to filter different artifact types on long duration EEG recordings. Comput Methods Programs Biomed 108(1):234–249
5. Tsuchimoto S, Shibusawa S, Iwama S, Hayashi M, Okuyama K, Mizuguchi N et al (2021) Use of common average reference and large-Laplacian spatial-filters enhances EEG signal-to-noise ratios in intrinsic sensorimotor activity. J Neurosci Methods 353:109089
6. Roy V, Shukla S, Shukla PK, Rawat P (2017) Gaussian elimination-based novel canonical correlation analysis method for EEG motion artifact removal. J Healthc Eng 2017(1):9674712
7. Harishvijey A, Raja JB (2022) Automated technique for EEG signal processing to detect seizure with optimized variable Gaussian filter and fuzzy RBFELM classifier. Biomed Signal Process Control 74:103450
8. Kawala-Sterniuk A, Podpora M, Pelc M, Blaszczyszyn M, Gorzelanczyk EJ, Martinek R, Ozana S (2020) Comparison of smoothing filters in analysis of EEG data for the medical diagnostics purposes. Sensors 20(3):807
9. Lyakhov PA, Kialdze MR, Kaplun DI, Voznesensky AS (2021) Removal of ocular artifacts from the electroencephalogram signal flow using median filtering. In: 2021 International conference automatics and informatics (ICAI). IEEE, pp 97–100
10. McFarland DJ, McCane LM, David SV, Wolpaw JR (1997) Spatial filter selection for EEG-based communication. Electroencephalogr Clin Neurophysiol 103(3):386–394

Chapter 6
Frequency Analysis

Frequency analysis for EEG is a fundamental technique that unveils the distribution of different frequency components within the brain's electrical activity [1]. This analysis involves transforming EEG signals from the time domain to the frequency domain, typically using the Fast Fourier Transform (FFT) algorithm. This transformation allows us to observe the intensity and prevalence of specific frequency bands, such as delta (0.5–4 Hz), theta (4–8 Hz), alpha (8–13 Hz), beta (13–30 Hz), and gamma (30–100 Hz) waves [2, 3].

Each frequency band corresponds to distinct neural processes and cognitive states. For instance, delta waves are associated with deep sleep and unconsciousness, while alpha waves often indicate a state of relaxed wakefulness. Beta waves are associated with active cognition and alertness, while gamma waves are connected to high-level information processing. Frequency analysis helps identify anomalies or irregularities in these patterns, aiding in the diagnosis of neurological conditions like epilepsy, sleep disorders, and cognitive impairments [3, 4].

6.1 Fast Fourier Transform (FFT)

FFT is a widely used method in signal processing and is particularly valuable in the field of neurophysiology for studying the frequency components present in EEG signals [5].

Positive

- **Frequency Representation**: EEG signals comprise complex patterns of neural oscillations at different frequencies. FFT breaks down these signals into their constituent frequency components, revealing the dominant frequencies present in the data.

I. Rakhmatulin and G. R. Naik, *EEG Signal Processing with Python*, Brain Informatics and Health, https://doi.org/10.1007/978-981-95-4177-5_6

- **Feature Extraction**: FFT generates a frequency spectrum that can be used for feature extraction. Different frequency bands (delta, theta, alpha, beta, gamma) are associated with distinct cognitive and neural processes, enabling the extraction of relevant features for analysis.
- **Brain Rhythms**: EEG signals are characterized by rhythmic patterns that are linked to specific brain functions. FFT enables the identification and quantification of these rhythmic components, aiding in the study of brain states and processes.
- **Event-Related Potentials (ERPs)**: FFT can be applied to segmented EEG epochs to examine event-related potentials, revealing time-locked neural responses to specific stimuli or events in the frequency domain.
- **Spectral Analysis**: The FFT provides power spectral density estimates, helping to analyze the distribution of signal power across different frequency bands and their variations over time or under various experimental conditions.
- **Artifact Detection**: FFT can help in detecting and addressing artifacts in EEG data. Artifacts often appear as broadband frequency components, making them distinguishable from genuine neural oscillations.
- **Temporal Resolution**: While EEG has excellent temporal resolution, it lacks frequency-specific information. FFT adds frequency specificity while preserving the time information, offering a comprehensive view of EEG signals [6, 7].

Negative

- **Temporal Resolution**: FFT sacrifices temporal resolution to provide frequency information. This can result in a loss of information regarding rapid changes and dynamic interactions between neural oscillations, which are essential for understanding certain cognitive processes.
- **Frequency Leakage**: FFT assumes that signals are periodic and stationary, which may not hold true for EEG data. This can result in "frequency leakage," where spectral energy can spread across adjacent frequency bins, making it challenging to isolate specific frequency components accurately.
- **Windowing Effects**: Applying FFT to short segments of EEG data, a common practice for event-related analysis, introduces windowing effects that can distort frequency representations, particularly for high-frequency oscillations.
- **Non-Stationarity**: EEG signals can exhibit non-stationarity, where frequency content changes over time. FFT assumes stationary signals, which can lead to misinterpretations of dynamic changes in neural activity.
- **Artifact Influence**: EEG signals often contain artifacts (e.g., eye blinks, muscle activity) that can introduce spurious frequency components, potentially compromising the accuracy of the analysis. FFT might not effectively separate these artifacts from genuine neural oscillations.
- **Choosing Frequency Bands**: Dividing EEG signals into predefined frequency bands using FFT might not capture individual variability in frequency ranges and can lead to arbitrary or oversimplified interpretations [6, 7].

FFT is a mathematical algorithm that converts time-domain EEG signals into the frequency domain. It does this by breaking down the EEG data into its constituent sinusoidal frequency components, revealing the strength of each frequency's presence in the signal. This process helps identify dominant frequencies and their distribution, offering insights into the underlying neural oscillations present in the EEG data [6, 7].

Below, we provide a Python implementation of FFT using the NumPy library. We should also mention the Nyquist frequency, which is half the sampling rate (fps/2) and represents the highest frequency that can be accurately captured without aliasing. In our code, we keep only the first half of the FFT output, corresponding to frequencies from 0 Hz up to the Nyquist limit.

```
data_len = len(data_filtered)                # detect length for the EEG data
fourier_transform = np.fft.fft(data_filtered) # compute FFT
fourier_transform = fourier_transform / data_len # normalize values
fourier_transform = fourier_transform[:int(data_len/2)] # take half of the data
time_period = data_len / fps                 # time period of the signal
values = np.arange(int(data_len/2)) # x-axis values up to Nyquist frequency
frequencies = values / time_period # x-axis values in Hz

# plot the frequency spectrum
plt.plot(frequencies, abs(fourier_transform))
plt.title("Frequency spectrum, Channel " + str(channel+1))
plt.xlabel('Frequency (Hz)')
plt.ylabel('Amplitude')
plt.xlim([0, 20])
plt.show()
```

Implementation of the FFT via the Matplotlib library is shown in Fig. 6.1.

The figure clearly illustrates the significance of various frequency ranges in EEG signal analysis. This delineation is crucial for interpreting brain states and conducting frequency-based assessments. By mapping specific frequency bands to their corresponding neurophysiological meanings, researchers and clinicians can gain valuable insights into brain activity and cognitive processes. This frequency-to-function correlation is particularly vital when performing spectral analysis of EEG data, enabling more precise identification of mental states, sleep stages, and potential neurological conditions.

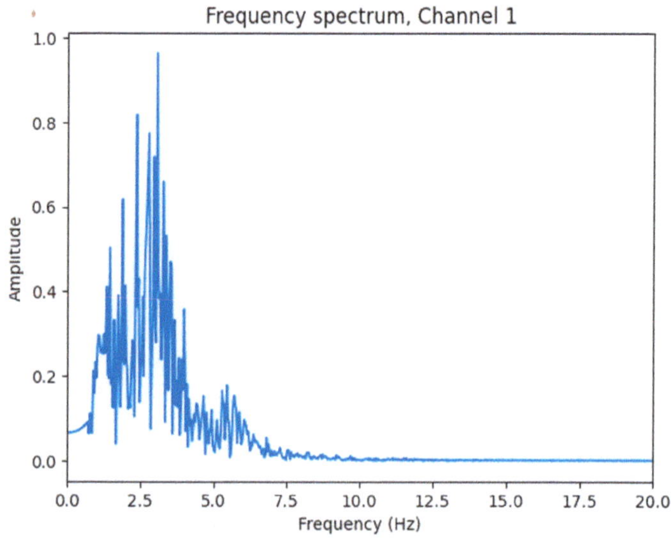

Fig. 6.1 Implementation of the FFT via the Matplotlib library

6.2 Wavelet Transform

Wavelet transform is another useful technique for dimensionality reduction in EEG data. It is particularly effective when applied to time-frequency analysis, allowing the extraction of relevant time-frequency features from EEG signals [8, 9].

Positive

- **Multiresolution Analysis**: Wavelet transform decomposes EEG signals into different scales, revealing details at various levels. This enables a selective representation of signal components, effectively highlighting relevant patterns while minimizing noise.
- **Adaptation to Non-Stationarity**: EEG signals often exhibit non-stationarity, with frequency characteristics changing over time. Wavelet's variable-sized window can adapt to these changes, ensuring accurate representation of dynamic neural processes.
- **Sparse Representation**: In wavelet decomposition, only a subset of coefficients is significant, resulting in a sparse representation. This sparsity can be leveraged for efficient dimensionality reduction while preserving essential signal characteristics.
- **Visualization**: Wavelet scalograms offer a visual representation of time-frequency dynamics, facilitating the identification of patterns and changes in neural oscillations [8, 9].

Negative

- **Feature Extraction Overload**: Wavelet coefficients generated from different scales can result in many features. If not managed carefully, this abundance of features can lead to overfitting and reduced interpretability.
- **Subjectivity in Wavelet Selection**: The choice of wavelet function and decomposition levels can be subjective and influence the outcomes. Different decisions might yield varying results, leading to difficulties in reproducibility.
- **Loss of Temporal Detail**: While the Wavelet transform captures time-frequency information, it might not retain fine-grained temporal details as effectively as time-domain methods. This could be a limitation when preserving precise timing is crucial.
- **Non-Linear Relationships**: The Wavelet transform assumes linear relationships between different scales and levels of EEG data, which may not hold true in all cases. This could lead to the oversimplification of complex neural interactions.
- **Choice of Scaling Functions**: Different wavelet functions are suited for different types of signals. Selecting an inappropriate wavelet could result in a poor representation of the EEG data, leading to suboptimal dimensionality reduction [8, 9].

The wavelet transform is a mathematical technique that analyses EEG data by decomposing it into different frequency components over time. It involves using a set of wavelet functions, which are like filters of varying scales, to capture both the time and frequency characteristics of the data. By applying these wavelets, the original EEG signal is transformed into a representation where different scales reveal different frequency information. This approach helps understand how frequencies change over time, which is essential in capturing the dynamic nature of EEG signals [10].

Below, we explain Python implementation of Wavelet via the PyWavelets (pywt), a free and open-source library for wavelet transforms in Python. In our code, db4 refers to the Daubechies 4 wavelet, which is one of the wavelet types provided by the PyWavelets (pywt) library.

Daubechies wavelets are a family of orthogonal wavelets, known for having good time-frequency localization. The "4" means it uses 4 coefficients in its filter, which gives it a specific shape and smoothness. With level = 3, for wavelet decomposition, how many times to recursively break the signal into approximation (low-frequency) and detail (high-frequency) components.

```
# define wavelet function and decomposition level
wavelet = 'db4'  #Daubechies wavelet
level = 3        # Number of recursively interrupted
# perform wavelet decomposition
coeffs = pywt.wavedec(channel_data_bp_filtered, wavelet, level=level)
# plot wavelet coefficients
fig, axs = plt.subplots(level+1, 1, figsize=(12, 6))
# plot approximation coefficients
axs[0].plot(coeffs[0], 'g')
axs[3].set_ylabel('Amplitude')
# Plot detail coefficients (higher-frequency components at each level)
for i, detail_coeffs in enumerate(coeffs[1:]):
    axs[i+1].plot(detail_coeffs, 'b')
axs[-1].set_xlabel('Sample')
plt.tight_layout()
plt.show()
```

Implementation of Wavelet via the PyWavelets is shown in Fig. 6.2.

The figure illustrates that the wavelet transform is highly effective in reducing the dimensionality of EEG data. This capability is particularly valuable in various EEG analysis applications. By compressing complex, high-dimensional EEG signals into more manageable representations, the wavelet transform facilitates more efficient data processing and analysis. This dimensionality reduction not only saves computational resources but also helps extract key features from EEG data, potentially improving the accuracy of subsequent analyses or classifications. This efficiency is crucial in both research settings and real-time EEG monitoring scenarios, where large volumes of neurophysiological data must be processed quickly.

6.3 Hilbert Transform

The Hilbert transform is a signal processing technique used to compute the analytic signal of a real-valued time-domain signal. The analytic signal provides the amplitude and instantaneous phase information of the original signal. The Hilbert transform is commonly used in EEG (Electroencephalography) data analysis to obtain the instantaneous phase and amplitude of brain oscillations, particularly in the context of time-frequency analysis [11].

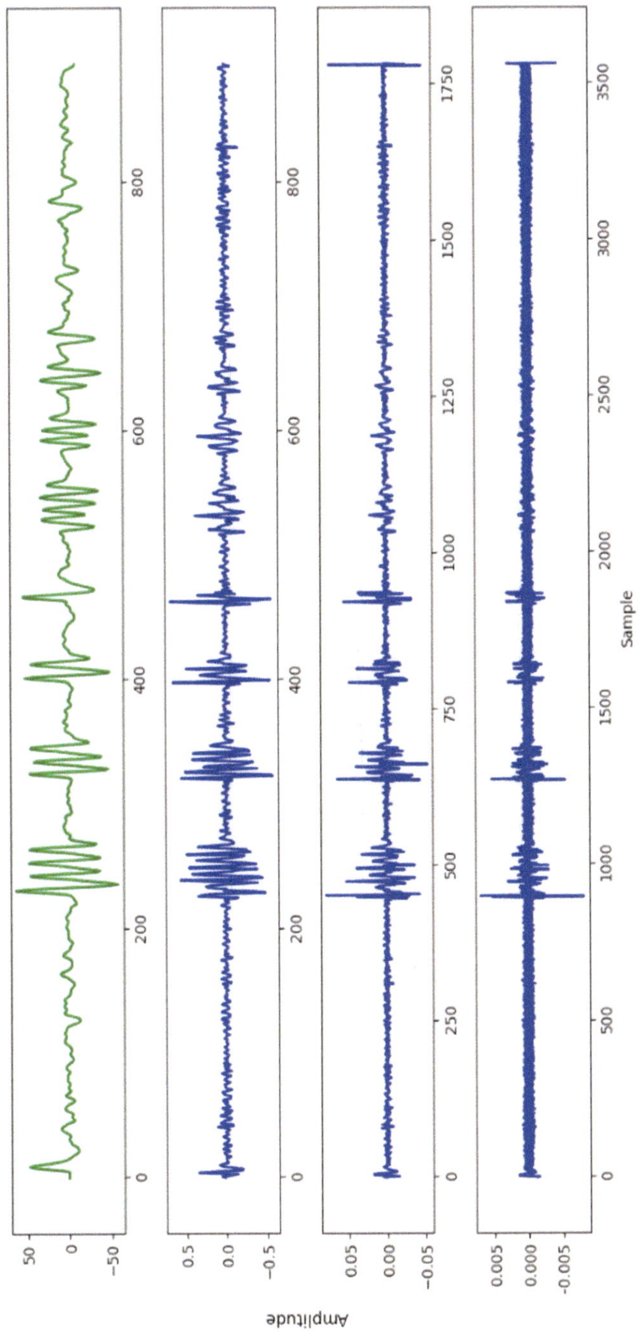

Fig. 6.2 Example of Wavelet transform via the PyWavelets

Positive

- **Time-Frequency Analysis**: EEG signals often contain oscillatory components that vary in amplitude and frequency over time. The Hilbert transform can be used to compute the instantaneous amplitude and phase of these oscillations at each time point, enabling detailed time-frequency analysis of brain activity.
- **Phase-Amplitude Coupling**: The Hilbert transform can uncover relationships between the phase of one frequency band and the amplitude of another. This is useful for investigating phase-amplitude coupling, which is implicated in various cognitive functions and neuronal communication.
- **Cross-Frequency Coupling**: EEG signals frequently exhibit interactions between different frequency bands, a phenomenon known as cross-frequency coupling. The Hilbert transform facilitates the quantification of these interactions, shedding light on the complex neural dynamics.
- **Improved Signal Interpretation**: Extracting the instantaneous phase can help differentiate between phase-locked and non-phase-locked components in EEG data, enhancing the interpretation of neural responses.
- **Connectivity Analysis**: The Hilbert transform is a fundamental tool for connectivity analysis, enabling the assessment of functional connectivity between brain regions by comparing phase relationships across electrodes [12, 13].

Negative

- **Filtering Artifacts**: Applying filters before the Hilbert transform can introduce phase distortion and affect the accuracy of the extracted phase information. The choice of filter parameters and the potential introduction of filter artifacts should be carefully considered.
- **Phase Ambiguity**: The Hilbert transform fails to differentiate between positive and negative phase angles, resulting in phase ambiguity. This can affect interpretations of phase relationships, particularly when analyzing cross-frequency coupling.
- **Amplitude Modulation**: The Hilbert transform assumes a sinusoidal waveform for the signal, which may not accurately capture complex waveform shapes, including amplitude modulations that are present in some EEG components.
- **Low Signal-to-Noise Ratio**: The Hilbert transform can be sensitive to noise and artifacts in EEG data. When the signal-to-noise ratio is low, extracted phase and amplitude information might be unreliable or biased.
- **Frequency Mixing**: The Hilbert transform assumes that the signal consists of a single dominant frequency. When multiple frequency components are present, the Hilbert transform can mix their phase and amplitude information, leading to inaccuracies.
- **Time Smoothing**: Applying the Hilbert transform inherently involves a degree of time smoothing, which can obscure rapid changes in the data and potentially mask important transient neural events [12, 13].

The Hilbert transform is a mathematical technique used in EEG analysis to extract time-varying amplitude and phase information from oscillatory signals. It transforms a real-valued signal into a complex signal by adding a 90-degree phase-shifted component. This complex representation enables the separation of amplitude and phase, facilitating tasks such as time-frequency analysis, phase-amplitude coupling, and connectivity studies [14, 15].

Belo, we explain the Python implementation of the Hilbert Transform via the SciPy library.

```
analytic_signal = scipy.signal.hilbert(channel_data_bp_filtered) # apply Hilbert
transform
amplitude_envelope = np.abs(analytic_signal) # compute amplitude envelope
# plot the amplitude envelope
plt.plot(amplitude_envelope)
plt.title("Hilbert Transform , Channel " + str(channel+1))
plt.ylabel('EEG, μV')
plt.xlabel('Sample')
plt.show()
```

Implementation of the Hilbert transform via the Matplotlib library in Fig. 6.3.

As observed in the image, applying the Hilbert transform to the EEG signal resulted in a significant change: the transformed signal now resides entirely in the

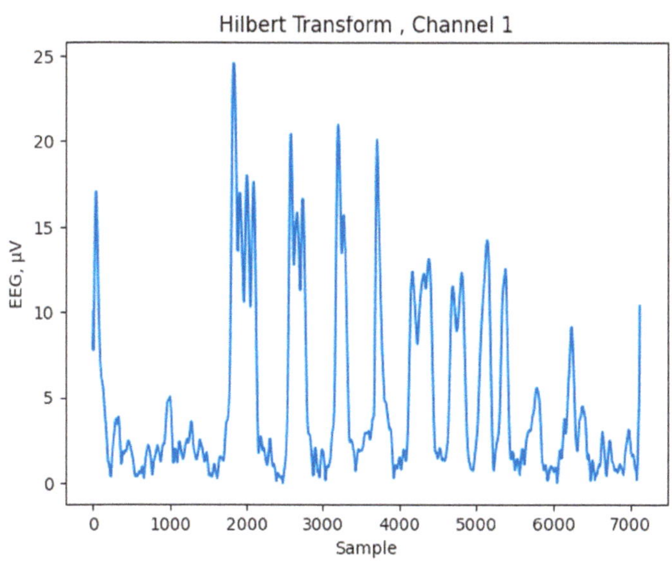

Fig. 6.3 Example of Hilbert transform

positive domain of the y-axis. This transformation offers several valuable applications and advantages in EEG signal analysis:

- **Envelope Detection**: The positive-only representation facilitates easier envelope detection of the EEG signal. This can be crucial for identifying overall amplitude trends and modulations in brain activity over time.
- **Instantaneous Frequency Analysis**: The Hilbert transform enables the calculation of instantaneous frequency, providing insights into moment-to-moment changes in the oscillatory behavior of brain waves.
- **Phase Information Extraction**: By converting the signal to its analytic form, the Hilbert transform enables the more straightforward extraction of phase information, which is vital for studying neural synchronization and communication between brain regions.
- **Visualization and Interpretation**: The positive-only nature of the transformed signal can make visual inspection and interpretation of EEG data more intuitive for researchers and clinicians.

6.4 Conclusion

This chapter explored key techniques for frequency analysis within the Python ecosystem. We began with the Fast Fourier Transform (FFT), implemented efficiently using the NumPy library. FFT excels at analyzing stationary signals, providing a comprehensive spectral representation. However, its fixed-resolution nature limits its ability to capture transient events effectively.

To address this limitation, we delved into Wavelet Transforms, implemented through the PyWavelets (pywt) library. Wavelets provide a multi-resolution framework, allowing for time-frequency localization and the identification of events with varying time scales. This flexibility makes them particularly valuable for analyzing non-stationary signals.

Finally, we examined the Hilbert Transform, leveraging the SciPy library for its implementation. The Hilbert Transform provides a powerful tool for analyzing the instantaneous frequency and amplitude of signals, enabling the characterization of time-varying spectral content.

This chapter has demonstrated the versatility of Python for frequency analysis. By combining the power of libraries like NumPy, PyWavelets, and SciPy, researchers and engineers can effectively analyze a wide range of signals, from simple audio signals to complex biomedical data. The choice of technique depends on the specific characteristics of the signal and the desired analysis goals.

References

1. Murugappan M, Rizon M, Nagarajan R, Yaacob S, Hazry D, Zunaidi I (2008) Time-frequency analysis of EEG signals for human emotion detection. In: 4th Kuala Lumpur international conference on biomedical engineering 2008: BIOMED, 25–28 June 2008. Springer, Kuala Lumpur, Malaysia, pp 262–265
2. Morales S, Bowers ME (2022) Time-frequency analysis methods and their application in developmental EEG data. Dev Cogn Neurosci 54:101067
3. Wagh KP, Vasanth K (2022) Performance evaluation of multi-channel electroencephalogram signal (EEG) based time frequency analysis for human emotion recognition. Biomed Signal Process Control 78:103966
4. Chiarion G, Sparacino L, Antonacci Y, Faes L, Mesin L (2023) Connectivity analysis in EEG data: a tutorial review of the state of the art and emerging trends. Bioengineering 10(3):372
5. Li M, Chen W (2021) FFT-based deep feature learning method for EEG classification. Biomed Signal Process Control 66:102492
6. Sanei S, Chambers JA (2013) EEG signal processing. Wiley
7. Díaz López JM, Curetti J, Meinardi VB, Farjreldines HD, Boyallian C (2025) FFT power relationships applied to EEG signal analysis: a meeting between visual analysis of EEG and its quantification. medRxiv. https://doi.org/10.1101/2025.03.14.25323563
8. Daud SNSS, Sudirman R (2022) Wavelet based filters for artifact elimination in electroencephalography signal: a review. Ann Biomed Eng 50(10):1271–1291
9. Grobbelaar M, Phadikar S, Ghaderpour E, Struck AF, Sinha N, Ghosh R, Ahmed MZI (2022) A survey on denoising techniques of electroencephalogram signals using wavelet transform. Signals 3(3):577–586
10. Khan DM, Masroor K, Jailani MFM, Yahya N, Yusoff MZ, Khan SM (2022) Development of wavelet coherence EEG as a biomarker for diagnosis of major depressive disorder. IEEE Sens J 22(5):4315–4325
11. Khare SK, Gaikwad NB, Bajaj V (2022) VHERS: a novel variational mode decomposition and Hilbert transform-based EEG rhythm separation for automatic ADHD detection. IEEE Trans Instrum Meas 71:1–10
12. Agarwal P, Kumar S (2024) EEG-based imagined words classification using Hilbert transform and deep networks. Multimed Tools Appl 83(1):2725–2748
13. Emara HM, Elwekeil M, Taha TE, El-Fishawy AS, El-Rabaie E-SM, Alotaiby T et al (2021) Hilbert transform and statistical analysis for channel selection and epileptic seizure prediction. Wirel Pers Commun 116:3371–3395
14. Liu C, Chen W, Zhang T (2023) Wavelet-Hilbert transform based bidirectional least squares grey transform and modified binary grey wolf optimization for the identification of epileptic EEGs. Biocybern Biomed Eng 43(2):442–462
15. Zheng J, Liang M, Sinha S, Ge L, Yu W, Ekstrom A, Hsieh F (2021) Time-frequency analysis of scalp EEG with Hilbert-Huang transform and deep learning. IEEE J Biomed Health Inform 26(4):1549–1559

Chapter 7
Navigating Noise: Strategies for EEG Artefact Removal

7.1 Biological Artefacts

The EEG signal, while providing valuable insights into brain activity through amplitude and frequency data, is often accompanied by undesirable components. These include various artifacts and noise that can obscure the underlying neural information. Effectively separating these unwanted elements from the genuine brain signals is crucial for accurate interpretation and analysis in neuroscience and clinical applications. Advanced signal processing techniques are typically employed to enhance the signal-to-noise ratio, allowing researchers and clinicians to extract meaningful data from the complex electrical patterns recorded by the EEG [1, 2].

Physiological artifacts in EEG refer to unwanted signals generated in the body that interfere with the measurement of brain activity. These artifacts can be caused by a variety of biological processes, such as eye movements, muscle activity, heart activity, and breathing [1, 2].

Eye movements, for example, can create artifacts in the EEG signal that resemble brain activity. Blinking, saccadic eye movements, and smooth pursuit eye movements are common sources of EEG artifacts. Figure 7.1 demonstrates blinking artifacts in EEG signals.

The next popular artifact is the jaw or making facial expressions, Fig. 7.2 shows a chewing artefact in order 4-3-2-1.

Cardiac activity, such as the electrical signals generated by the heartbeat, can also create artifacts in EEG recordings. These artifacts are usually rhythmic and can be removed by filtering out frequencies associated with the heart rate [3].

Respiration can also create artifacts in EEG recordings, especially if the subject is breathing heavily or irregularly [4]. To minimize physiological artifacts in EEG recordings, it is crucial to properly prepare the subject and carefully monitor their physiological signals during the recording. Post-processing techniques such as filtering and artifact suppression can also be used to remove physiological artifacts

I. Rakhmatulin and G. R. Naik, *EEG Signal Processing with Python*, Brain Informatics and Health, https://doi.org/10.1007/978-981-95-4177-5_7

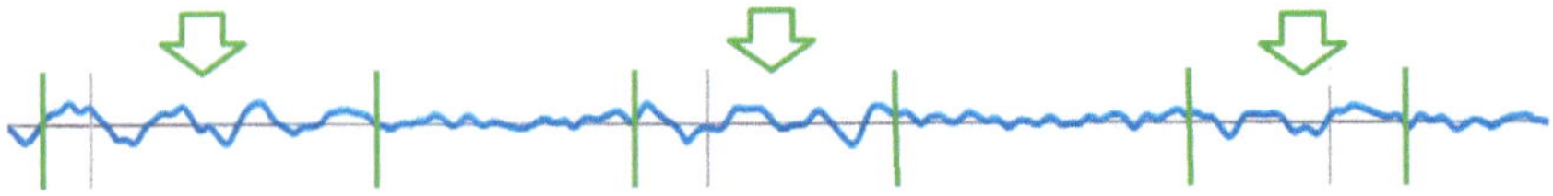

Fig. 7.1 Blinking artifacts in the EEG signal

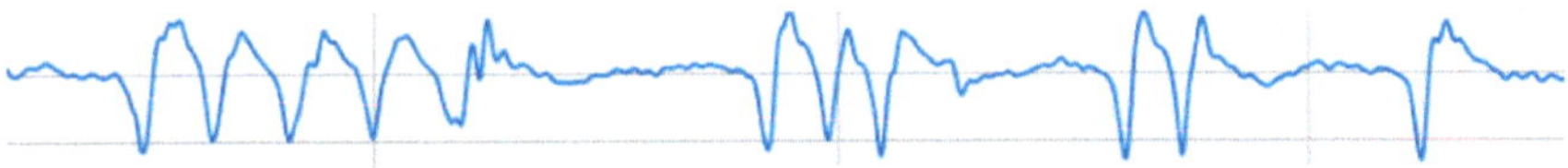

Fig. 7.2 Chewing artifacts in the EEG signal

from EEG recordings. However, it is crucial to carefully evaluate and interpret the data to ensure that any artifact removal does not remove valid brain activity [2, 5].

7.2 Electromagnetic Noise

We live in a world surrounded by electronic devices that generate electromagnetic fields (EMFs), which can significantly affect the quality of data recording. EMFs can induce interference in EEG signals through various mechanisms:

- **Induction of voltages**: Fluctuating magnetic fields from devices can induce voltages across stationary electrodes and cables used in EEG recordings. This induction can occur at the level of neurons, electrodes, and cables, potentially creating artifacts in the EEG data.
- **Electromagnetic interference (EMI)**: Electronic devices emit EMFs that can cause unwanted noise or interference in electrical paths or circuits8. This interference can affect the EEG signal, resulting in data corruption or misinterpretation of results.
- **Power line interference**: Common household appliances and power lines generate low-frequency (50 or 60 Hz) electromagnetic fields that can interfere with EEG recordings.
- **High-frequency radiation**: Electronic devices such as mobile phones, Wi-Fi routers, and other wireless technologies emit high-frequency electromagnetic radiation that can potentially affect EEG measurements.

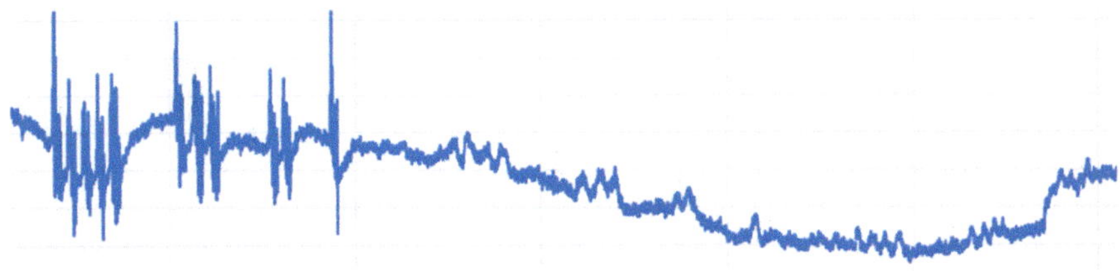

Fig. 7.3 50 Hz interference in the EEG signal

The EEG recording exhibits prominent 50 Hz interference, manifesting as a persistent, high-frequency oscillation superimposed on the underlying neural activity. This artifact is readily apparent in the graph, characterized by rapid, regular fluctuations that create a distinctive "sawtooth" pattern throughout the EEG trace [6]. The presence of this interference not only obscures the genuine neurophysiological signals but also potentially compromises the accuracy of subsequent data analysis and interpretation, underscoring the importance of implementing robust noise reduction techniques in EEG signal processing (Fig. 7.3).

For example, to avoid any electromagnetic noise, PiEEG has the following recommendations:

- Use as short an EEG electrode cable as possible.
- Position the device away from sources of disruptive noise such as computers, Wi-Fi routers, and phones.
- Ensure there's effective insulation between the device and its resting surface, such as a rubber mat or even a book.
- Ground contact with your feet can introduce noise; consider using foot insulation or avoiding contact with the floor during measurements or avoid using it altogether. Additionally, avoid using a metal stool.
- Body movements can generate artifacts; hence, electrodes need to establish good skin contact (without causing discomfort to the subject) and remain stationary.
- Applying gel can enhance the electrode-to-skin contact area; although unpleasant, it helps reduce noise from electrode micro-movements.
- Before starting the measurement, confirm that the connections between the electrodes and the skin are good. It is better not to corrupt data during measurement, as the band-pass filter takes time to adjust [7, 8].

7.3 Current Stage in Science

While numerous artifact removal techniques employing algorithms and machine learning exist, we advocate for algorithm-based approaches in EEG signal processing that do not rely on deep learning. This preference stems from the enhanced control and transparency they offer researchers, allowing for a more nuanced understanding of the processing steps. Algorithm-based methods also provide greater flexibility, enabling easier adjustments to accommodate new research objectives or varying recording conditions. The adaptability of these techniques is particularly valuable in the dynamic field of EEG analysis, where experimental protocols and data characteristics can differ significantly. Figure 7.4 illustrates several widely adopted algorithmic and learning algorithm methods for artifact removal in academic EEG research, highlighting their prevalence and effectiveness in addressing signal contamination issues.

Removing muscle artifacts from EEG (Electroencephalography) data is a critical preprocessing step to obtain clean and reliable brain signals. Physiological artifacts in EEG, a common issue in all EEG recordings, will be addressed in this chapter with a focus on eliminating blinking and chewing artifacts from EEG data. Next, we will consider practical methods for removing artifacts in practice.

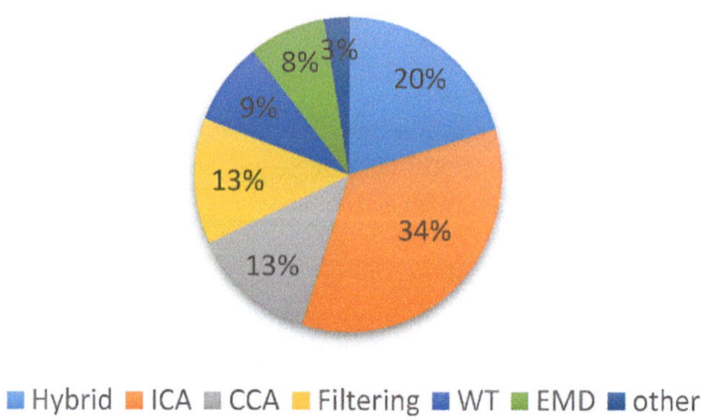

Fig. 7.4 A popular method for removing artifacts from EEG in the percentage of the number of references [2]

7.4 Independent Component Analysis (ICA)

Independent Component Analysis (ICA) is a widely used signal-processing technique for separating mixed sources in EEG data. It is beneficial for decomposing EEG signals into their underlying independent components, which can represent different brain sources or artifacts. ICA helps to remove artifacts and identify specific brain-related activity, making it an essential tool for EEG data analysis. Generally, this method works well for 32 channels and above. In our example, we use 8 channels, which allows us to more clearly demonstrate the basics of this method in practice [9].

Positive

- Statistical Independence: ICA is designed to decompose mixed signals into components that are statistically independent of each other. Muscle artifacts, which often have distinct temporal patterns and different frequency characteristics from neural signals, can be modeled as separate independent components.
- Multichannel Data: EEG signals are recorded from multiple channels, capturing spatially distributed neural and artifact sources. ICA's ability to simultaneously analyze multichannel data helps in separating spatially localized muscle artifacts.
- Unmixing Overlapping Sources: EEG signals are a mixture of various sources, including neural activity, noise, and artifacts. ICA can unmix these overlapping sources by identifying their unique statistical properties, effectively isolating the muscle artifacts.
- Adaptive Filtering: ICA adaptively identifies artifact sources without relying on predefined templates or assumptions about their characteristics. This makes it versatile and effective in capturing a wide range of muscle artifact patterns.
- Reduced Dependence on Reference Electrodes: Unlike methods that rely on reference electrodes, ICA does not require specific electrode placements or reference strategies. This makes it helpful for removing muscle artifacts even in scenarios where reference electrode placement might be suboptimal.
- Non-stationary Artifacts: Muscle artifacts can exhibit non-stationary characteristics, such as changes in amplitude or frequency. ICA's flexibility in capturing time-varying source patterns makes it suitable for removing such non-stationary artifacts.
- Enhanced Data Quality: By separating muscle artifacts from neural signals, ICA improves the overall quality of the EEG data, making subsequent analyses more accurate and reliable [10, 11].

Negative

- Assumption Violations: ICA assumes statistical independence of sources, which might not hold true for all types of artifacts. Muscle artifacts, in particular, can sometimes exhibit temporal or spectral correlations that violate this assumption.
- Modeling Complex Artifacts: Muscle artifacts can exhibit complex and variable patterns that the linear assumptions of ICA may not adequately capture. This can lead to incomplete removal or misidentification of artifact components.
- Source Mixing: EEG signals often arise from a mixture of neural, noise, and artifact sources. ICA can sometimes mix artifact components with neural sources, leading to challenges in isolating and removing artifacts without affecting neural signals.
- Lack of Gold Standard: There is no "gold standard" for verifying the accuracy of ICA-based artifact removal. Validation typically involves visual inspection and expert judgment, which can introduce subjectivity.
- Over- or Under-Removal: ICA may over-remove or under-remove artifact components depending on how well the assumptions align with the actual data. Over-removal can distort the underlying neural activity, while under-removal leaves artifacts in the data.
- Varying Muscle Patterns: Muscle artifacts can vary between individuals and sessions, and ICA might not generalize well across different datasets or recording conditions.
- Component Validation: Identifying which extracted components are truly artifact-related and which are neural can be challenging. Manual validation requires expertise and can be time-consuming.
- Additional Preprocessing Steps: ICA is often combined with other preprocessing steps, such as band-pass filtering and rejection of contaminated components. These steps introduce complexity and may create additional artifacts [10, 11].

A common example used to illustrate this method is a room full of people talking simultaneously. While we typically hear only the general noise, this method can isolate and extract each voice from the overall cacophony. Similarly, this approach can be applied to EEG data. ICA for removing muscle artifacts from EEG involves decomposing mixed EEG signals into statistically independent components. It identifies components that correspond to various sources, including muscle artifacts. By isolating and excluding these artifact-related components, ICA aims to enhance the quality of the EEG data, Fig. 7.5.

To begin, we visualize the data by displaying each channel with vertical offsets to separate them, setting tick marks and y-axis labels for clarity, and adding labels and a title to facilitate a clear presentation of the data before independent component analysis (ICA), Fig. 7.6.

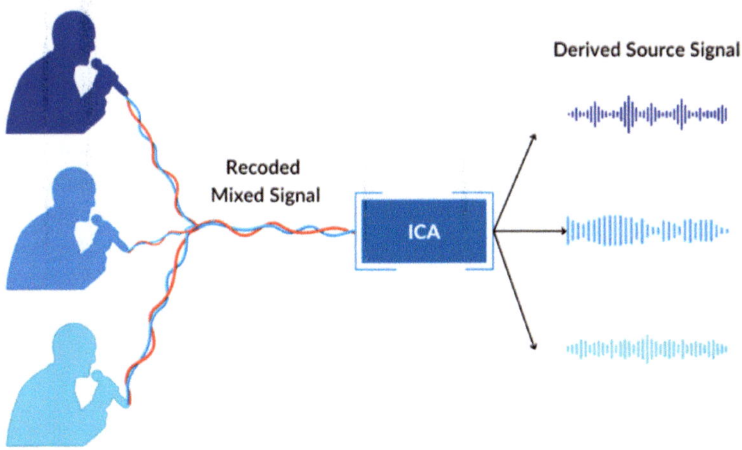

Fig. 7.5 Examples of ICA

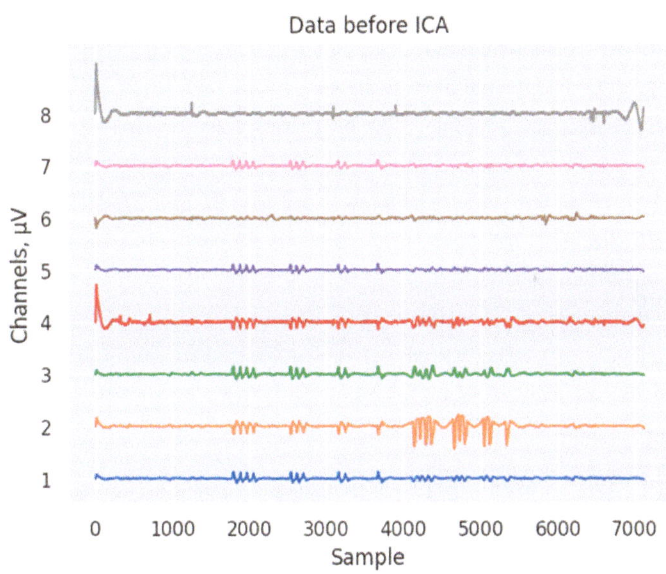

Fig. 7.6 EEG data before the implementation of the ICA method

The code first creates an instance of the FastICA class from the scikit-learn library, specifying the number of components to be extracted as 8. The fit method is then called on the data_bp_filtered data, which performs the ICA decomposition and learns the unmixing matrix. The transform method applies the learned unmixing matrix to the original data, resulting in the independent components stored in the components variable. Next, the code plots the independent components using plt.plot, with each element vertically offset by adding a constant value from the range(1, 1*n_channels+1, 1) sequence. This separation makes it easier to visualize the individual components.

The following script implements the ICA method using the open-source scikit-learn library and the FastICA method.

```
# Initialize the FastICA model to extract 8 independent components
ica=FastICA(n_components=8)
# Perform ICA: fit the model and transform the data in one step
out_ica=ica.fit_transform(eeg_data    )
# Alternatively: fit the ICA model first, then transform data separately
ica = FastICA(n_components=8)
ica.fit(data_after_band_pass_filter_reshape)
components = ica.transform(data_after_band_pass_filter_reshape)

offset = 5  # Adjust this value to increase or decrease the spacing
plt.figure(figsize=(12, 10))  # Increase figure size for better visibility
for i in range(8):
    plt.plot(components[:, i] + offset * i)
     plt.yticks(range(0, offset * 8, offset), range(0, 8))
plt.ylabel('Components, µV')
plt.xlabel('Sample')
plt.title('Components data')
plt.show()
```

Ultimately, we aim to obtain graphs (components) that will ideally contain only EEG signals and artifacts, such as those from wrinkling and chewing, as shown in Fig. 7.7.

After plotting the ICA components, we can visually inspect them to identify which contain EEG signals, noise, or artifacts. In this case, component 7 includes a chewing artifact. To remove it:

- We set all values in component 7 to 0, leaving the other components unchanged.
- We then call the inverse_transform method of the ICA object.

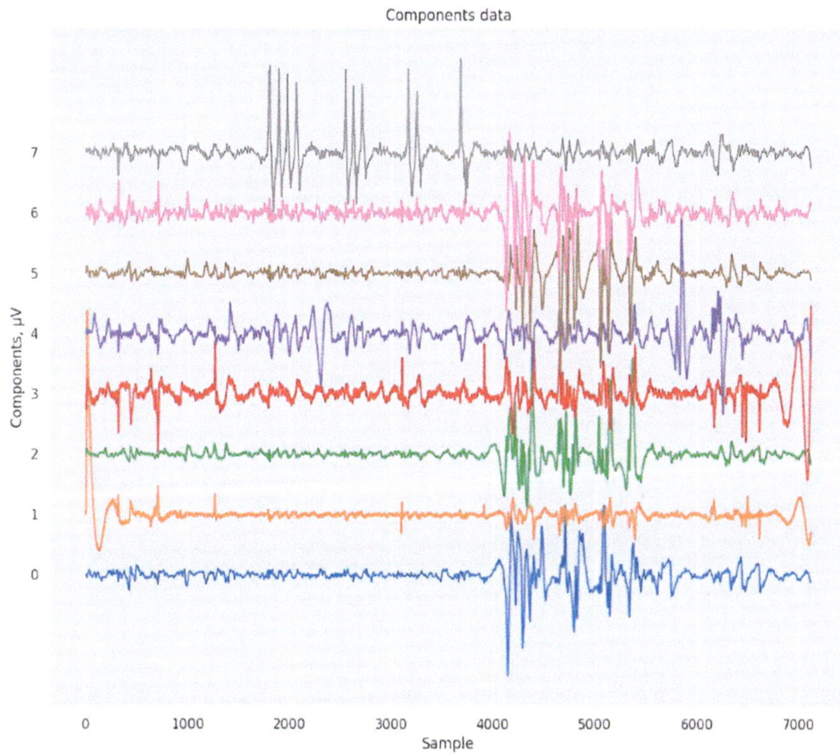

Fig. 7.7 Components after ICA method for 8 ch EEG data

- This reconstructs the EEG signal by applying the inverse of the ICA unmixing matrix.
- The reconstructed signal (stored in restored) is the original EEG with the chewing artifact removed.

Finally, we plot the restored EEG data:

- Each channel is vertically offset using values from the range (1000, 1000 * n_ channels + 1000, 1000) so that individual traces are separated and easier to interpret.

```
# remove all components except for the eye blink component (component 7     )
#components[:, 0] = 0
#components[:, 1] = 0
#components[:, 2] = 0
#components[:, 3] = 0
#components[:, 4] = 0
#components[:, 5] = 0
#components[:, 6] = 0
components[:, 7] = 0
# reconstruct EEG without blinks
restored = ica.inverse_transform(components)

plt.plot(restored + range(1000, 1000*n_channels+1000, 1000))
plt.yticks(range(1000, 1000*n_channels+1000, 1000), range(1, n_channels+1))
plt.ylabel('Channel')
plt.xlabel('Sample')
plt.title("Data after ICA")
plt.show()
```

Thus, we can now observe that the chewing artifact has been effectively removed.

The next one, as shown in Fig. 7.8, blinking artefacts are observed in the 6, 3, 2, 1, and 0 components. We need to modify only the parts with components as it was done before.

```
components[:, 0] = 0
components[:, 1] = 0
components[:, 2] = 0
components[:, 3] = 0
#components[:, 4] = 0
#components[:, 5] = 0
components[:, 6] = 0
#components[:, 7] = 0
```

Therefore, if we save only components 4 and 5, we can obtain the next result for channel 1, as shown in Fig. 7.9, with data before and after the implementation of the ICA method to remove artifacts.

As shown in Fig. 7.4, the following popular method is Canonical correlation analysis (CCA).

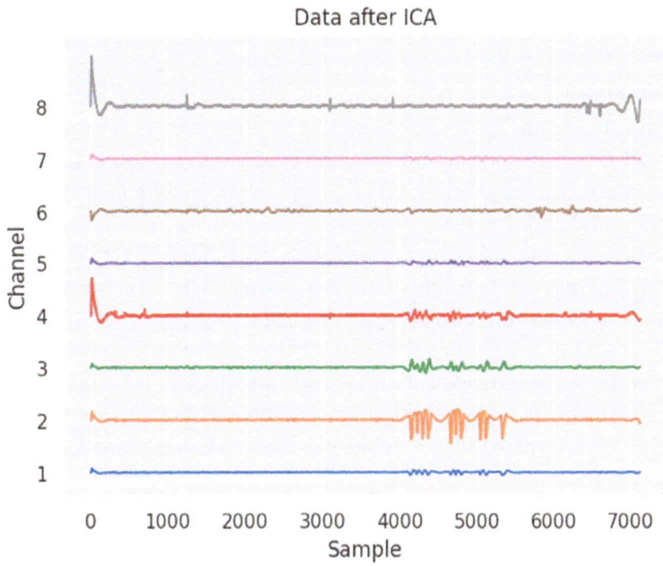

Fig. 7.8 EEG data after chewing artefacts from EEG data

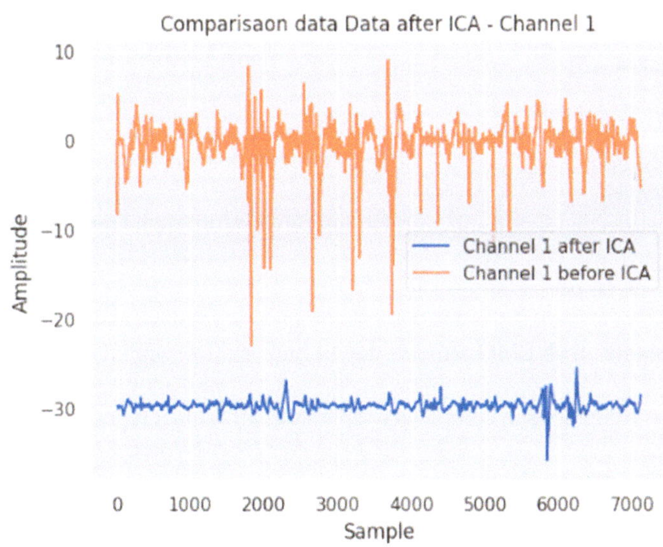

Fig. 7.9 Channel 1 before and after ICA method implementation

7.5 Canonical Correlation Analysis

Canonical correlation analysis (CCA) examines the relationship between two sets of variables, specifically the EEG signals and the artifact signals. The method assumes that the true EEG and artifacts are uncorrelated, enabling their separation. CCA transforms the original EEG data into a set of components that are maximally correlated with the artifact reference signals [12, 13].

The components that show high correlation with the artifact signals are identified as artifactual and can be removed or attenuated. After removing the artifactual components, the remaining components are used to reconstruct the cleaned EEG signal.

Independent component analysis (ICA) and canonical correlation analysis (CCA) are similar methods, as both are blind source separation methods used to remove artifacts from EEG signals [12, 13]. However, they differ in several key respects.

Effectiveness:

- ICA is more widely used, with approximately 45% of studies using it for artifact removal.
- CCA is particularly effective in reducing muscle artifacts due to its lower autocorrelation.
- CCA does not consistently outperform ICA in removing EMG, ocular, or cardiac artifacts [14, 15].

Algorithmic Approach:

- ICA decomposes signals into independent components to separate artifacts and brain signals.
- CCA focuses on identifying correlations between different signal components to remove artifacts [14, 15].

Challenges:

- ICA struggles with EMG artifacts due to high spatiotemporal overlap with EEG signals.
- CCA has limitations in completely separating all artifact types from brain signal [14, 16].

To implement the CCA method, a script can be used similarly to the ICA script, via the same library, sklearn, with the process in this case being CCA.

```
from sklearn.cross_decomposition import CCA
# Define the number of components to extract
n_components = 8 # Number of canonical variables to compute
# Initialize the CCA model with the specified number of components
cca = CCA(n_components=n_components)
# Fit the CCA model to the EEG data
# Here the same dataset is used for both X and Y (self-correlation),
# but typically CCA is used to find relationships between two different datasets
cca.fit(data_after_band_pass_filter_reshape, data_after_band_pass_filter_reshape)
```

The results for 8 channels are quite similar, so the choice of method will ultimately depend on the specific task requirements.

7.6 Empirical Mode Decomposition (EMD)

Empirical Mode Decomposition (EMD) is a data analysis method used to explore the intrinsic oscillatory components present in EEG signals. EMD decomposes a complex EEG time series into simpler components called Intrinsic Mode Functions (IMFs) based on the data itself, without requiring any predefined basis functions [17].

Positive

- Adaptive Decomposition: EMD adaptively decomposes a signal into a set of intrinsic mode functions (IMFs) based on the local characteristics of the signal. This is beneficial for handling muscle artifacts, as they can vary in amplitude and frequency over time.
- Localized Frequency Decomposition: Muscle artifacts often manifest as high-frequency oscillations in EEG signals. EMD's ability to decompose signals into IMFs with distinct frequency ranges can help separate the muscle-related components from the neural activity of interest.
- Separation of Components: EMD can effectively separate the different components present in the EEG signal, including muscle artifacts, neural activity, and other noise sources. This separation can aid in the selective removal of unwanted elements.
- Preservation of Temporal Features: EMD retains the temporal features of the original signal within each IMF, allowing it to capture both rapid and gradual changes caused by muscle artifacts.
- Non-Parametric Approach: EMD doesn't rely on predefined models or assumptions about the signal's structure, making it well-suited for handling the complex and non-stationary nature of muscle artifacts [18, 19].

Negative

- Mode Mixing: EMD can suffer from mode mixing, where the intrinsic mode functions (IMFs) obtained may not cleanly separate the muscle artifacts from the neural signals. This can lead to incomplete or inaccurate artifact removal.
- Complexity of EEG Signals: EEG signals are complex and encompass a range of neural activities across various frequency ranges. EMD might not always effectively distinguish between muscle artifacts and neural components, especially when they overlap in frequency.
- Baseline Wander: EMD might not handle baseline wander effectively, which is a common low-frequency artifact in EEG signals. This can impact the accuracy of artifact removal.
- Subjectivity in Decomposition: EMD requires the selection of stopping criteria for the decomposition process, and these choices can be somewhat subjective. This subjectivity can lead to variations in results between different researchers or datasets.
- Artifact Variability: Muscle artifacts can vary widely in terms of amplitude, frequency, and time duration. EMD's adaptability might not guarantee consistent artifact removal across different EEG recordings or individuals.
- Computational Complexity: EMD can be computationally intensive, especially for longer EEG recordings. This can limit its practicality for real-time or large-scale applications [18, 19].

In simple terms, EMD decomposes a signal into components called Intrinsic Mode Functions (IMFs) by identifying local maxima and minima, creating upper and lower envelopes via interpolation, and finding their average. The advantage of this method is its simplicity of implementation, which does not require large computational values, allowing for its use in real-time applications. Figure 7.10 show an example of how the EMD method works, where Raw data interpolation is performed for the upper peaks and the lower peaks of the raw data. The arithmetic mean of these peaks results in data that is less sensitive to artifacts. This approach reduces the amplitude component of the artifacts while preserving the frequency component of the raw signal [20]. This operation can be performed several times.

The first step of this method is finding the peaks, which can be done through the find_peaks method of the SciPy library, via the following script:

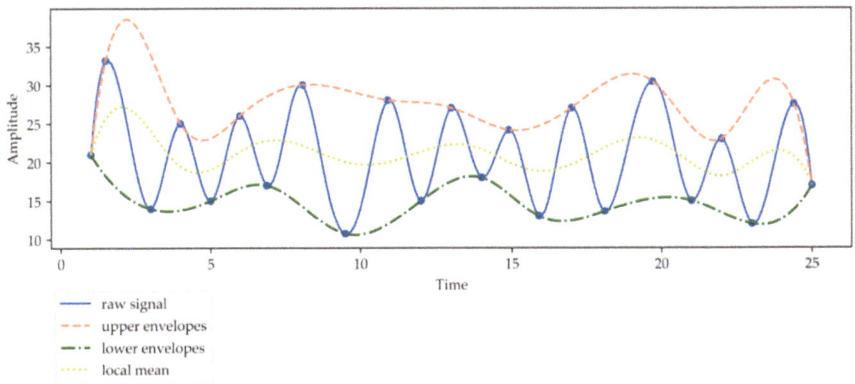

Fig. 7.10 Example of EMD method implementation

```
import numpy as np
import matplotlib.pyplot as plt
from scipy.signal import find_peaks

# Create some data (for example, a sine wave with noise)
x = np.linspace(0, 10, 100)
y = np.sin(x) + np.random.normal(0, 0.1, size=x.shape)

# Use scipy's find_peaks function
peaks, _ = find_peaks(y)
# Plotting the data
plt.plot(x, y, label='Data')
plt.plot(x[peaks], y[peaks], 'ro', label='Peaks')
plt.legend()
plt.show()
```

The visualization of the script is shown in Fig. 7.11.

After identifying the peaks and gathering the necessary information, we can proceed to implement the EMD method. However, it is inefficient to apply the EMD method to all EEG data. A more effective approach is first to identify the positions of artifacts and then use the EMD method only within those specific time domains, leaving the clear EEG data untouched. One of the simple methods for identifying artifacts is K-Nearest Neighbors (KNN).

Fig. 7.11 Example of finding peaks in data

7.6.1 K-Nearest Neighbors (KNN) to Detect Artifacts in EEG Data

K-Nearest Neighbors (KNN) is a simple, yet robust supervised machine learning algorithm used for classification and regression tasks. It operates on the principle of similarity, predicting the label or value of a new data point by considering the labels or values of its K nearest neighbors in the training dataset [21].

The KNN algorithm works as follows:

- The algorithm stores the entire dataset without any initial training.
- When a new data point needs to be classified, KNN calculates the distance between this point and all existing data points in the dataset.
- It then selects the K nearest neighbors based on the calculated distances.
- For classification tasks, the algorithm assigns the most frequent class among the K neighbors to the new data point.
- For regression tasks, it predicts the average value of the K neighbors [22, 23].

In the context of detecting artifacts in EEG data, KNN can be applied as follows:

- Feature Extraction: Various features are extracted from EEG signals, such as root mean square (RMS), polynomial fitting, and Hjorth descriptors.
- Training Data: A dataset of EEG signals with labeled artifacts is used as the training set.
- Classification: When a new EEG segment needs to be classified, KNN calculates its distance to all training samples and identifies the K nearest neighbors. The segment is then classified as an artifact or clean EEG based on the majority class of these neighbors.

- Artifact Types: KNN has been successfully used to classify various types of EEG artifacts, including those related to facial muscle movements, eye blinks, and head movements [22, 23].

The implementation of KNN algorithm using the provided sklearn library is presented below:

```
from sklearn.preprocessing import StandardScaler
from sklearn.preprocessing import StandardScaler
from sklearn.cluster import Kmeans

EMD_data = eeg_data
 #Duplicate for visualization later
just_for_graph = data_for_wave = EMD_data
sc_X = StandardScaler()                          # Create a StandardScaler object
data_for_wave = data_for_wave.reshape(-1,1) # Reshape into 2D array (samples,
features)
scaler = sc_X.fit_transform(data_for_wave)      # Scale to zero mean and unit
variance

# Keep the scaled values in a simple list for plotting
scaler_wave = []
for a in scaler:
   scaler_wave.append(a[0])
# Apply K-Means clustering
# n_clusters=2 because we want to separate "artifact" vs "clean" EEG
# init='k-means++' helps to speed up convergence
# max_iter=3 means the algorithm will only run 3 iterations (very fast, but not
very accurate)
# tol=1000.001 is an extremely loose tolerance (practically no early stopping)
# verbose=10 will print iteration details
# random_state=1 ensures reproducibility
# n_init=10 means run k-means 10 times with different initializations, keep the
best
# algorithm='elkan' is efficient for low-dimensional data

kmeans = KMeans(
   n_clusters=2, init='k-means++', max_iter=3, tol=1000.001,
   verbose=10, random_state=1, n_init=10,  copy_x=True,
```

```
    algorithm='elkan')   #algorithm= 'auto', 'full' or 'elkan
X = scaler          # Use standardized EEG data
kmeans.fit(X)  # Train K-Means model
y_kmeans = kmeans.predict(X) #Get cluster labels for each sample

plt.plot(scaler)
plt.plot(y_kmeans)
plt.legend(["EEG, μV","KNN to detect artefacts"])
plt.ylabel('EEG, μV')
plt.title("KNN to detact muscle artefacts, Channel " +str(channel + 1))
plt.xlabel('Sample')
plt.show()
```

As shown in Fig. 7.12, pronounced artifacts are identified with high accuracy. The orange line in an elevated position indicates the presence of an artifact.

In certain applications, particularly those involving real-time tasks, the execution time of a task is paramount. Consequently, understanding the implementation of methods without relying on external libraries can prove to be invaluable. Such knowledge ultimately empowers you to optimize program execution time and achieve notable speed enhancements. Here, we demonstrate how to use Empirical Mode Decomposition (EMD) to remove muscle artifacts without a high-level EMD library. This code estimates the baseline oscillatory structure of an EEG signal using

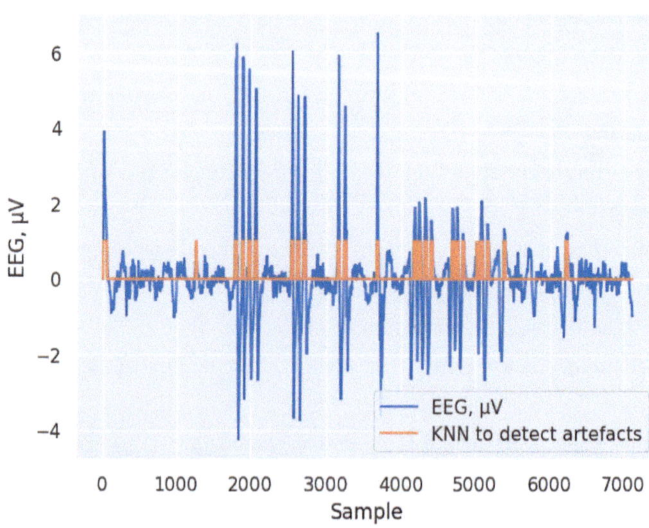

Fig. 7.12 KNN for detecting muscle artifacts in EEG

an envelope-averaging approach inspired by Empirical Mode Decomposition (EMD). First, it identifies all local maxima and minima in the bandpass-filtered EEG data. Then, it constructs smooth upper and lower envelopes by cubic interpolation through these peaks and valleys. The mean of these two envelopes represents the local baseline of the signal, isolating slow variations from faster oscillations. This baseline can be subtracted or analyzed to help separate intrinsic oscillatory components, detect trends, or prepare the data for further decomposition.

```
from scipy.interpolate import interp1d
from scipy.signal import find_peaks

# --------------------------------------------------

# 1. Detect peaks and valleys in the bandpass-filtered EEG data

# --------------------------------------------------

# 'high_peaks' are the local maxima in the EEG signal
high_peaks, _ = find_peaks(channel_data_bp_filtered)
# 'low_peaks' are the local minima (found by inverting the signal)
low_peaks, _ = find_peaks(-channel_data_bp_filtered)

# --------------------------------------------------

# 2. Create interpolation functions for the envelope curves
# --------------------------------------------------
# Interpolation for the high envelope (maxima curve)
# kind='cubic' produces a smooth spline interpolation
# fill_value="extrapolate" ensures values are generated outside the peak range

f_high = interp1d(high_peaks, channel_data_bp_filtered[high_peaks],
kind='cubic', fill_value="extrapolate")
# Create a new x-axis with 1-sample spacing
x_new = np.arange(0, len(channel_data_bp_filtered), 1)
# Compute the interpolated high envelope
y_high_inter = f_high(x_new)
```

```
# Interpolation for the low envelope (minima curve)
f_low = interp1d(low_peaks, channel_data_bp_filtered[low_peaks], kind='cubic',
fill_value="extrapolate")
 # Compute the interpolated low envelope
 y_low_inter = f_low(x_new)

# --------------------------------------------------

# 3. Calculate the mean envelope curve (similar to EMD)

# --------------------------------------------------

# 'EMD_Y is the average of the high and low envelopes
# In Empirical Mode Decomposition (EMD), this is used to extract intrinsic mode
functions
 EMD_Y = (y_high_inter + y_low_inter) / 2
plt.xlabel('Sample')
plt.plot(EMD_Y - 10)
plt.plot(channel_data_bp_filtered)
plt.legend(["After interpolation", "Before interpolation"])
plt.show()
```

Figure 7.13 shows all calculated values for a 100-sample segment, including the detected high peaks with their interpolated curve, and the detected low peaks with their interpolated curve. The blue line in the middle represents the original EEG data, the green line at the top is the interpolation through the high peaks, and the violet line at the bottom is the interpolation through the low peaks.

After this step, only the high and low interpolations are retained, and their average is calculated by summing the corresponding values and dividing them by two. The resulting waveform is shown in Fig. 7.14.

The raw signal, represented by the orange trace, exhibits large artefacts. After interpolation, the blue trace reflects a smoother signal with reduced peak amplitudes, indicating that high- and low-frequency disturbances have been effectively suppressed while the overall waveform structure is preserved, resulting in a cleaner and more reliable EEG signal for subsequent analysis.

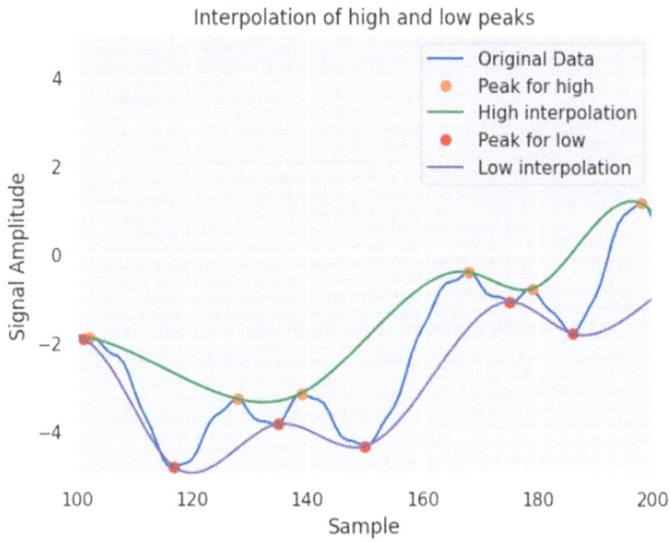

Fig. 7.13 Process of EMD method for EEG

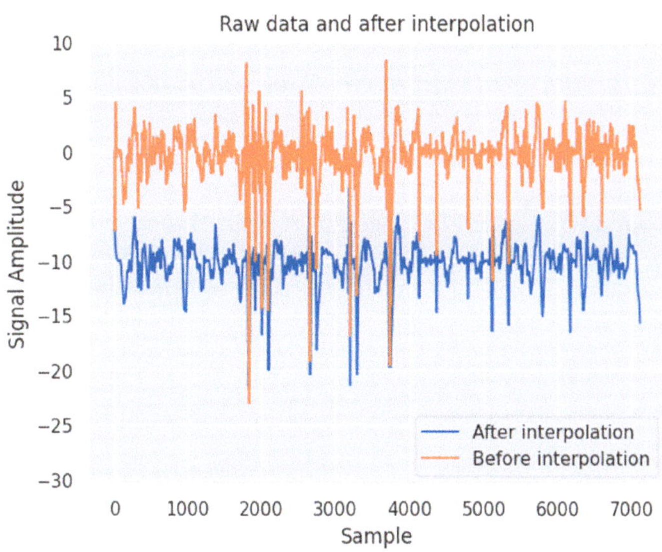

Fig. 7.14 Data EEG before and after implementation of EMD method

7.7 Evaluation of Artifact Removal

The challenge in removing artifacts lies not merely in eliminating the artifact itself, but in ensuring that valuable information within the EEG signal is preserved.

Therefore, artifact removal verification algorithms should always be used in conjunction with the artifact removal algorithm. Evaluation of artifact removal methods for EEG typically involves comparing the correlation between EEG signals and artifact-representing channels before and after applying removal algorithms. The effectiveness of a technique is quantified by the extent to which it reduces this correlation across different artifact-inflicting tasks [24, 25].

However, it is crucial to consider the frequency range in which your feature extraction operates and where your artifact falls.

For example, chewing and blinking typically occur in specific frequency ranges:

- Blinking frequency range: 0.5–3 Hz
- Chewing frequency range: 13–30 Hz 7.7.1 Evaluation via Fast Fourier Transform.

If your task involves stress control, which falls within the frequency range of 8–12 Hz, it is crucial to ensure that this range remains unaffected after artifact removal.

7.7.1 Evaluation via Fast Fourier Transform (FFT)

This script is designed to evaluate the effectiveness of artifact removal in time-series data by performing a Fast Fourier Transform (FFT) analysis on signals before and after the removal process for EEG data from a single channel, after the implementation of the EMD method. The primary objective is to visualize and compare the frequency spectra of the data, allowing for a clear assessment of the impact of artifact removal on signal integrity [26, 27].

```
import numpy as np
import matplotlib.pyplot as plt

sample_rate = 250  # Sampling rate in Hz
# Define a function to compute and plot the Fourier Transform (FFT) of a signal
def furie (data,channel):
   # Perform the Fast Fourier Transform (FFT) on the input signal
  fft_result = np.fft.fft(data)
  # Compute the magnitude spectrum (absolute value of FFT),
  # normalized by the length of the signal
  fft_magnitude = np.abs(fft_result) / len(data)  # Normalize magnitude

  # Number of samples in the signal
 N = len(data)
# Plot data
 plt.figure(figsize=(6, 4))
 data_for_graph =  fft_magnitude[:N//2]
 plt.plot(data_for_graph)
 plt.xlim(0, 100)
 plt.title('Frequency Spectrum. ' + channel)
 plt.xlabel('Frequency [Hz]')
 plt.ylabel('Magnitude')
 plt.show()

furie(EMD_Y[1500:2500], "After artefact removed")
furie(channel_data_bp_filtered[1500:2500], "After artefact removed")
```

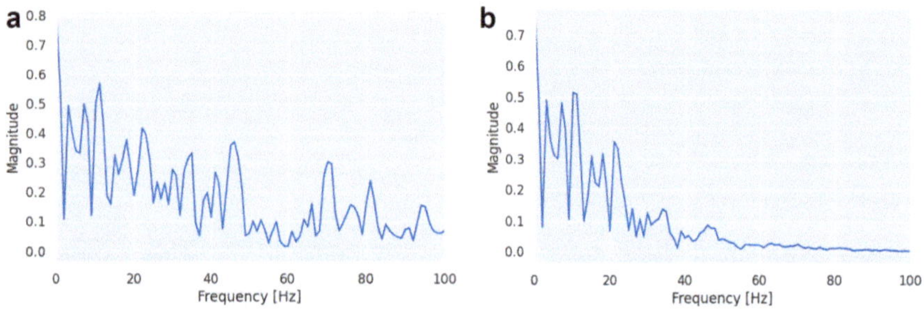

Fig. 7.15 Checking the removal of artifacts by frequency component, after EMD was implemented (**a**), and before (**b**)

Figure 7.15 illustrates the test results.

The frequency spectrum analysis demonstrates that muscle artifacts introduce substantial broadband high-frequency activity (above ~ 20 Hz), thereby elevating the noise floor and obscuring low-frequency physiological signals. After artifact removal, these high-frequency components are markedly reduced, revealing a spectrum dominated by low-frequency peaks (0–15 Hz) with a cleaner baseline. This confirms that the applied processing method effectively suppresses artefact contamination while preserving the essential low-frequency structure of the signal.

7.7.2 Evaluation via Signal-to-Noise Ratio (SNR)

The Signal-to-noise ratio (SNR) represents the ratio of the desired signal (brain activity) to the background noise (unwanted electrical activity). A higher SNR indicates that the brain signals are more precise and more distinguishable from noise, which is essential for accurate analysis. Poor SNR can lead to misinterpretation of EEG data. If noise is not adequately separated from the signal, researchers may falsely conclude that specific neural responses are occurring when, in fact, they are simply noise artifacts. Understanding and improving SNR is, therefore, important to designing experiments that yield valid and reliable results [28, 29].

```
import numpy as np
# Calculate average power of the EEG signal before denoising
P_signal_before = np.mean(channel_data_bp_filtered**2)
# Calculate average power of the EEG signal after applying EMD (Empirical
Mode Decomposition)
P_signal_after = np.mean(EMD_Y**2)
# Load noise data from an Excel file
noise = pd.read_excel("    Noise.xlsx")
# Load noise data from an Excel file
P_noise = np.mean(    noise**2)

#  Calculate Signal-to-Noise Ratio (SNR) before denoising
SNR_before = 10 * np.log10(P_signal_before / P_noise)
# Calculate Signal-to-Noise Ratio (SNR) after denoising
SNR_after = 10 * np.log10(P_signal_after / P_noise)
# Print SNR values in decibels (dB)
print(f"SNR: {SNR_before:.2f} dB")
print(f"SNR: {SNR_after:.2f} dB")
```

SNR: − 68.48 dB—Before EMD was implemented.

SNR: − 69.39 dB—After EMD was implemented.

The SNR before artifact removal is generally lower due to the presence of muscle artifacts, which can dominate the EEG signal. Therefore, we can conclude that the removal of these artifacts was successful.

7.8 Conclusion

In conclusion, the accurate interpretation of electroencephalography signals is critically dependent on the effective identification and removal of various contaminating artefacts. This chapter has highlighted the pervasive nature of both biological artefacts (such as ocular, muscular, and cardiac activity) and electromagnetic noise, which can significantly obscure genuine neural oscillations. To address these challenges, we explored several advanced signal processing techniques. Independent Component Analysis and Canonical Correlation Analysis were presented as powerful blind source separation methods capable of isolating and eliminating artefact components. Furthermore, the utility of Empirical Mode Decomposition combined with K-Nearest

Neighbors was discussed as a robust approach for adaptively decomposing and classifying signal components for artefact rejection. The effectiveness of these sophisticated methods was quantitatively evaluated using metrics such as Signal-to-Noise Ratio (SNR) and through analysis of the Fast Fourier Transform (FFT), confirming their ability to restore signal fidelity. The practical implementation and application of these techniques, facilitated by the flexibility and extensive libraries available in Python, underscore their importance in achieving clean and reliable EEG data. Ultimately, mastering these artefact removal techniques is paramount for ensuring the validity and interpretability of EEG-based research and clinical findings.

References

1. Islam MK, Rastegarnia A, Yang Z (2016) Methods for artifact detection and removal from scalp EEG: a review. Neurophysiol Clin Clin Neurophysiol 46(4–5):287–305
2. Jiang X, Bian G-B, Tian Z (2019) Removal of artifacts from EEG signals: a review. Sensors 19(5):987
3. Debener S, Kranczioch C, Gutberlet I (2010) EEG quality: origin and reduction of the EEG cardiac-related artefact. In: EEG-FMRI: physiological basis, technique, and applications, pp 135–151
4. Littmann L, Rennyson SL, Wall BP, Parker JM (2008) Significance of respiratory artifact in the electrocardiogram. Am J Cardiol 102(8):1090–1096
5. Sethi N, Sethi J, Torgovnick E, Arsura E (2007) Physiological and non-physiological EEG artifacts. Internet J Neuromonitoring 5(1)
6. Lai CQ, Ibrahim H, Abdullah MZ, Abdullah JM, Suandi SA, Azman A (2018) Artifacts and noise removal for electroencephalogram (EEG): a literature review. In: 2018 IEEE symposium on computer applications & industrial electronics (ISCAIE). IEEE, pp 326–332
7. Kramarenko AV, Tan U (2003) Effects of high-frequency electromagnetic fields on human EEG: a brain mapping study. Int J Neurosci 113(7):1007–1019
8. Fiedler P, Haueisen J, Alvarez AMC, Cheron G, Cuesta P, Maestú F et al (2023) Noise characteristics in spaceflight multichannel EEG. PLoS ONE 18(2):e0280822
9. Vigário RN (1997) Extraction of ocular artefacts from EEG using independent component analysis. Electroencephalogr Clin Neurophysiol 103(3):395–404
10. Iriarte J, Urrestarazu E, Valencia M, Alegre M, Malanda A, Viteri C et al (2003) Independent component analysis as a tool to eliminate artifacts in EEG: a quantitative study. J Clin Neurophysiol 20(4):249–257
11. Chaumon M, Bishop DV, Busch NA (2015) A practical guide to the selection of independent components of the electroencephalogram for artifact correction. J Neurosci Methods 250:47–63
12. De Clercq W, Vergult A, Vanrumste B, Van Paesschen W, Van Huffel S (2006) Canonical correlation analysis applied to remove muscle artifacts from the electroencephalogram. IEEE Trans Biomed Eng 53(12):2583–2587
13. Gao J, Zheng C, Wang P (2010) Online removal of muscle artifact from electroencephalogram signals based on canonical correlation analysis. Clin EEG Neurosci 41(1):53–59
14. Janani AS, Grummett TS, Lewis TW, Fitzgibbon SP, Whitham EM, DelosAngeles D et al (2018) Improved artefact removal from EEG using Canonical Correlation Analysis and spectral slope. J Neurosci Methods 298:1–15
15. Somers B, Bertrand A (2016) Removal of eye blink artifacts in wireless EEG sensor networks using reduced-bandwidth canonical correlation analysis. J Neural Eng 13(6):066008
16. Roy V, Shukla S, Shukla PK, Rawat P (2017) Gaussian elimination-based novel canonical correlation analysis method for EEG motion artifact removal. J Healthc Eng 2017(1):9674712

17. Alam ME, Samanta B (2017) Performance evaluation of empirical mode decomposition for EEG artifact removal. In: ASME international mechanical engineering congress and exposition: American society of mechanical engineers, p V04BT5A024
18. Teng C, Zhang Y, Wang G (2014) The removal of EMG artifact from EEG signals by the multivariate empirical mode decomposition. In: 2014 IEEE international conference on signal processing, communications and computing (ICSPCC). IEEE, pp 873–876
19. Roy V, Shukla S (2016) Enhanced empirical mode decomposition approach to eliminate motion artifacts in EEG using ICA and DWT. Int J Signal Process Image Process Pattern Recognit 9(5):321–338
20. Rakhmatulin I (2024) Encoder with the empirical mode decomposition (EMD) to remove muscle artefacts from EEG signal. arXiv preprint arXiv:240914571
21. Ghosh R, Phadikar S, Deb N, Sinha N, Das P, Ghaderpour E (2023) Automatic eyeblink and muscular artifact detection and removal from EEG signals using k-nearest neighbor classifier and long short-term memory networks. IEEE Sens J 23(5):5422–5436
22. Hamid H, Mujab AS, Pramudita BA, Rizal A (2024) Empirical mode decomposition and k-nearest neighbors combination for removing ocular artifact in EEG signals. In: 2024 8th International conference on information technology, information systems and electrical engineering (ICITISEE). IEEE, pp 17–22
23. Hamidi AA, Robertson B, Ilow J (2023) A new approach for ECG artifact detection using fine-KNN classification and wavelet scattering features in vital health applications. Procedia Comput Sci 224:60–67
24. Chang C-Y, Hsu S-H, Pion-Tonachini L, Jung T-P (2018) Evaluation of artifact subspace reconstruction for automatic EEG artifact removal. In: 2018 40th Annual international conference of the IEEE engineering in medicine and biology society (EMBC). IEEE, pp 1242–1245
25. Urigüen JA, Garcia-Zapirain B (2015) EEG artifact removal—state-of-the-art and guidelines. J Neural Eng 12(3):031001
26. Münch B, Trtik P, Marone F, Stampanoni M (2009) Stripe and ring artifact removal with combined wavelet—Fourier filtering. Opt Express 17(10):8567–8591
27. Islam MK, Rastegarnia A, Sanei S (2020) Signal artifacts and techniques for artifacts and noise removal. In: Signal processing techniques for computational health informatics. Springer, pp 23–79
28. Daly I, Nicolaou N, Nasuto SJ, Warwick K (2013) Automated artifact removal from the electroencephalogram: a comparative study. Clin EEG Neurosci 44(4):291–306
29. Mahmood F, Toots M, Öfverstedt L-G, Skoglund U (2015) 2D discrete Fourier transform with simultaneous edge artifact removal for real-time applications. In: 2015 International conference on field programmable technology (FPT). IEEE, pp 236–239

Chapter 8
Real-Time Signal Processing in EEG

8.1 Introduction

Real-time signal processing in electroencephalography (EEG) is paramount for a multitude of advanced applications and fundamental research endeavors. Its criticality stems from the immediate insights it offers into ongoing brain dynamics, which is crucial across several domains.

Positive Aspects of Real-Time EEG Processing:
One of the most significant advantages, or what we can consider a **"positive" or "real-time" benefit**, is that it provides **immediate analysis and interpretation of brain activity**. This capability is indispensable for:

- **Neurofeedback**: In neurofeedback training, individuals learn to self-regulate specific brainwave patterns. Real-time processing enables instantaneous feedback, allowing users to consciously modify their brain activity as they observe its fluctuations, thereby facilitating the learning process and improving therapeutic outcomes.
- **Brain-Computer Interfaces (BCI)**: BCIs rely on translating real-time brain signals into commands for external devices. Here, **responsiveness** is key: real-time processing minimizes latency, making BCIs significantly more effective and user-friendly by providing quick, natural responses to user inputs. This immediacy directly enhances the user experience, leading to a smoother and more intuitive interaction.

Real-time monitoring of neurological conditions: For conditions like epilepsy, continuous and immediate analysis of EEG can detect the onset of seizures or other critical neurological events, allowing for timely intervention and improved patient safety. In surgical settings, real-time EEG monitoring can assess the depth of anesthesia and detect potential neurological complications [1].

Additionally, a crucial positive aspect is that real-time processing enables **adaptive algorithms** that can dynamically adjust to changing brain states, thereby

I. Rakhmatulin and G. R. Naik, *EEG Signal Processing with Python*, Brain Informatics and Health, https://doi.org/10.1007/978-981-95-4177-5_8

enhancing the accuracy and effectiveness of interventions. The human brain is a highly dynamic system, with brainwave patterns constantly evolving. **Adaptive algorithms** can dynamically adjust to ongoing changes in brain activity and applications. This allows systems to continuously optimize their performance by adapting to individual variability and fluctuating brain states [2].

Challenges of Real-Time EEG Processing (Negative Aspects):

Despite these substantial advantages, real-time EEG processing is not without its challenges. These can be considered the "negative" aspects that require careful consideration in system design:

- **Signal Noise**: A pervasive issue is that EEG signals are inherently susceptible to contamination from various sources of noise. These include biological artifacts such as muscle movements (e.g., electromyography, EMG), eye blinks and movements (electrooculography, EOG), and cardiac activity (electrocardiography, ECG), as well as environmental factors like electrical interference from power lines or other electronic devices. This inherent "noise" can significantly complicate real-time processing, potentially reducing the accuracy and reliability of the extracted brain signals. Robust real-time noise reduction techniques are thus essential.
- **Computational Load**: Implementing real-time processing demands complex EEG data promptly, sophisticated algorithms and powerful hardware are often required. This can lead to high **computational load**, necessitating careful optimization of algorithms and potentially limiting the complexity of analyses that can be performed within strict time constraints. Balancing accuracy with computational efficiency is a continuous challenge in designing real-time EEG systems [3].

While the immediate analysis, enhanced responsiveness, and adaptive capabilities afforded by real-time EEG processing offer profound benefits for a range of critical applications, developers must also contend with significant challenges posed by signal noise and the substantial computational demands that this presents. Overcoming these hurdles is key to unlocking the full potential of EEG for neurofeedback, BCI, and clinical diagnostics [4].

8.2 How It Works

When working in real-time, the primary difference is the need to create a data buffer. It's crucial to determine the length of data that will be fed into the filter for processing and subsequent visualization. For instance, with a frame rate of 250 FPS (meaning we receive 250 EEG data points from each channel per second), data processing and visualization would occur once per second. However, for bandpass filters, it is essential to supply data with a margin, as the filter requires time to adjust.

The primary purpose of the buffer is to address a specific issue during the processing of EEG data. When we read EEG data into an array, we cannot simply apply a band-pass filter and use the resulting data immediately. This is because the band-pass filter distorts the initial data points in the array as it adjusts and calibrates itself using these early samples.

To mitigate this issue, we feed the filter an array containing not only the current data but also data from previous sessions. For instance, if we read 250 samples every second, we might input data from the last 3 s into the band-pass filter. After processing, we receive filtered data for the entire 3-s period. Although the first portion of this data was affected by the filter's initialization, we are primarily interested in the data from the most recent second.

Consequently, from the processed array of 750 data points (3 s * 250 samples/second), we extract only the last 250 samples. These final samples have been filtered adequately after the initial calibration period, providing us with accurate, filtered data for our analysis. This process repeats indefinitely, simulating a real-time data processing pipeline. The structure of the buffer is shown in Fig. 8.1.

This script streams EEG data from an Excel file, maintains a rolling window of past and new samples, applies a Butterworth band-pass filter to isolate a target frequency range, and refreshes a live plot displaying both the filtered and raw signals in real-time.

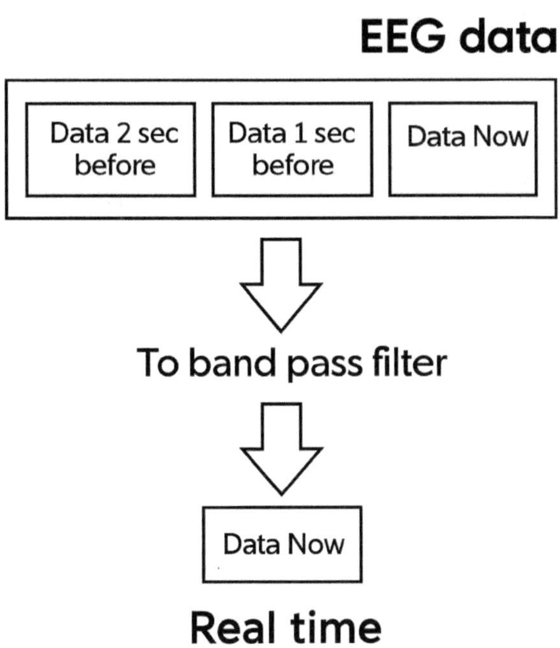

Fig. 8.1 Structure of buffer for real-time signal processing

```
def butter_bandpass(lowcut, highcut, fs, order=5):
    nyq = 0.5 * fs
    low = lowcut / nyq
    high = highcut / nyq
    b, a = signal.butter(order, [low, high], btype='band')
    return b, a
def butter_bandpass_filter(data, lowcut, highcut, fs, order=5):
    b, a = butter_bandpass(lowcut, highcut, fs, order=order)
    data = signal.lfilter(b, a, data)
    return data

#Load EEG dataset. We will read data every sec 250 samples to simulate real-time
dataset_y = pd.read_excel("/dataset.xlsx")
channel = 0  # Select which EEG channel to process
# Extract data for chosen channel
dataset_y = dataset_y.iloc[channel]
# ------------------------
# Initialize buffers and parameters
# ------------------------
just_one_time = 0 # Flag to fill 'data_before' only once
data_before = []  # Holds previously read chunks
data_after = []  # Holds most recent chunks
fps = 250        # Sampling frequency
cutoff = 1       # Low cutoff frequency for filter
cutoffs = 30      # High cutoff frequency for filter
start = 0        # Start index for reading
total_lenght = end = 500 # End index & total plot length

# ------------------------
# Main loop: read data, filter, plot
# ------------------------

while 1:
# Step 1: Fill the 'before' buffer only at the start
        if just_one_time == 0:
```

```
            # Read past data in nested loops
        for b in range (0,data_lenght_for_Filter,1):
            for a in range (0,read_data_lenght_one_time,1):
                data_read = dataset_y[start:end]
                start = start + 250
                end = end + 250
                data_before.append(data_read)

        just_one_time = 1
            # Remove oldest chunk to keep buffer size consistent
        data_before = data_before[read_data_lenght_one_time:]
# Step 2: Read the 'after' buffer (new incoming data)
    for c in range (0,read_data_lenght_one_time,1):
        data_read = dataset_y[start:end]
        start = start + 250
        end = end + 250
        data_after.append(data_read)
# Step 3: Flatten the buffered lists into single lists of samples
    data_before_for_sum = data_before
    data_after_for_sum = data_after
# Combine past and new samples into one dataset
    data_before_for_sum = [item for sublist in data_before for item in sublist]
    data_after_for_sum = [item for sublist in data_after for item in sublist]
    dataset =  data_before_for_sum + data_after_for_sum #+ data_after_flip
    dataset = [int(x) for x in dataset]
# Step 4: Update 'before' buffer to include most recent data
    dataset_before = data_before + data_after
    data_before = dataset_before[read_data_lenght_one_time:]
# Step 5: Apply band-pass filter
    data = butter_bandpass_filter(dataset, cutoff, cutoffs,fps)
# Step 6: Clear temporary buffers for next loop
    data_after = []
    dataset = []
# Step 7: Plot filtered data and raw data
    pl.clf()
```

```
        pl.plot(data[-total_lenght:],label='Data after band-pass filter')
        data_for_graph = np.array(data_read)
        pl.title("Real-time for band-pass filter , Channel " + str(channel + 1))
        pl.ylabel('EEG, μV')
        pl.xlabel('Sample')
        pl.plot(data_for_graph - np.average(data_for_graph), label='Raw data')
        pl.legend()
# Step 8: Display in notebook and update
        display.display(pl.gcf())
        display.clear_output(wait=True)
        time.sleep(1)  # Simulation for real time, read for 1 sec 250 samples
```

This script simulates real-time operation using previously written data. We simulate reading 250 samples every second using a timer. This is done so that, without connecting to a real device, you can see how the timer works in real time. As a result, the graph shown in Fig. 8.2 will be updated every second.

The graph shows that the band-pass filter effectively removes high-frequency noise from the raw EEG signal, resulting in a smoother waveform that preserves the slower brainwave activity within the target frequency range.

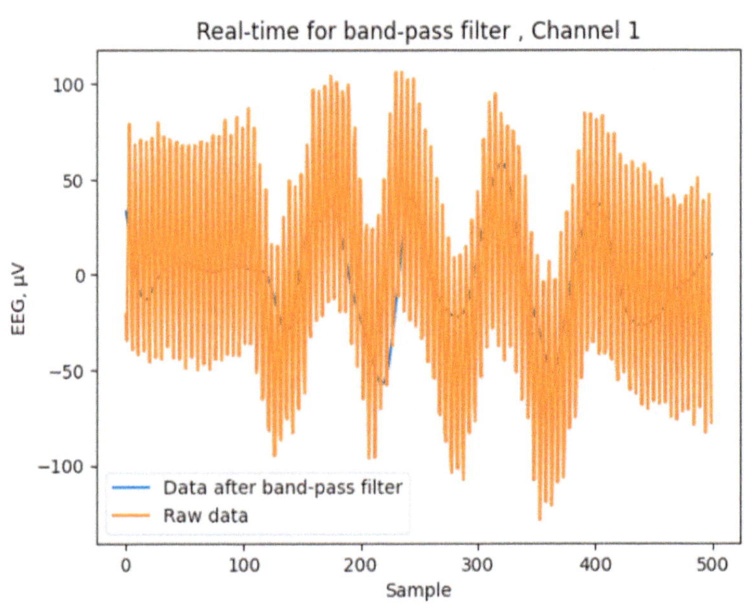

Fig. 8.2 Example of implementation of a band-pass filter

8.3 Conclusion

When processing real-time EEG data, it is essential to understand that a buffer is needed when using bandpass filters. However, this is not the case for the Fast Fourier Transform (FFT) analysis or most other methods. In other words, if you are using FFT without a bandpass filter, you can read the data and send it directly to the processing method without needing a buffer.

In EEG signal analysis, especially for BCI applications, implementing real-time processing capabilities is a complex task that requires careful attention to code optimization. This need is even more evident when using Python, a language known for its user-friendly nature and versatility, but inherently lagging behind performance-oriented languages such as C in terms of pure computational efficiency. It is essential to realize that the optimization challenge extends well beyond the initial data processing stage. Subsequent stages, including real-time analysis and feature extraction, typically occur concurrently with data acquisition, adding to the computational burden. This cascading complexity elevates real-time EEG tasks to a significantly higher level of complexity compared to traditional post-processing methodologies. It is therefore critical to understand how data is buffered to optimize code for real-time tasks.

References

1. Feng W, Wang X, Xie J, Liu W, Qiao Y, Liu G (2024) Real-time EEG-based driver drowsiness detection based on convolutional neural network with gumbel-softmax trick. IEEE Sens J
2. Zanetti R, Arza A, Aminifar A, Atienza D (2021) Real-time EEG-based cognitive workload monitoring on wearable devices. IEEE Trans Biomed Eng 69(1):265–277
3. Dávila-Montero S, Dana-Lê JA, Bente G, Hall AT, Mason AJ (2021) Review and challenges of technologies for real-time human behavior monitoring. IEEE Trans Biomed Circuits Syst 15(1):2–28
4. An Y, Wong J, Ling SH (2024) Development of real-time brain-computer interface control system for robot. Appl Soft Comput 159:111648

Chapter 9
Application Without Machine Learning

9.1 Introduction

The utilization of skills in data processing and the subsequent application of this knowledge in practice without relying on machine learning offers two key advantages. Firstly, it enables individuals to acquire a more fundamental and in-depth understanding of working with EEG data. Secondly, it allows for effective work even in scenarios where a comprehensive dataset for training ML is not available.

As an example for this chapter, we choose stress control since it is a good indicator for EEG feature extraction, because EEG signals contain rich information about mental states and conditions, including stress levels. EEG-based stress monitoring is crucial for the early detection and prevention of stress-related disorders. This non-invasive method offers a comprehensive and real-time understanding of mental states, addressing one of the most significant challenges we face today [1]. By providing continuous insights into brain activity, EEG-based stress control enables timely interventions and personalized stress management strategies, ultimately contributing to improved mental health and well-being in our increasingly demanding world [2].

9.2 Entropy for Stress Control

Entropy can serve as an intriguing and, according to science publications, grounded indicator for stress control. Entropy describes the degree of disorder, randomness, or uncertainty in a system [3, 4].

I. Rakhmatulin and G. R. Naik, *EEG Signal Processing with Python*, Brain Informatics and Health, https://doi.org/10.1007/978-981-95-4177-5_9

Several types of entropy are used to analyze EEG signals for stress level assessment:

- Approximate Entropy (ApEn) and Sample Entropy (SampEn): These time-domain entropies have performed well in detecting burst suppression patterns in EEG.
- Shannon Entropy (SE): This measures EEG signal irregularity and quantifies energy distribution in the power spectrum. It can be applied to detect alterations in sleep EEGs related to stress disorders like ASD and PTSD3.
- Spectral Entropy: Used in commercial EEG monitoring, it includes Response Entropy (RE) and State Entropy (SE). RE covers frequencies from 0.8 to 47 Hz, while SE focuses on frequencies from 0.8 to 32 Hz.
- Shannon Wavelet Entropy (SWE): This indicates signal variation at each frequency scale in the wavelet domain.

These entropy measures provide various ways to quantify the complexity and irregularity of EEG signals, offering insights into stress levels and brain states.

We chose ApEn because it is the method most commonly used in scientific publications. ApEn analyses time series data from EEG recordings, typically using segments of the data points (a few seconds of the EEG signal). It calculates the probability that similar patterns of observations will remain identical in the next incremental comparisons. ApEn measures the likelihood that patterns within a dataset that are like each other will remain similar when additional data points are included. It is often used to assess the regularity or predictability of EEG signals. Lower ApEn values suggest more regular patterns [1, 5, 6].

Entropy is useful for monitoring brain activity in real-time, providing insights into how the brain responds to various stimuli or conditions.

The following script, via the SciPy library, iterates over increasing data segments, calculates their differential entropy, and stores these values. It then fits a polynomial regression to the entropy data and plots both the entropy values and the fitted polynomial curve to visualize the relationship between the EEG data at different times and entropy.

```
from scipy.stats import differential_entropy, norm
data_ent_graph = [] # list to store entropy values at different sample sizes
# Loop through data in chunks of 1000, compute entropy for increasing sample
sizes
for a in range (1000, len(eeg_data), 1000):
    values = eeg_data[:a] # take data up to index a
    data_ent_final = differential_entropy(values) # compute differential entropy
    data_ent_graph.append(data_ent_final) # store result
# X-axis values corresponding to entropy measurements
x_inter_removed_high = []
for data_x in range (0, len(data_ent_graph),1):
    x_inter_removed_high.append(data_x)
degree = 5 # Degree of polynomial to fit
# Polynomial regression: fit polynomial of chosen degree
coefficients = np.polyfit(x_inter_removed_high, data_ent_graph, degree)
# Evaluate polynomial fit at given x-values
y_poly = np.polyval(coefficients, x_inter_removed_high)
# Plotting
plt.xlabel('Data step')
plt.ylabel('Entropy')
plt.plot(x_inter_removed_high, data_ent_graph, 'o', label='Data Points')
plt.plot(x_inter_removed_high, y_poly, 'r', label=f'Polynomial Regression (Degree
{degree})')
plt.legend()
plt.show()
```

The results of the entropy calculations are provided in Fig. 9.1. Each calculation was performed over a total of 4 s, using 1000 samples. Longer data lengths generally yield more accurate results. Currently, there is no universally agreed-upon optimal length; researchers should consider the specific entropy measure, the characteristics of their EEG data, and the trade-offs between accuracy and stationarity assumptions when selecting the sample length for entropy calculation in EEG.

It's difficult to determine the stress level solely from this data. While some differences in entropy between stressed and non-stressed states may be visually detectable, additional contextual knowledge is required to interpret the values accurately. Specifically, understanding what constitutes a stressed state versus a non-stressed state, as well as identifying the threshold, is essential. Only with this information can a definitive conclusion be made. In these cases, we can visualize the stress level in real-time without having to confirm what that level is in percentage terms.

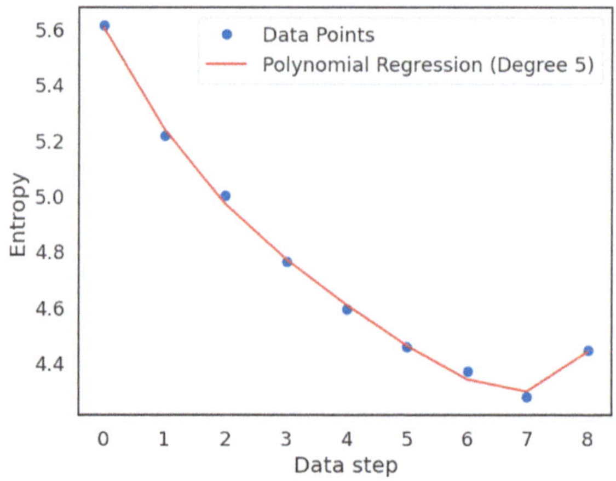

Fig. 9.1 Result of entropy with ApEn

9.3 Power Spectral Density (PSD)

Power Spectral Density (PSD) is highly effective for stress monitoring using EEG, as it enables the quantification and analysis of brain activity across different frequency bands. By identifying changes in neural oscillations associated with stress, PSD provides valuable insights for assessing and managing stress. This method is relatively straightforward to implement, requires minimal computational resources compared to more complex techniques, and has been extensively utilized in scientific research and publications due to its reliability and practicality [7, 8].

To implement power spectral density, one needs to calculate the power within the specified frequency range. Before, we used the Fast Fourier Transform, and now we would like to show how to use Welch's Method. Welch's Method is a technique for estimating the power spectral density (PSD) of a signal. It improves upon the basic periodogram method by reducing noise in the estimated spectrum. Welch's process involves the following steps:

Welch's Method: By averaging the FFTs of overlapping segments, Welch's method provides a smoother and more reliable estimate of the PSD, reducing variance. FFT: A single FFT of the entire signal can be noisy and less trustworthy, particularly for short or non-stationary signals.

Both Welch's method and FFT are valuable tools in EEG analysis, each with its own strengths. Welch's method is preferred for its accuracy and reliability in estimating power spectral densities, while the FFT is favored for its computational efficiency and speed. The choice between the two depends on the specific requirements of the EEG analysis task at hand. However, for us, accuracy is essential here.

The following script calculates and visualizes the power spectral density (PSD) of a data segment using Welch's method, highlights the alpha frequency band, and computes the absolute power within this band.

```
from scipy import signal
from scipy.integrate import simps
# Define window length (4 seconds)
sf = 250
win = 4 * sf
freqs, psd = signal.welch(eeg_data      , sf, nperseg=win)
# Plot the power spectrum
sns.set(font_scale=1.2, style='white')
# Define delta lower and upper limits
low, high = 8, 13  # Delta Waves: Up to 4 Hz
                   # Alpha Waves: 8 - 13 Hz
                   # Theta Waves: 4-7 Hz
                  # Gamma Waves: 30-100 Hz

# Find intersecting values in frequency vector
idx_delta = np.logical_and(freqs >= low, freqs <= high)

# Plot the power spectral density and fill the delta area
plt.plot(freqs, psd, lw=2, color='k')
plt.fill_between(freqs, psd, where=idx_delta, color='green')
plt.xlabel('Frequency (Hz)')
plt.ylabel('Power spectral density (uV^2 / Hz)')
plt.title("Welch's periodogram")
plt.show()
# Frequency resolution
freq_res = freqs[1] - freqs[0]  # = 1 / 4 = 0.25
# Compute the absolute power by approximating the area under the curve
delta_power = simps(psd[idx_delta], dx=freq_res)
print('Absolute delta power: %.3f uV^2' % delta_power)
```

In Fig. 9.2 the calculated area is clearly shown in green. This area is an indicator of the delta power in EEG.

This script calculates the area within a specified range of the power spectral density (PSD), representing the Absolute Delta Power. For this script, the result is: Absolute delta power = 8.324 μV2. By computing the Absolute Delta Power for each time range, it serves as a potential indicator of stress. However, this method shares a similar limitation with entropy-based approaches. It is crucial to accurately

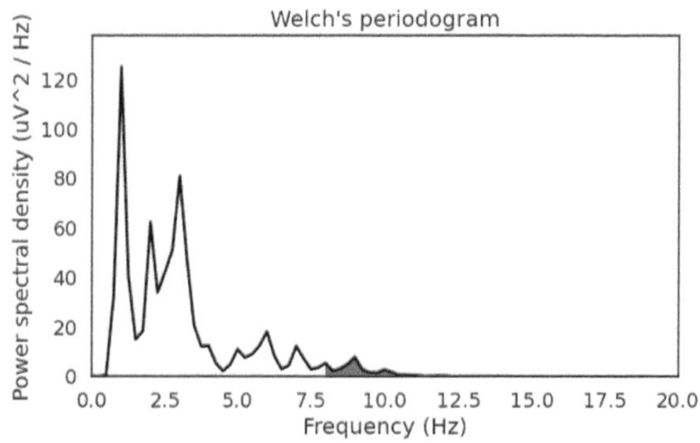

Fig. 9.2 Result of Absolute delta power, the shaded area shows our area of interest

distinguish between stressed and non-stressed states and establish a clear threshold to ensure that meaningful and reliable results are obtained.

9.4 Conclusion

Calculating the Power Spectral Density (PSD) for EEG signals is crucial for various applied tasks, as it provides valuable information about the distribution of power across different frequency components of the signal. This analysis can also be used for several contexts:

- Sleep Studies Sleep Stages Classification: Different sleep stages (e.g., REM, NREM) are characterized by distinct frequency patterns. PSD helps identify these stages by highlighting the dominant frequencies associated with each stage.
- Mental State Analysis: Different cognitive states (e.g., attention, relaxation) are associated with specific EEG frequency bands (e.g., alpha, beta). PSD helps in quantifying these states by analyzing the power in these frequency bands.
- Mental Health Assessment: Conditions like depression and anxiety can manifest as specific changes in EEG frequency content. PSD analysis can aid in the assessment and understanding of these mental health conditions.

Finally, on one hand, we see that it is possible to do without machine learning for some EEG tasks; on the other hand, we need to make algorithms more stationary and find thresholds to indicate stress level. The data received in this chapter will be useful as input for the machine learning model. Which we will consider in the following chapters.

References

1. Katmah R, Al-Shargie F, Tariq U, Babiloni F, Al-Mughairbi F, Al-Nashash H (2021) A review on mental stress assessment methods using EEG signals. Sensors 21(15):5043
2. Attar ET (2022) Review of electroencephalography signals approaches for mental stress assessment. Neurosci J 27(4):209–215
3. Zavala-Yoé R, Iqbal HM, Parra-Saldívar R, Ramírez-Mendoza RA (2023) Stress response analysis via dynamic entropy in EEG: caregivers in view. Int J Environ Res Public Health 20(10):5913
4. Keshmiri S (2021) Conditional entropy: a potential digital marker for stress. Entropy 23(3):286
5. Liu L, Ji Y, Gao Y, Li T, Xu W (2022) A novel stress state assessment method for college students based on EEG. Comput Intell Neurosci 2022(1):4565968
6. Su C-H, Ko L-W, Jung T-P, Onton J, Tzou S-C, Juang J-C, Hsu C-Y (2024) Extracting stress-related EEG patterns from pre-sleep EEG for forecasting slow-wave sleep deficiency. IEEE Trans Neural Syst Rehabil Eng 32:1817–1827
7. Yang B, Huang Y, Li Z, Hu X (2023) Management of post-stroke depression (PSD) by electroencephalography for effective rehabilitation. Eng Regen 4(1):44–54
8. Redwan SM, Uddin MP, Ulhaq A, Sharif MI, Krishnamoorthy G (2024) Power spectral density-based resting-state EEG classification of first-episode psychosis. Sci Rep 14(1):15154

Chapter 10
Machine Learning: EEG Perspective

10.1 Introduction to ML

In recent years, Machine Learning (ML) has revolutionized numerous scientific and engineering disciplines, and its impact on the analysis and interpretation of electroencephalography (EEG) signals has been particularly profound. Traditionally, EEG signal processing relied heavily on conventional methods characterized by handcrafted features and rule-based logic. These approaches often involved extensive domain expertise to manually design filters, extract specific frequency bands (e.g., alpha, beta, theta), and define thresholds or patterns indicative of brain states or neurological events. While effective to a degree, these traditional methods could be rigid, labor-intensive, and sometimes struggled to capture the subtle, complex, and highly non-linear dynamics inherent in brain activity.

The emergence of Machine Learning has presented a powerful paradigm shift. Unlike their traditional counterparts, ML algorithms possess the unique ability to learn patterns and structures directly from data. This data-driven approach means that instead of relying on pre-defined rules, ML models can automatically discover intricate relationships within large volumes of EEG data, identifying features and patterns that might be too subtle or complex for human observation or explicit rule formulation. This inherent adaptability and capacity for automatic feature learning enable more adaptive, accurate, and scalable analysis of EEG signals.

This innovative capability of ML has opened new avenues for understanding brain function, diagnosing neurological disorders, and developing advanced neurotechnologies. For precision and the automatic detection of subtle biomarkers for diseases such as epilepsy or Alzheimer's, classify different cognitive states with higher precision, and significantly enhance the performance and robustness of Brain-Computer Interfaces (BCIs). The ability of ML algorithms to adapt to inter-individual variability in EEG signals, a notorious challenge in neurophysiology, further underscores their transformative potential.

I. Rakhmatulin and G. R. Naik, *EEG Signal Processing with Python*, Brain Informatics and Health, https://doi.org/10.1007/978-981-95-4177-5_10

This chapter serves as an essential introduction to the fundamental concepts of ML, applied explicitly within the context of EEG signal processing. It will lay the groundwork by exploring the basic principles of how ML algorithms operate on raw or minimally preprocessed EEG data, highlighting key differences from traditional signal processing pipelines. By understanding these foundational concepts, readers will be well-equipped to delve into the more advanced applications and cutting-edge research discussed in subsequent chapters, where ML's power in deciphering the complexities of the human brain truly comes to the fore.

10.2 Why Use Machine Learning for EEG

The integration of ML into EEG analysis is driven by its capacity to overcome significant limitations inherent in traditional methods, offering enhanced objectivity, efficiency, and diagnostic precision. Firstly, EEG signals are inherently complex, highly susceptible to various artifacts (e.g., eye blinks, muscle movements, electrical interference), and exhibit substantial inter- and intra-individual variability, making manual interpretation subjective, time-consuming, and prone to human error, especially in long-term recordings [1, 2]. ML algorithms, particularly deep learning models, excel at processing vast quantities of noisy, high-dimensional data, automatically learning intricate, non-linear patterns and features that might be imperceptible to the human eye or conventional signal processing techniques [1, 3]. This automated feature extraction and classification capability significantly reduces the laborious effort of manual analysis, enabling researchers to explore subtle biomarkers associated with neurological conditions such as epilepsy, Alzheimer's disease, and schizophrenia with greater accuracy and scalability [2, 4]. Furthermore, ML enables the development of real-time monitoring and brain-computer interface (BCI) applications, which require rapid and reliable decoding of brain states that traditional, offline analysis cannot provide [4, 5]. The availability of increasingly large EEG datasets also provides a fertile ground for training sophisticated ML models, fostering a virtuous cycle where more data leads to better models, which in turn encourages more data collection and research [6].

EEG signals are inherently non-linear, non-stationary, and often noisy. Traditional statistical and signal processing approaches, while valuable, may fall short in extracting complex patterns, especially when dealing with high-dimensional datasets or subject variability. Machine learning methods excel in such scenarios by:

- Learning from large volumes of data.
- Discovering non-obvious patterns.
- Adapting to inter-subject and intra-subject variability.
- Enabling real-time decision-making (e.g., in Brain-Computer Interfaces).

10.3 Introduction to Machine Learning for EEG

The application of ML to EEG data analysis is a rapidly evolving field, leveraging various ML paradigms to extract meaningful insights from complex neural signals. These paradigms can be broadly categorized into supervised and unsupervised learning approaches, each offering distinct advantages for different EEG tasks.

Supervised Machine Learning for EEG analysis involves training models on labelled data, where each EEG segment is associated with a known outcome or state (e.g., presence of a seizure, specific motor imagery, emotional state). Supervised learning involves training models on labelled data, making it suitable for tasks where ground truth is available. Common applications in EEG analysis include:

- Event Classification: Distinguishing between different types of brain activity, such as motor imagery or cognitive tasks.
- Mental Workload Estimation: Assessing cognitive load based on EEG patterns.
- Sleep Stage Detection: Automatically identifying various sleep stages from EEG recordings.

This approach aims to learn a mapping function from inputting EEG features to their corresponding labels, enabling the model to predict labels for new, unseen data. Common algorithms in this category include:

- **Support Vector Machines (SVMs)**: Known for their ability to find optimal hyperplanes that maximize the margin between different classes, SVMs have been widely used in EEG classification tasks, such as distinguishing between different mental states or detecting epileptic seizures [2, 7]. Their effectiveness often relies on robust feature engineering.
- **K-Nearest Neighbors (KNN)**: This non-parametric, instance-based learning algorithm classifies a data point based on the majority class among its 'k' nearest neighbors in the feature space. KNN is conceptually simple and has been applied to various EEG classification problems, including motor imagery and anxiety detection [1, 7].
- **Random Forests (RF)**: As an ensemble learning method, RF constructs multiple decision trees during training and outputs the mode of the classes for classification. RFs are robust to overfitting and excel at handling high-dimensional EEG data, demonstrating superior performance in tasks like visual stimulation-induced EEG classification and anxiety detection [7, 8].
- **Linear Discriminant Analysis (LDA)**: A classic statistical method that finds a linear combination of features that separates two or more classes. While often used for dimensionality reduction, it can also serve as a classifier for EEG signals, particularly in brain-computer interfaces (BCIs), due to its computational efficiency [2].

Unsupervised Machine Learning for EEG focuses on finding hidden patterns or structures within unlabeled EEG data, without prior knowledge of outcomes. This is particularly useful for tasks like artifact removal, anomaly detection, and data exploration. Key unsupervised techniques include:

- **Clustering Algorithms (e.g., K-Means, Hierarchical Clustering)**: These algorithms group similar EEG segments or features into clusters. They can be used to identify distinct brain states, segment EEG recordings, or detect unusual patterns that might indicate artifacts or pathological activity without requiring manual annotation [2].
- **Dimensionality Reduction Techniques (e.g., Principal Component Analysis (PCA), Independent Component Analysis (ICA))**: PCA, a dimensionality reduction technique that simplifies EEG data by extracting the most informative features. PCA is commonly used for artifact removal and preprocessing. ICA separates mixed EEG signals into independent components, enabling advanced artifact removal (such as eye blink correction) and improving signal quality in preprocessing pipelines. PCA identifies orthogonal components that capture the maximum variance in the data, while ICA aims to separate a multivariate signal into independent non-Gaussian components. These are crucial for reducing the high dimensionality of EEG data, making subsequent analysis more manageable, and effectively removing artifacts like eye blinks and muscle movements by isolating their independent sources [9].
- **Autoencoders (AEs)**: As neural networks trained to reconstruct their input, AEs learn compressed, latent representations of the data. They are particularly effective for unsupervised artifact detection and correction in EEG, by learning the normal patterns and identifying deviations as artifacts [9, 10]. Variational Autoencoders (VAEs), a generative variant, can also be used for unsupervised seizure identification by training on non-seizure activity and detecting seizures based on reconstruction errors [11].

By leveraging both supervised and unsupervised learning, researchers can maximize the insights gained from EEG data, whether for classification, exploration, or signal enhancement.

In EEG-based machine learning, tasks generally fall into two main categories: classification and numerical prediction, like other domains in the field. Deep learning approaches, particularly those using recurrent neural networks (RNNs) and attention-based models, are often employed for numerical prediction tasks due to their ability to capture temporal dependencies in EEG signals.

However, classification remains a powerful tool even when the goal is to estimate a numerical value. By discretizing a continuous variable into defined intervals or levels, classification models can approximate underlying numerical values. For example, if you partition a continuous measurement into three ranges, such as $< 10\%$ (class 1), $< 50\%$ (class 2), and $< 90\%$ (class 3), a classification model can predict which interval a given EEG segment falls into. This approach enables the estimation of numerical values through categorical predictions, providing a practical solution when direct regression is challenging or when labelled data is limited.

Such discretization strategies are commonly used in EEG analysis to translate complex, continuous brain signal features into actionable categories for brain-computer interfaces and clinical applications.

10.4 Challenges and Considerations

The integration of ML into EEG analysis, while transformative, is accompanied by a unique set of challenges and critical considerations that must be addressed from an academic standpoint to ensure robust, reliable, and ethically sound applications.

One of the foremost challenges stems from the inherent characteristics of EEG data itself. EEG signals are notoriously noisy and exhibit a low signal-to-noise ratio (SNR) due to various sources of artifacts, including physiological (e.g., eye blinks, muscle activity, and heartbeats) and non-physiological (e.g., electrical interference and electrode movement) contributions [12]. Effectively pre-processing and removing these artifacts without distorting the underlying neural activity remains a significant hurdle, often requiring sophisticated signal processing techniques or dedicated ML models for denoising [13, 14]. Furthermore, EEG signals are non-stationary, meaning their statistical properties change over time, and exhibit considerable inter-subject and intra-subject variability [13, 15]. This variability implies that ML models trained on data from one individual or session may not generalize well to others, necessitating extensive calibration or the development of advanced transfer learning and domain adaptation techniques to improve model robustness across diverse populations and recording conditions [15]. The raw, high-dimensional nature of EEG data also presents a challenge, demanding effective feature extraction and dimensionality reduction to render it suitable for ML algorithms and to avoid the "curse of dimensionality" [16].

Another significant consideration is the availability and quality of EEG datasets. Compared to domains like computer vision or natural language processing, publicly available, large-scale, and well-annotated EEG datasets are relatively scarce. This scarcity, coupled with the expensive and time-consuming nature of data collection, often leads to limitations in model generalizability and the potential for overfitting in deep learning models. Moreover, data annotation in EEG, especially for complex cognitive or neurological states, requires expert knowledge and is often subjective, leading to potential inconsistencies and errors that can propagate through the ML pipeline. The lack of standardization in EEG acquisition protocols (e.g., electrode placement, sampling rates, experimental paradigms) across different research groups and clinical settings further complicates data integration and the development of universally applicable ML models [16, 17].

Beyond data challenges, the interpretability and explainability (XAI) of ML models in EEG analysis are crucial academic and clinical considerations. Many powerful deep learning models, while achieving high performance, operate as "black boxes," making it difficult to understand how they arrive at their predictions or classifications [18]. In clinical applications, such as seizure detection or neurological disorder diagnosis, a lack of transparency can hinder trust among clinicians, impede error analysis, and pose significant challenges for regulatory approval [18]. Researchers are actively exploring methods to make these models more interpretable, such as visualizing learned features or using intrinsically interpretable models, to bridge the gap between algorithmic complexity and clinical utility.

Finally, significant ethical considerations surround the use of ML in EEG, particularly given the sensitive nature of brain data. Data privacy and security are paramount, requiring robust anonymization techniques and adherence to regulations like HIPAA and GDPR, especially when dealing with large, potentially identifiable datasets [19, 20]. The potential for algorithmic bias is another critical concern; if ML models are trained on unrepresentative or biased datasets, they could lead to inequitable or inaccurate diagnoses and treatments for certain demographic groups, exacerbating existing health disparities. Furthermore, questions of accountability arise when AI-driven decisions impact patient care, raising complex legal and ethical dilemmas regarding responsibility in cases of misdiagnosis or adverse outcomes. As ML-EEG systems move towards real-time applications and brain-computer interfaces, considerations around user autonomy, mental privacy, and the potential for unintended cognitive or psychological effects also come into sharper focus [21]. Addressing these multifaceted challenges requires interdisciplinary collaboration among neuroscientists, computer scientists, clinicians, ethicists, and policymakers to develop robust, equitable, and responsible ML solutions for EEG. While machine learning holds significant promise for EEG analysis, several challenges continue to hinder its full potential. One major issue is the scarcity of data and the high cost associated with labelling it accurately. Additionally, subject variability makes it challenging to generalize models across different individuals, limiting the robustness of results. EEG data is also highly susceptible to noise and artifacts, which can obscure meaningful signals and reduce model accuracy. In clinical settings, the interpretability of machine learning models becomes especially important, yet remains a persistent challenge. Furthermore, the computational demands of deep learning models can be substantial, posing barriers to real-time applications and broader accessibility [22].

10.5 Applications

Machine learning has become indispensable for EEG analysis due to its capacity to extract complex, non-linear patterns from inherently noisy and high-dimensional brain signals, transcending the limitations of traditional methods. It has opened the door to a wide array of applications in EEG research and practice. In the field of neurology, machine learning has shown promise in the detection and prediction of seizures, offering potential improvements in patient care and safety. Briefly, the primary applications of ML in EEG include:

- **Diagnosis and Prognosis of Neurological and Psychiatric Disorders**: ML algorithms excel at identifying subtle, long-range temporal and spatial patterns in EEG that are indicative of various conditions. For instance, deep learning models are widely used for the automated detection and classification of epileptic seizures, even in long-term recordings, by learning distinct ictal and interictal signatures. Similarly, ML aids in the early diagnosis and severity assessment of neurodegenerative diseases, such as Alzheimer's and Parkinson's, by pinpointing characteristic alterations in brain oscillations, and in differentiating various sleep disorders through automated sleep stage classification [1, 2].
- **Brain-Computer Interfaces (BCIs)**: ML algorithms are fundamental to BCIs, translating user-intended brain activity into control commands for external devices. Supervised learning models (e.g., SVMs, CNNs, LSTMs) decode motor imagery, P300 evoked potentials, or steady-state visually evoked potentials (SSVEPs) into actionable signals, enabling individuals with severe motor disabilities to communicate or control prosthetics. Reinforcement learning is also emerging to optimize BCI adaptation based on user feedback [1, 2].
- **Cognitive State Monitoring and Emotion Recognition**: ML is applied to infer various cognitive states, such as attention levels, mental workload, fatigue, and engagement, by recognizing specific EEG features (Hosseini et al., 2021). Furthermore, emotion recognition from EEG leverages ML to classify distinct emotional states (e.g., happy, sad, angry) based on brain activity patterns across different channels and frequency bands [8].
- **Artifact Removal and Signal Enhancement**: Unsupervised ML techniques, particularly Independent Component Analysis (ICA) and Autoencoders, are crucial for identifying and effectively removing artifacts (e.g., eye blinks, muscle movements) from raw EEG data, thereby improving the signal-to-noise ratio and enhancing the reliability of subsequent analyses [9, 23]. Generative Adversarial Networks (GANs) are also explored for synthesizing realistic EEG data, which can be used for data augmentation in ML training or for generating artifact-free signals [24, 25].

10.6 Conclusion

This chapter provides a foundational understanding of both real-time EEG signal processing and the application of ML in EEG analysis. It first establishes the criticality of real-time EEG, highlighting its direct benefits for applications like neurofeedback and BCI. These advantages stem from immediate analysis, leading to enhanced responsiveness, improved user experience through reduced latency, and the ability to implement adaptive algorithms for greater accuracy. However, the chapter also acknowledges the inherent "negative" challenges of real-time processing, specifically signal noise and the significant computational load.

The discussion then transitions to the transformative role of ML in modern EEG analysis. It emphasizes how ML algorithms, by learning complex patterns directly from data rather than relying on predefined rules, offer more adaptive, accurate, and scalable interpretations of brain activity.

For readers, particularly those working with Python in the field of neuroscience, this chapter serves as a vital steppingstone. It equips them with the theoretical knowledge and practical skills to utilize powerful Python libraries (like MNE-Python, Scikit-learn, and deep learning frameworks) to conduct cutting-edge research, develop innovative neurotechnologies, and effectively address complex analytical challenges in the field of EEG. The insights gained here provide a robust foundation for a deeper exploration of specific models and advanced applications in subsequent chapters.

References

1. Hosseini M-P, Hosseini A, Ahi K (2020) A review on machine learning for EEG signal processing in bioengineering. IEEE Rev Biomed Eng 14:204–218
2. Khalfallah S, Peuch W, Tlija M, Bouallegue K (2025) Exploring the effectiveness of machine learning and deep learning techniques for EEG signal classification in neurological disorders. IEEE Access
3. Akhtar ZB, Rozario VS (2025) AI perspectives within computational neuroscience: EEG integrations and the human brain. In: Artificial intelligence and applications, pp 145–60
4. Campos MSR, McCracken HS, Uribe-Quevedo A, Grant BL, Yielder PC, Murphy BA (2024) A machine learning approach to classifying EEG data collected with or without haptic feedback during a simulated drilling task. Brain Sci 14(9):894
5. Li G, Lee CH, Jung JJ, Youn YC, Camacho D (2020) Deep learning for EEG data analytics: a survey. Concurr Comput: Pract Exp 32(18):e5199
6. Hurley D, Automated AI (2023) Program interprets EEG as accurately as experts, study finds. Neurol Today 23(15):1–5
7. Zuo M, Chen X, Sui L (2025) Evaluation of machine learning algorithms for classification of visual stimulation-induced EEG signals in 2D and 3D VR videos. Brain Sci 15(1):75
8. Murugappan M, Rizon M, Nagarajan R, Yaacob S, Hazry D, Zunaidi I (2008) Time-frequency analysis of EEG signals for human emotion detection. In: 4th Kuala Lumpur international conference on biomedical engineering 2008: BIOMED 2008 25–28 June 2008 Kuala Lumpur, Malaysia: Springer, p 262–265
9. Saba-Sadiya S, Chantland E, Alhanai T, Liu T, Ghassemi MM (2021) Unsupervised EEG artifact detection and correction. Front Digit Health 2:608920
10. Yıldız İ, Garner R, Lai M, Duncan D (2022) Unsupervised seizure identification on EEG. Comput Methods Programs Biomed 215:106604
11. Zhang W, Tang X, Wang M (2024) Attention model of EEG signals based on reinforcement learning. Front Hum Neurosci 18:1442398
12. Utoft S, Dou J, Wu J (2024) Enhancing EEG data quality: a comprehensive review of outlier detection and cleaning methods
13. Huang G, Zhao Z, Zhang S, Hu Z, Fan J, Fu M et al (2023) Discrepancy between inter-and intra-subject variability in EEG-based motor imagery brain-computer interface: Evidence from multiple perspectives. Front Neurosci 17:1122661
14. Kalita B, Deb N, Das D (2024) AnEEG: leveraging deep learning for effective artifact removal in EEG data. Sci Rep 14(1):24234
15. Krumpe T, Baumgaertner K, Rosenstiel W, Spüler M (2017) Non-stationarity and inter-subject variability of EEG characteristics in the context of BCI development. In: 7th Graz brain-computer interface conference 2017, Graz, Austria: Verlag der TU Graz

16. Da Silva CP, Tedesco S, O'Flynn B (2024) EEG datasets for healthcare: a scoping review. IEEE Access
17. Peres da Silva C, Tedesco S, O'Flynn B (2024) EEG datasets for healthcare: a scoping review
18. Gatfan SK (2024) A review on deep learning for electroencephalogram signal classification. J Al-Qadisiyah Comput Sci Math 16(1):137–151
19. Herington J, McCradden MD, Creel K, Boellaard R, Jones EC, Jha AK et al (2023) Ethical considerations for artificial intelligence in medical imaging: data collection, development, and evaluation. J Nucl Med 64(12):1848–1854
20. Kundu T, Bardhan M (2025) Artificial intelligence in neurology, ethics, recent guideline, and law-an Indian perspective. Front Neurol 16:1515041
21. Ienca M, Ignatiadis K (2020) Artificial intelligence in clinical neuroscience: methodological and ethical challenges. AJOB Neurosci 11(2):77–87
22. Kellmeyer P (2019) Artificial intelligence in basic and clinical neuroscience: opportunities and ethical challenges. Neuroforum 25(4):241–250
23. Sunny MSH, Hossain S, Afroze N, Hasan MK, Hossain E, Rahman MH (2021) Understanding the nonlinear behavior of EEG with advanced machine learning in artifact elimination. Biomed Phys Eng Express 8(1):015017
24. Barua S, Begum S (2014) A review on machine learning algorithms in handling EEG artifacts. The Swedish AI Society (SAIS) Workshop SAIS, 14, 22–23 May 2014, Stockholm, Sweden
25. Mumtaz W, Rasheed S, Irfan A (2021) Review of challenges associated with the EEG artifact removal methods. Biomed Signal Process Control 68:102741

Chapter 11
Dataset for Machine Learning

11.1 Introduction

In this chapter, we consider datasets [1] under the Creative Commons Attribution 4.0 International (CC BY 4.0) license, available via the next link https://archive.ics.uci.edu/dataset/121/eeg+database. This dataset originates from an extensive research project investigating the relationship between genetic susceptibility to alcoholism and electroencephalogram (EEG) patterns. The study collected data using a network of 64 electrodes positioned across participants' scalps, recording electrical activity at a sampling rate of 256 Hz (256 times per second).

The dataset comprises neurological recordings from two distinct groups: individuals with alcoholism and a control group. These recordings were obtained using 64 electrodes positioned on the participants' scalps, capturing data at a rate of 256 Hz (equivalent to a 3.9-ms epoch) over a one-second duration.

The successful application of machine learning methods to detect alcoholism using EEG signals demonstrates the potential for using similar approaches in diagnosing and monitoring other health problems [1, 2]. The algorithms applicable to this method can be adapted for other tasks in the field of neuroscience, enabling the extraction of meaningful features from EEG data and the application of advanced algorithms that can be transferred to other health problems manifesting through changes in brain activity [3]. This opens the possibility of creating objective, fast, and non-invasive diagnostic tools for a wide range of health problems.

I. Rakhmatulin and G. R. Naik, *EEG Signal Processing with Python*, Brain Informatics and Health, https://doi.org/10.1007/978-981-95-4177-5_11

11.2 Dataset Format

We converted the original dataset to a more readable format in Excel, which is available as a single file on GitHub https://github.com/Ildaron/EEG-Signal-Processing-with-Python/tree/main/Dataset/Machine_Learning, Fig. 11.1.

Trials—A record number, 1 s, resulting in 256 record values from each channel.

Identifier—An Indicator of whether he is an alcoholic (1) or not (0).

Following that, the electrodes are positioned according to the International 10–20 EEG electrode system, with measurements recorded in microvolts. The electrode placements include:

- Frontal region: AF1, AF2, AF7, AF8, AFz, F1, F2, F3, F4, F5, F6, F7, F8, Fp1, Fp2, Fpz, Fz
- Central region: C1, C2, C3, C4, C5, C6, Cz
- Temporal region: T7, T8, T3, T4, T5, FT7, FT8
- Parietal region: P1, P2, P3, P4, P5, P6, P7, P8, Pz
- Occipital region: O1, O2, Oz
- Fronto-central region: FC1, FC2, FC3, FC4, FC5, FC6, FCz
- Centro-parietal region: CP1, CP2, CP3, CP4, CP5, CP6, CPz
- Parieto-occipital region: PO1, PO2, PO7, PO8, POz
- Temporo-parietal region: TP7, TP8

This comprehensive electrode array enables the detailed mapping of electrical activity across various brain regions, allowing for a thorough analysis of neural processes and patterns (see Figs. 11.2 and 11.3).

Trials	Identifier	AF1	AF2	AF7	AF8	AFZ	C1	C2	C3	C4
0	1	-6.083	-7.64	-0.682	6.46	-4.71	7.762	-0.773	24.017	-2.319
1	1	-4.618	-9.593	0.295	2.065	-3.733	-7.375	-0.285	-21.881	0.61
2	1	-2.177	-7.151	-1.17	-5.259	-1.292	-2.981	1.18	-3.815	2.075
3	1	1.241	0.173	-3.611	-8.189	1.638	2.391	1.668	-5.28	-1.343
4	1	2.706	8.962	-5.564	-4.283	4.079	2.391	1.18	0.58	-1.343
5	1	2.706	14.333	-6.541	3.53	5.056	-0.539	-2.726	1.068	-1.343
6	1	1.729	13.357	-5.076	9.389	4.567	2.879	-0.773	5.463	-0.854
7	1	1.241	7.009	-0.682	10.854	4.079	3.855	-0.773	6.439	-2.808

Fig. 11.1 Format of the dataset

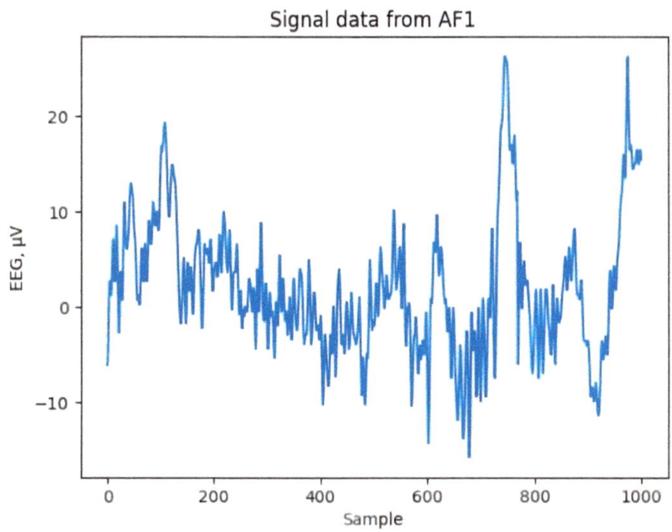

Fig. 11.2 Example of the dataset for the channel AF1 alco

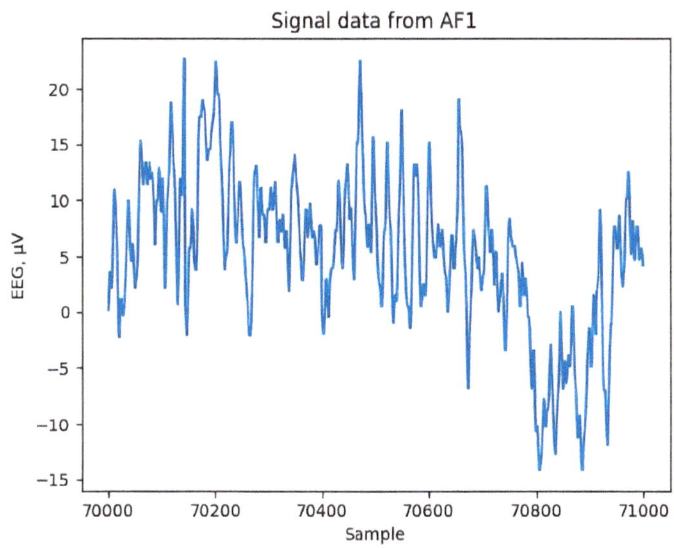

Fig. 11.3 Example of the dataset for the channel AF1—not Alco

```
# Select the data from the first channel for demo
channel = "AF1"
channel_data = eeg_data[channel]
# Plot the EEG data
plt.plot(channel_data[0:1000])
plt.title("Signal data from "+channel)
plt.ylabel('EEG, µV')
plt.xlabel('Sample')
plt.show()
```

Obviously, just by looking at the waveforms, one cannot directly say whether a person has consumed alcohol or not.

However, visual inspection still plays an important role as a first step:

- Check signal quality: By plotting the EEG data, we can quickly see if the signal looks like a real EEG or if it has major distortions.
- Assess amplitude and components: EEG has characteristic rhythms (delta, theta, alpha, beta). A glance confirms that the recorded amplitudes and frequency ranges are reasonable.
- Identify artifacts: Eye blinks, muscle movements, or electrode noise often appear clearly in raw EEG. Removing or marking them is crucial before training a model.
- Get a general impression: Even though visual inspection alone cannot classify alcohol use, it provides confidence that the dataset is meaningful, consistent, and worth analyzing further.

11.3 Visualization of the Dataset

First, let's start with a 3D visualization of all channels on the graph. 3D visualization of EEG data is essential for deepening our understanding of brain activity. It enables researchers to intuitively grasp the complex spatial and temporal relationships within the brain, offering a clearer view of how different regions interact over time. By adding a spatial dimension, 3D visualization makes it easier to detect patterns, trends, and anomalies that might be missed in traditional 2D representations, leading to improved diagnostic accuracy and greater insight. Moreover, it enhances interactive exploration, allowing users to rotate, zoom, and focus on specific areas of interest, making data analysis more dynamic and revealing hidden structures that static views may overlook. The script is provided below, and the results are presented in Figs. 11.4 and 11.5.

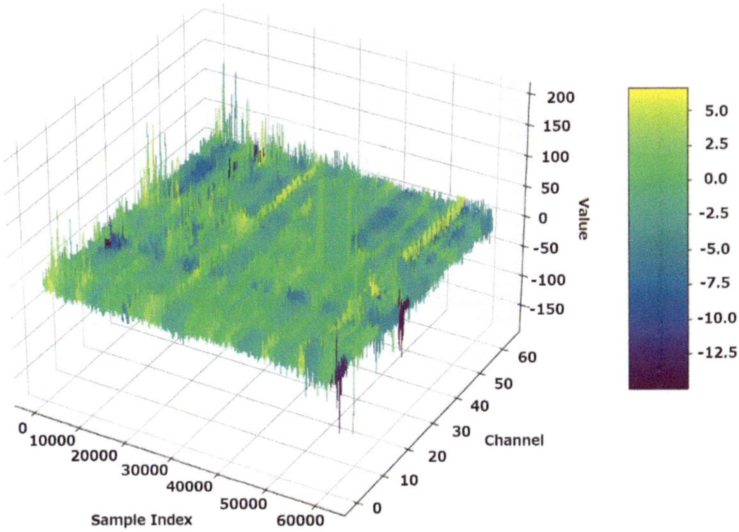

Fig. 11.4 3D visualization of the dataset alco

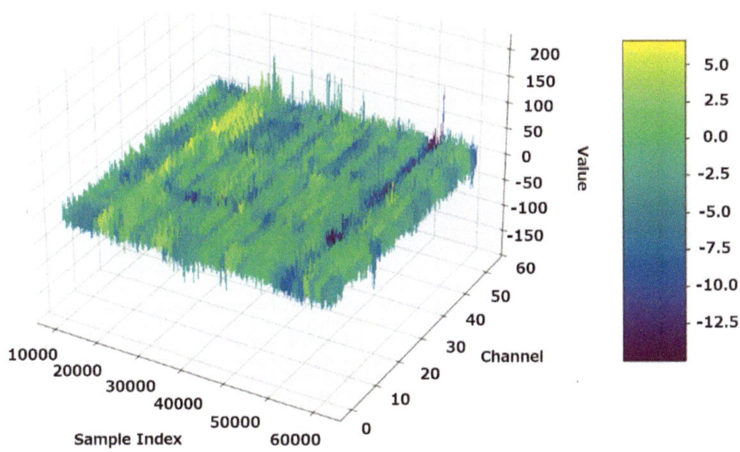

Fig. 11.5 3D visualization of the dataset not alco

```
import pandas as pd
import numpy as np
import matplotlib.pyplot as plt
from mpl_toolkits.mplot3d import Axes3D
df = eeg_data_final #pd.DataFrame(np.random.randn(122880, 64))
# Create the 3D plot
fig = plt.figure(figsize=(20, 10))
ax = fig.add_subplot(111, projection='3d')
# Create Y and X coordinates for the surface
Y = np.arange(df.shape[1])
X = np.arange(df.shape[0])
Y, X = np.meshgrid(Y, X)
# Plot the surface
surf = ax.plot_surface(X, Y, df.values, cmap='viridis', linewidth=0,
antialiased=False)
# Customize the plot
ax.set_title('3D Surface Plot of 64 Channels')
ax.set_ylabel('Channel')
ax.set_xlabel('Sample Index')
ax.set_zlabel('Value')
# Add a color bar
fig.colorbar(surf, shrink=0.5, aspect=5)
plt.show()
```

At first glance, both "Alco" and "Not Alco" conditions appear broadly similar. This is expected: the EEG signal does not contain obvious, large-scale patterns that directly indicate alcohol consumption. Both datasets contain amplitudes within a comparable range (roughly − 200 μV to + 200 μV).

However, closer inspection suggests slightly different variability patterns across channels:

- In the Alco condition, some channels show more frequent sharp deflections (spikes), suggesting increased irregularities. In the Not Alco condition, the signals appear slightly smoother and more consistent across channels.
- Both conditions show evidence of artifacts (e.g., eye blinks, muscle noise, electrode disturbances).
- The "Not Alco" condition looks more structured across channels, while the "Alco" condition seems to have more irregular fluctuations. This could be related to how alcohol affects neural synchronization and EEG rhythms.

11.4 Correlation Matrix

The correlation matrix offers insights into how strongly each EEG channel and the others, facilitating the identification of patterns of functional connectivity within the brain. Channels with high correlation values often indicate similar brain activity, while low or negative correlations suggest distinct or even opposing activity between regions. Differences in correlation between channels on the left and right hemispheres can highlight potential functional imbalances. Additionally, channels showing unusually low correlations may point to issues such as external noise or poor electrode contact. Figures 11.6 and 11.7 contain a correlation matrix for 64 EEG channels generated using the following script.

```
# Plot correlation matrix of EEG data
# Each cell in the matrix shows how strongly two EEG channels are correlated
plt.matshow(eeg_data_final.corr()) # compute correlation across all channels and display as a matrix
plt.colorbar() # add color scale to interpret correlation values (-1 to 1)
plt.show()
```

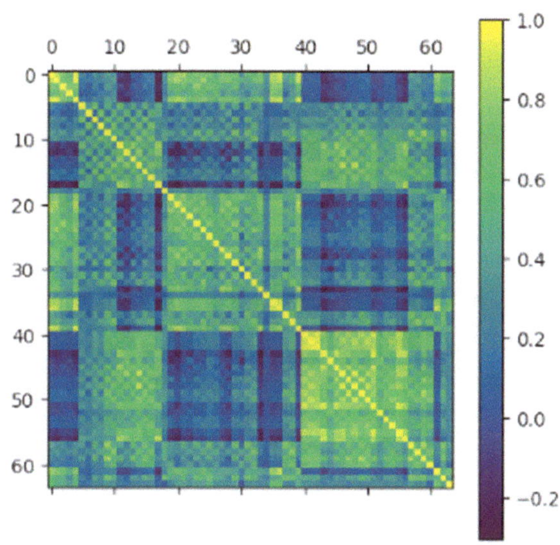

Fig. 11.6 Correlation matrix for 64 EEG channels alco

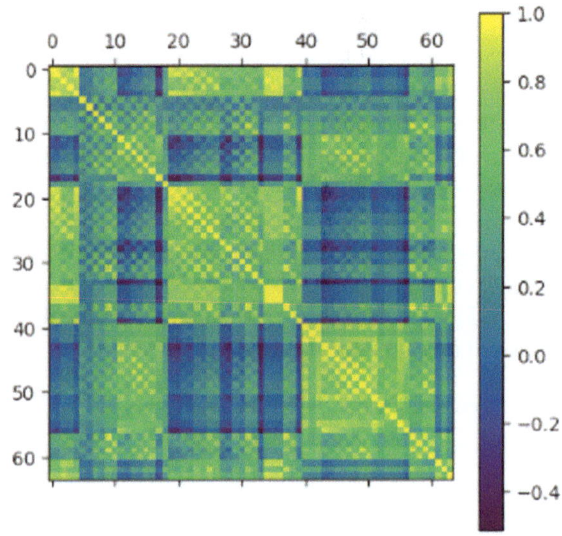

Fig. 11.7 Correlation matrix for 64 EEG channels not alco

Each element of the matrix represents the correlation between two channels (from – 1 to + 1), where:

- Yellow (~ 1.0): Strong positive correlation (signals move together).
- Dark purple (~ 0.0 or negative): Weak or negative correlation (signals move independently or oppositely).

Both conditions show strong diagonal dominance (self-correlation = 1), as expected. In the Not Alco case, the off-diagonal structure appears more consistent and evenly distributed, suggesting stronger global coherence across electrodes. In the Alco case, correlation values are more fragmented with more scattered low-correlation blocks.

It's essential since visualizing connectivity matrices provides insights that raw EEG plots cannot:

- It reveals relationships between brain regions rather than just local signal fluctuations.
- It highlights systematic disruptions under alcohol that could be key for machine learning models.

11.5 Cap Visualization

Figure 11.8 presents EEG heatmaps comparing brain activity patterns between two groups: individuals with alcoholism (left) and individuals without alcoholism (right). Each heatmap illustrates the distribution of EEG power across different scalp regions, with color intensity representing levels of neural activity. Red areas indicate higher activity, while blue areas correspond to lower activity.

By analyzing these spatial patterns, it becomes possible to observe how alcoholism may alter brain function and electrical activity compared to healthy individuals.

```
import numpy as np
import matplotlib.pyplot as plt
import mne
# Extract Alco EEG data (skip metadata columns)
eeg_data_alco = eeg_data.iloc[:, 3:]
# Extract not Alco EEG data
# eeg_data_alco = eeg_data_alco.iloc[:61442]

# Must match the standard 10-20/10-10 system for visualization
channel_names = ['AF1', 'AF2', 'AF7', 'AF8', 'AFz', 'C1', 'C2', 'C3', 'C4', 'C5', 'C6',
'CP1', 'CP2', 'CP3', 'CP4', 'CP5', 'CP6', 'CPz', 'Cz', 'F1', 'F2', 'F3', 'F4', 'F5', 'F6',
'F7', 'F8', 'FC1', 'FC2', 'FC3', 'FC4', 'FC5', 'FC6', 'FCz', 'Fp1', 'Fp2', 'Fpz', 'FT7',
'FT8', 'Fz', 'O1', 'O2', 'Oz', 'P1', 'P2', 'P3', 'P4', 'P5', 'P6', 'P7', 'P8', 'PO1', 'PO2',
'PO7', 'PO8', 'POz', 'Pz', 'T7', 'T8', 'TP7', 'TP8', 'T3', 'T4', 'T5']
# Create a montage (standard electrode positions)
montage = mne.channels.make_standard_montage('standard_1020')
```

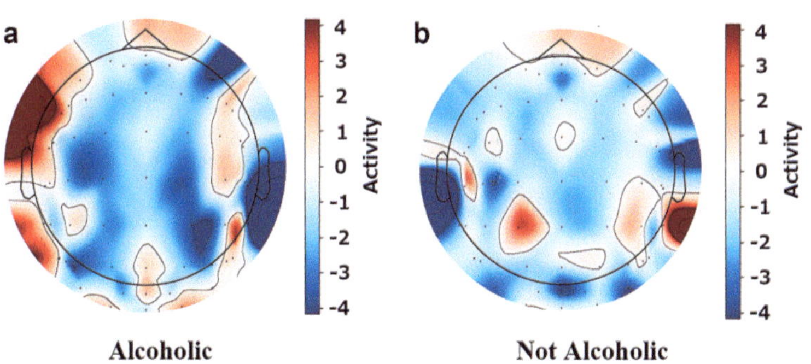

Fig. 11.8 Heat map of the Alcoholic (**a**) and not Alcoholic groups (**b**)

```
# Filter channel names to only those present in the montage
valid_channel_names = [ch for ch in channel_names if ch in montage.ch_names]
invalid_channel_names = [ch for ch in channel_names if ch not in
montage.ch_names]
# Create random values for demonstration (replace with your actual data)
eeg_data_alco = np.array(eeg_data_alco)
reshaped_array = eeg_data_alco.reshape(64, -1).mean(axis=1)
values = np.array(reshaped_array)
# Extract positions for valid channels
positions = montage.get_positions()['ch_pos']
pos = np.array([positions[ch][:2] for ch in valid_channel_names])
# Plot the topomap (heatmap on the head)
fig, ax = plt.subplots()
im, cn = mne.viz.plot_topomap(values, pos=pos, axes=ax, show=False,
cmap='RdBu_r', contours=6)
plt.title("EEG Heatmap")
# Add colorbar
cbar = plt.colorbar(im, ax=ax)
cbar.set_label('Activity')
plt.show()
```

From the visual comparison, it is evident that there are noticeable differences in EEG activity between the alcoholic and non-alcoholic groups. The alcoholic group shows more localized regions of elevated or suppressed brain activity, particularly in the frontal and temporal regions. In contrast, the non-alcoholic group demonstrates a more balanced and diffuse pattern of brain activity.

These distinctions suggest that alcoholism may lead to specific disruptions in neural processing, which could potentially be used as biomarkers for diagnosis and further research in neurophysiology [4, 5].

11.6 Conclusion

In conclusion, the meticulous preparation and insightful exploration of datasets are paramount, forming the bedrock upon which robust and reliable machine learning models are built. As detailed in this chapter, understanding the Dataset Format is the initial, critical step, ensuring data compatibility and structured readiness for algorithmic processing.

Beyond mere formatting, the power of visualization proved indispensable. The 3D Visualization of the Dataset offered a profound ability to discern intricate spatial and temporal patterns, particularly vital for complex neurophysiological signals like

EEG. This macroscopic view enables the identification of global trends and potential anomalies that might otherwise be hidden within raw numerical data. Complementing this, the Cap Visualization, exemplified by the clear distinctions observed between individuals with alcoholism and those without alcoholism, underscored its efficacy in revealing group-specific topographical differences in brain activity. Such visualizations provide intuitive, qualitative insights into the underlying neural dynamics, guiding hypothesis generation and feature selection.

Furthermore, the Correlation Matrix served as a quantitative compass, mapping the interdependencies between various features. This analysis is crucial for identifying highly correlated variables, informing feature engineering decisions, mitigating multicollinearity, and ensuring that subsequent machine learning models are trained on an optimized and informative feature set.

References

1. Mumtaz W, Kamel N, Ali SSA, Malik AS (2018) An EEG-based functional connectivity measure for automatic detection of alcohol use disorder. Artif Intell Med 84:79–89
2. Mumtaz W, Vuong PL, Malik AS, Rashid RBA (2018) A review on EEG-based methods for screening and diagnosing alcohol use disorder. Cogn Neurodyn 12:141–156
3. Mumtaz W, Vuong PL, Xia L, Malik AS, Abd Rashid RB (2016) Automatic diagnosis of alcohol use disorder using EEG features. Knowl-Based Syst 105:48–59
4. Mumtaz W, Vuong PL, Xia L, Malik AS, Rashid RBA (2017) An EEG-based machine learning method to screen alcohol use disorder. Cogn Neurodyn 11:161–171
5. Rodrigues JdC, Rebouças Filho PP, Peixoto Jr E, Kumar A, de Albuquerque VHC (2019) Classification of EEG signals to detect alcoholism using machine learning techniques. Pattern Recognit Lett 125:140–149

Chapter 12
Dataset Preprocessing

Processing of raw Electroencephalography (EEG) data is a crucial step in EEG signal processing and Machine Learning (ML) analysis. EEG signals are noisy and often contaminated by various artifacts. A standard preprocessing analysis of EEG for ML involves several key stages, which include: (i) prepare dataset, (ii) channel selection, (iii) Signal to Noise Ratio (SNR) measurements, etc. This chapter explains the key steps involved in data preparation for EEG-ML analysis.

12.1 Prepare Dataset

The issue with the dataset is that it is not shuffled. The first 61,440 rows correspond to alcoholic data, while the next 61,440 rows correspond to non-alcoholic data. This lack of shuffling creates a problem.

In most cases, shuffling a dataset is straightforward when each row represents a single independent value. However, in our case, the dataset consists of EEG data collected over 1 s, with each second containing 250 samples. We cannot randomly shuffle individual samples within these 1-s intervals because EEG data relies on time-dependent patterns. Therefore, for proper feature extraction, we should shuffle the data in 1-s blocks (i.e., groups of 250 samples) rather than shuffling all rows individually.

Also, shuffling data in scikit-learn is quite important for several reasons:

- Reduce Bias and Improve Model Generalization: Shuffling helps prevent the model from learning the order of the data instead of learning the underlying patterns. This is especially important when the data is sorted or has a specific order, as it ensures that the model learns the overall patterns rather than memorizing the sequence.
- Ensuring representative splits: When splitting data into training and test sets, shuffling ensures that both sets contain a representative sample of the overall data

I. Rakhmatulin and G. R. Naik, *EEG Signal Processing with Python*, Brain Informatics and Health, https://doi.org/10.1007/978-981-95-4177-5_12

distribution. This is especially important for balanced data sets or when the data is ordered by class or target variable.

- Improving model accuracy: By presenting data in different orders during training, shuffling helps the model learn more robust features and improves its ability to generalize to new, unseen data.

To implement it, we used the following script via the Pandas library.

```
import pandas as pd
# Shuffle the DataFrame by 'file_num'
# Get unique file_nums and shuffle them
unique_file_nums = eeg_data['file_num'].unique()
np.random.shuffle(unique_file_nums)
#    Reorder the DataFrame based on the shuffled file_nums
shuffled_data = pd.concat([eeg_data[eeg_data['file_num'] == file_num] for
file_num in unique_file_nums])
# Reset the index (optional)
shuffled_data.reset_index(drop=True, inplace=True)
print(shuffled_data)
```

After the shuffle has the next format (Fig. 12.1).

The next step is to clarify which data is responsible for X and which for Y. that is, what data are responsible for the water indicators, EEG data—X, and those that are responsible for the classification (alcohol or not alcohol)—Y.

```
        file_num  sample_num  subje0t_identifier    AF1    AF2    AF7    AF8
0            260           0                   0 -2.268 -1.149 -3.815  0.010
1            260           1                   0 -1.292 -0.173 -1.373  1.963
2            260           2                   0 -0.804 -1.149  1.068  1.475
3            260           3                   0 -0.804 -2.126  1.068 -1.943
4            260           4                   0 -1.780 -3.591 -0.885 -5.849
...          ...         ...                 ...    ...    ...    ...    ...
122875       431         251                   0 -2.431 -2.523  1.261  4.690
122876       431         252                   0 -1.943 -2.035  4.191  3.713
122877       431         253                   0 -0.966 -2.035  7.121  2.736
122878       431         254                   0 -0.478 -2.523  8.097  1.760
122879       431         255                   0 -0.478 -3.011  7.121  1.272
```

Fig. 12.1 Dataset format after shuffle

	AF1	AF2	AF7	AF8	AFZ	C1	C2	C3	C4	C5	...	PO8	POZ	PZ	T7	T8	TP7	TP8
0	-2.268	-1.149	-3.815	0.010	-1.923	-0.671	0.387	5.717	-4.964	9.003	...	2.920	3.347	6.073	4.384	1.414	5.646	3.387
1	-1.292	-0.173	-1.373	1.963	-1.434	-4.089	1.851	3.764	-5.452	8.514	...	1.943	6.276	7.538	6.337	4.832	6.622	5.341
2	-0.804	-1.149	1.068	1.475	-1.434	-4.578	-3.031	1.322	-5.452	5.585	...	2.431	7.741	8.026	7.314	6.297	7.111	3.876
3	-0.804	-2.126	1.068	-1.943	-1.434	-4.578	-1.567	-1.119	-5.941	1.190	...	-4.893	8.718	9.003	5.361	4.344	6.134	0.946
4	-1.780	-3.591	-0.885	-5.849	-1.923	-2.625	-1.567	-3.560	-6.429	-2.228	...	0.966	9.694	10.468	0.478	0.926	3.204	-1.495

Fig. 12.2 Dataset format X

0	0
1	0
2	0
3	0
4	0

Fig. 12.3 Dataset format Y

```
# Select all columns except the first three from the shuffled_data DataFrame
(assumed EEG signal columns)
eeg_data_final = shuffled_data.iloc[:, 3:]
# Display the first few rows of the EEG data to verify selection
display(eeg_data_final.head())
# Extract the 'subject_identifier' column from shuffled_data as the target/status
variable
status_y = shuffled_data["subje0t_identifier"]
display(status_y.head())
```

Finally, dataset X (EEG data) has the following format, Fig. 12.2.
Dataset Y (alco—1, not alco—0), the next format, Fig. 12.3

12.2 Channel Selection

The current dataset consists of 64 channels, each with 250 samples, totaling 122,880 rows. However, the dataset could be even larger. Unfortunately, not all channels provide clean EEG signals due to issues like impedance problems. Therefore, it's essential to identify which channels are reliable and usable. Besides this, the appropriate EEG channels for feature extraction are crucial for several reasons:

1. Dimensionality reduction: EEG recordings often involve multiple channels, which can lead to high-dimensional data. By selecting the most relevant channels, we can reduce the dimensionality of the data, making it more manageable for machine learning algorithms and reducing computational complexity.
2. Improved classification accuracy: Focusing on the most informative channels can enhance the signal-to-noise ratio and improve the overall classification accuracy of the machine learning model.
3. Efficient processing: Channel selection helps in reducing the amount of data to be processed, leading to faster computation times and more efficient use of resources.
4. Removal of redundant information: Not all EEG channels provide equally valuable information for a given task. Channel selection helps in identifying and removing redundant or irrelevant channels, which can potentially introduce noise or confound the analysis.
5. Task-specific optimization: Different brain regions are involved in various cognitive tasks or neurological conditions. Selecting channels relevant to the specific task or condition being studied can lead to more targeted and accurate analysis.
6. Hardware optimization: In real-time applications or hardware implementations, using fewer channels can lead to more efficient and cost-effective systems.

12.2.1 Signal-to-Noise Ratio (SNR)

SNR is a crucial factor in EEG analysis before applying machine learning (ML), as it determines the quality and reliability of the recorded brain signals [1, 2]. EEG data is highly susceptible to noise from muscle movements, eye blinks, and environmental interference, which can significantly affect the performance of ML models. A low SNR means that useful brain signals are hidden under noise, making it challenging for ML algorithms to extract meaningful features and resulting in inaccurate or misleading results [3]. Pre-processing techniques such as filtering, artifact removal, and signal enhancement are necessary to improve SNR, ensuring that the ML model learns from relevant neural patterns and not from noise [4, 5]. Therefore, understanding and optimizing SNR before applying ML is essential to achieve reliable and interpretable results in EEG-based applications such as brain-computer interfaces, medical diagnostics, and cognitive research. For our dataset, we calculated SNR using the following scripts and the Pandas library.

```
import pandas as pd
import matplotlib.pyplot as plt
# Assuming eeg_data_final is already loaded as a DataFrame
# Define assumed noise power level (can be improved by empirical noise
estimation)
P_noise = 1  # Assuming unit noise power
# Initialize dictionary to store SNR values per channel
SNR_values = {}
# Calculate SNR for each EEG channel
for column in eeg_data_final.columns:
    channel_data = eeg_data_final[column]
    # Estimate signal power as mean squared amplitude of channel data
    P_signal = np.mean(channel_data**2)  # Power of the signal
     # Convert ratio to decibels (dB) for interpretability
    SNR_values[column] = 10 * np.log10(P_signal / P_noise)  # SNR calculation
# Convert dictionary to DataFrame for easier manipulation and visualization
SNR_df = pd.DataFrame.from_dict(SNR_values, orient='index', columns=['SNR
(dB)'])
# Plot the SNR values
plt.figure(figsize=(24, 6))
plt.bar(SNR_df.index, SNR_df['SNR (dB)'], color='skyblue', edgecolor='black')
# Formatting the plot
plt.xlabel("EEG Channels")
plt.ylabel("SNR (dB)")
plt.title("Signal-to-Noise Ratio (SNR) for Each EEG Channel")
```

For our dataset, we received the following the result, Fig. 12.4.

The bar graph you generated shows the Signal-to-Noise Ratio (SNR) in decibels (dB) across EEG channels. Overall, the SNR values vary substantially between channels, indicating differences in signal quality. Channels such as Cz and AF7/AF8 exhibit the highest SNR values (above 22–25 dB), suggesting these locations capture relatively strong and clean EEG signals. In contrast, channels like C3, C4, and CP6 show lower SNR values (around 10–12 dB), indicating more noise or weaker signal power in those regions. Most other channels cluster between 15 and 20 dB, indicating moderate signal quality. This variability could be due to electrode placement, contact quality, or physiological differences in brain activity across scalp regions. In practical terms, high-SNR channels may be more reliable for downstream EEG analysis, while low-SNR channels might require preprocessing techniques (e.g., filtering, artifact removal) to improve interpretability.

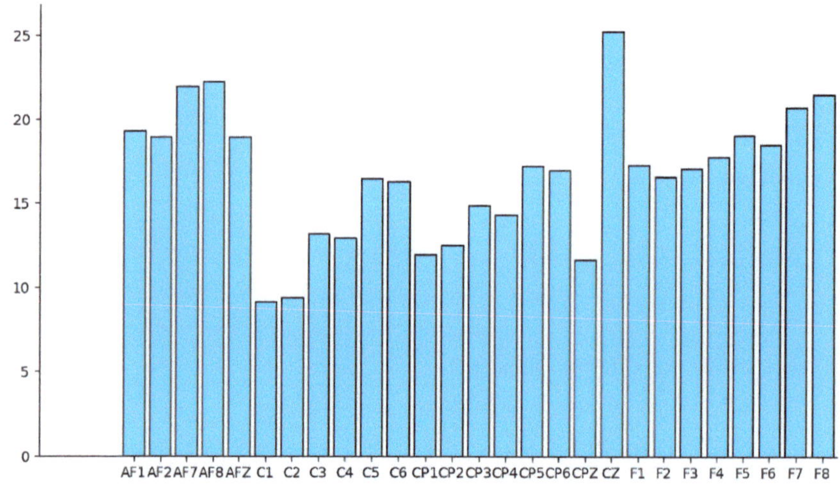

Fig. 12.4 Signal-to-noise ratios for EEG channels

12.2.2 Preprocessing EEG Data Recursive Feature Elimination

Preprocessing EEG data using recursive feature elimination (RFE) offers advantages over the signal-to-noise ratio (SNR) method for identifying optimal EEG channels [6]. RFE iteratively eliminates less important features while evaluating model performance using cross-validation, allowing for a more comprehensive assessment of channel importance [7]. This approach enables the integration of multiple evaluation methods, such as random forest, gradient boosting, and logistic regression, to provide a more robust channel selection. RFE helps improve the generalization ability of the model while reducing the risk of overfitting, making it particularly useful for cross-subject EEG analysis, where individual differences can significantly influence channel selection [8].

```
from sklearn.feature_selection import RFE
from sklearn.linear_model import LogisticRegression
model = LogisticRegression()
# create the RFE model and select 3 attributes
x = eeg_data_final
y = status_y
rfe = RFE(estimator=model, n_features_to_select=30)
    rfe = rfe.fit(x[:1000], y[:1000])
# Get the feature ranking
feature_ranking = rfe.ranking_
# Get the column names of your original dataset
feature_names = x.columns
# Create a list of selected features
selected_features = [feature for feature, rank in zip(feature_names,
feature_ranking) if rank == 1]
```

The following script provides for the following relevant channels.

AF1, C1, C4, C5, CP1, CP2, CP3, CZ, F1, F2, F3, F4, FC1, FC2, FC3, FC4, FC5, FCZ, O1, O2, P1, P3, P4, P5, P7, P8, PO7, PO8, TP7, as an example which channel is more correlated with the output value, Fig. 12.5.

The y-axis shows the ranking values assigned to each channel, where lower numbers represent higher importance. Only the top channels (rank = 1) were retained as most relevant for classification, while higher-ranked channels were progressively eliminated.

From the figure, channels such as AFZ, F2, CP5, Y, FPZ are ranked lower (17–21), indicating less contribution to model performance, while channels like F6, AF7, FT7, OZ, F5 rank highest (32–34), meaning they are the most influential features for classification in the EEG dataset.

The RFE procedure reduced dimensionality by prioritizing channels with stronger discriminative power. The highest-ranked channels (e.g., F5, OZ, FT7) are critical for the classification task, while lower-ranked ones (e.g., AFZ, F2) provide comparatively less useful information.

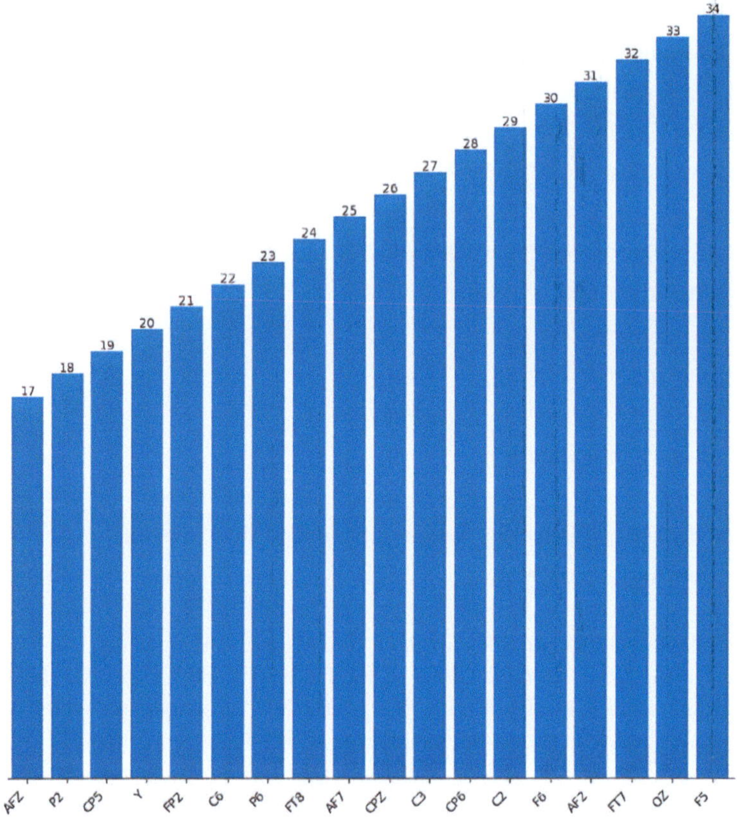

Fig. 12.5 Selected channels via RFE

12.2.3 Pearson Correlation

Pearson correlation, unlike Recursive Feature Elimination (RFE), which iteratively removes less important features based on model performance, Pearson correlation provides a direct statistical measure of similarity, allowing for a faster and more interpretable feature selection process [9, 10].

Implementation via the Pandas Library is provided below.

```
import pandas as pd
import numpy as np
# Compute the correlation between each feature (EEG channel) in x and the target
variable y
# This provides a measure of linear relationship between channel signals and the
classification target
correlations = x.corrwith(y)
# extract channel names (feature labels) and their correlation values into separate
lists
channels = correlations.index.tolist()
values = correlations.values.tolist()
# Create a DataFrame combining channels and their correlation values for easier
manipulation and plotting
df = pd.DataFrame({'Channel': channels, 'Value': values})

# Plot
plt.bar(df['Channel'], df['Value'], color='skyblue')
plt.title('EEG Channel Correlations with Target')
plt.xticks(rotation=90)
plt.tight_layout()
plt.show()
```

Graph visualization, Fig. 12.6

Each bar corresponds to an EEG channel labeled on the x-axis, while the y-axis shows the absolute strength of the linear relationship with the target. The chart reveals notable variability across channels in the strength of their signals' correlation with the target. Some channels, such as FC1, FT8, and AF4, exhibit relatively higher absolute correlation values (close to or above 0.10), indicating stronger associations with the target variable. Conversely, other channels show very low correlations near zero, suggesting a minimal linear relationship. This pattern indicates that certain EEG channels may carry more relevant information for predicting or classifying the target, while others contribute less.

12.2.4 *Feature Importance via Machine Learning*

Feature importance, as determined by machine learning, Pearson correlation, and RFE, serves as methods for feature selection, but they differ in their methodology and effectiveness [11]. Feature importance in ML assigns weights to variables

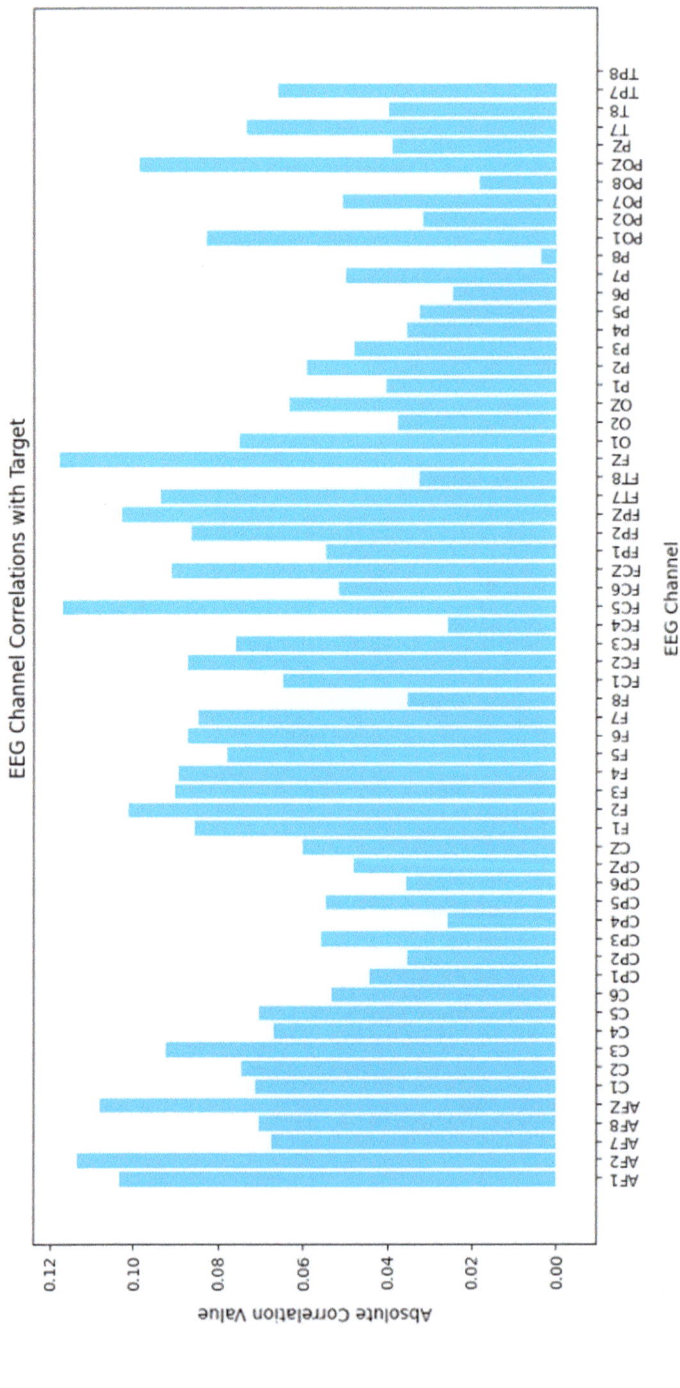

Fig. 12.6 Selected channels via pearson correlation

based on their impact on model performance, capturing complex, nonlinear interactions, but requiring high computation. Pearson correlation is a straightforward statistical approach that identifies linear dependencies between features, making it effective for redundancy removal, but it is limited in capturing intricate relationships [12]. RFE iteratively removes the least significant features using a model-based approach, preserving interactions, but this approach is computationally intensive. While ML-based feature importance provides deeper insights, Pearson correlation offers quick filtering, and RFE strikes a balance between interpretability and model-driven selection.

Implementation via sklearn is provided below:

```
from sklearn.ensemble import RandomForestClassifier
import pandas as pd
# Initialize Random Forest model with 100 trees and fixed random state for
reproducibility
rf = RandomForestClassifier(n_estimators=100, random_state=42)
# Fit the model on the first 1000 samples of features (x) and target labels (y)
rf.fit(x[:1000], y[:1000])
# Extract feature importance scores from the trained model
#  Map these importance scores to the feature names from the DataFrame columns
feature_importances = pd.Series(rf.feature_importances_, index=x.columns)
# Create a new pandas Series for feature importances (already created above but
repeated here
feature_importances = pd.Series(rf.feature_importances_, index=x.columns)
# Plot
plt.figure(figsize=(12, 8))
plt.title('Feature Importances in Random Forest Model', fontsize=16)
plt.xlabel('Features', fontsize=12)
plt.ylabel('Importance', fontsize=12)
plt.show()
```

The result is provided in Fig. 12.7.

A few channels stand out with significantly higher importance, particularly channel FP1, which exhibits the highest contribution. Other notable channels include F4 and PZ, indicating their strong influence in differentiating between the two groups. The presence of high importance attributed to frontal and central regions aligns with existing research suggesting altered neural activity in these areas due to alcohol consumption.

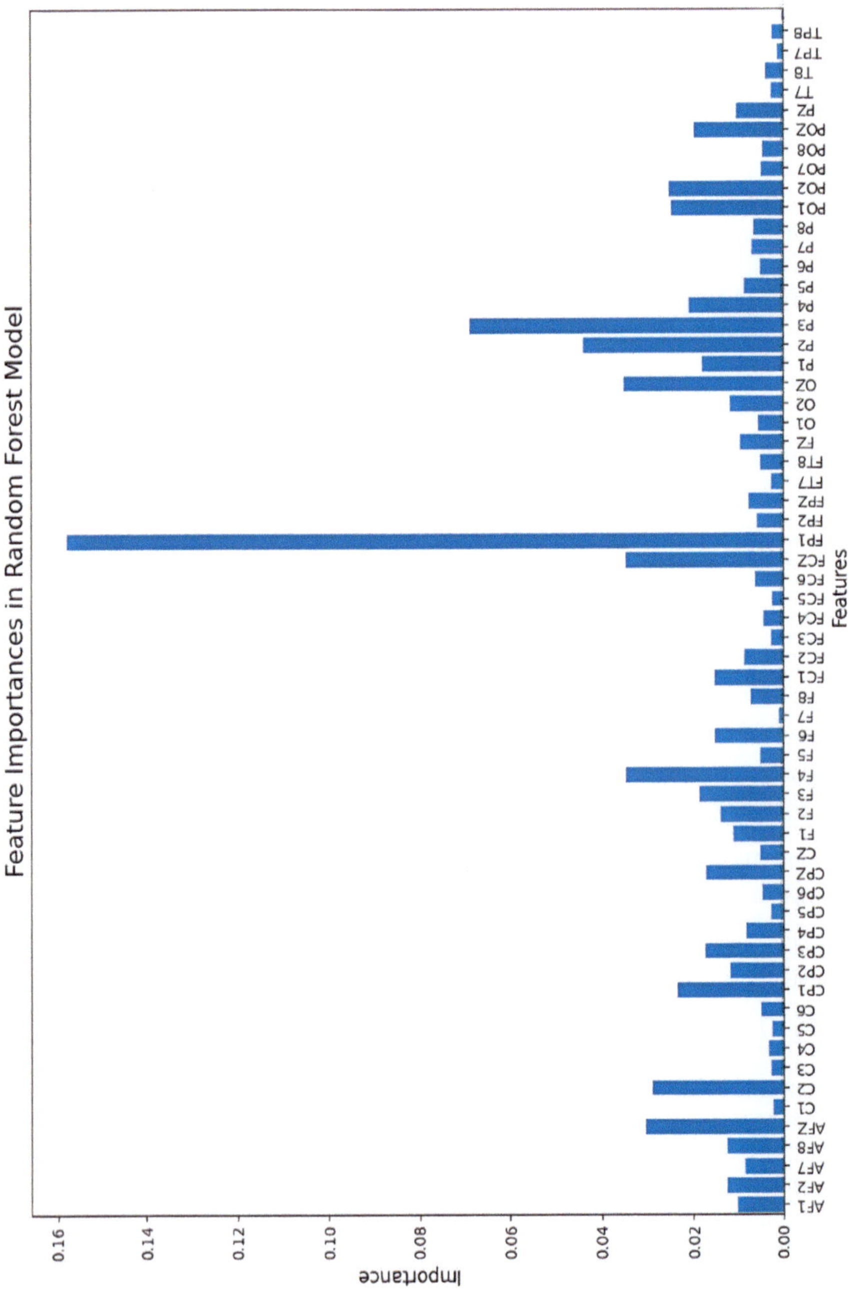

Fig. 12.7 Selected channels via feature importance

12.3 Conclusion

Identifying the most informative channels is critical for building reliable models. In this study, four complementary approaches—signal-to-noise ratio (SNR), recursive feature elimination (RFE), Pearson correlation, and feature-importance ranking—were applied to evaluate the discriminative power of different electrodes. The results revealed that certain regions consistently emerged as highly informative across methods, particularly electrodes over the frontal and central cortices, with additional contributions from parietal areas. These regions are neurobiologically relevant, as they reflect impaired executive control, disrupted cortical integration, and altered attentional processing associated with alcohol consumption. This demonstrates the importance of integrating multiple feature-selection strategies: it reduces reliance on a single statistical or model-driven criterion, enhances classification accuracy, and ensures that the selected electrodes are both data-driven and physiologically meaningful.

This chapter has provided a comprehensive exploration of essential techniques for preparing and preprocessing datasets in Python, a critical phase often underestimated yet fundamental to the success of any machine learning endeavor. We began by establishing the importance of a well-prepared dataset, delving into methodologies for channel selection to distil relevant information while mitigating noise and redundancy. A significant focus was placed on understanding and enhancing data quality through the calculation and improvement of the Signal-to-Noise Ratio (SNR), a vital metric particularly relevant for biological signals, such as EEG data.

The intricacies of preprocessing EEG data were specifically addressed, highlighting domain-specific challenges and solutions to transform raw neural signals into a clean, usable format. Furthermore, we investigated powerful feature engineering and selection strategies. Recursive Feature Elimination (RFE) was presented as a robust method for systematically identifying optimal feature subsets. At the same time, the utility of Pearson Correlation was demonstrated for understanding linear relationships and reducing multicollinearity among features. Finally, we explored how Feature Importance via Machine Learning models can provide invaluable insights into the predictive power of individual features, guiding more informed decisions about feature inclusion.

In essence, mastering these preprocessing techniques—from meticulous data preparation and strategic channel selection to advanced feature engineering and selection—empowers data scientists to unlock the true potential of their datasets. By systematically addressing data quality, relevance, and dimensionality, we not only improve the performance and interpretability of machine learning models but also build more robust and reliable predictive systems. As you progress in your data science journey, remember that the time invested in thorough data preprocessing is an investment in the accuracy, efficiency, and ultimately, the success of your machine learning applications.

References

1. Sadiya S, Alhanai T, Ghassemi MM (2021) Artifact detection and correction in EEG data: a review. In: 2021 10th International IEEE/EMBS conference on neural engineering (NER): IEEE, pp 495–498
2. Väisänen O, Malmivuo J (2009) Improving the SNR of EEG generated by deep sources with weighted multielectrode leads. J Physiol-Paris 103(6):306–314
3. Goldenholz DM, Ahlfors SP, Hämäläinen MS, Sharon D, Ishitobi M, Vaina LM, Stufflebeam SM (2009) Mapping the signal-to-noise-ratios of cortical sources in magnetoencephalography and electroencephalography. Hum Brain Mapp 30(4):1077–1086
4. Bast T, Boppel T, Rupp A, Harting I, Hoechstetter K, Fauser S et al (2006) Noninvasive source localization of interictal EEG spikes: effects of signal-to-noise ratio and averaging. J Clin Neurophysiol 23(6):487–497
5. Übeyli ED (2009) Measuring saliency of features representing EEG signals using signal-to-noise ratios. Expert Syst Appl 36(1):501–509
6. Yin Z, Wang Y, Liu L, Zhang W, Zhang J (2017) Cross-subject EEG feature selection for emotion recognition using transfer recursive feature elimination. Front Neurorobot 11:19
7. Cai J, Chen W, Yin Z (2019) Multiple transferable recursive feature elimination technique for emotion recognition based on EEG signals. Symmetry 11(5):683
8. Yin Z, Liu L, Liu L, Zhang J, Wang Y (2017) Dynamical recursive feature elimination technique for neurophysiological signal-based emotion recognition. Cogn Technol Work 19:667–685
9. Dhiman R (2023) Electroencephalogram channel selection based on pearson correlation coefficient for motor imagery-brain-computer interface. Meas Sens 25:100616
10. Šverko Z, Vrankić M, Vlahinić S, Rogelj P (2022) Complex Pearson correlation coefficient for EEG connectivity analysis. Sensors 22(4):1477
11. Mera-Gaona M, López DM, Vargas-Canas R (2021) An ensemble feature selection approach to identify relevant features from EEG signals. Appl Sci 11(15):6983
12. Shen K-Q, Ong C-J, Li X-P, Hui Z, Wilder-Smith EP (2007) A feature selection method for multilevel mental fatigue EEG classification. IEEE Trans Biomed Eng 54(7):1231–1237

Chapter 13
ML and EEG

Machine Learning (ML) has become an important tool for analyzing complex brain activities, such as Electroencephalography (EEG). EEG signals are complex, noisy and high-dimensional, making them difficult to analyze manually [1]. ML algorithms can identify subtle patterns in EEG data, making them suitable for various applications, such as Brain-Computer Interface (BCI) and Epilepsy detection [2]. The ML process involves three major steps, which include: (i) preprocessing, (ii) feature extraction and (iii) classification/regression. This chapter explains the use of ML and EEG in Python, starting with normalization, followed by ML features, and then regression and classification methods.

13.1 Standardize and Normalize Data

Normalizing and standardizing EEG data using scikit-learn preprocessing features is essential for improving the performance of machine learning models. EEG signals often have different amplitudes and scales across channels and subjects, which can introduce bias into model training (Fig. 13.1).

```
from sklearn import preprocessing
# Apply normalization to the dataset "x".
# Normalization rescales each row (sample) so that its vector norm (length) is 1.
normalized_x = preprocessing.normalize(x)
# Convert the normalized NumPy array back into a Pandas DataFrame
normalized_x = pd.DataFrame(normalized_x)
print (normalized_x )
```


I. Rakhmatulin and G. R. Naik, *EEG Signal Processing with Python*, Brain Informatics and Health, https://doi.org/10.1007/978-981-95-4177-5_13

```
             AF1       AF2       AF7       AF8       AFZ        C1        C2  \
0       0.577766  0.738289  0.752625  0.764557  0.577404  0.948091  0.234816
1       0.524765  0.682797  0.477631  0.499860  0.521902  0.437055 -0.095369
2       0.365654  0.516207  0.202637  0.197294  0.410899  0.607284  0.565001
3       0.206543  0.294125  0.006167  0.008258  0.244280  0.948091  1.059773
4       0.100433  0.127535 -0.033094 -0.029534  0.133163  0.096598  0.565001
...          ...       ...       ...       ...       ...       ...       ...
122875  0.848417  1.295938  1.026733  1.512957  1.291305  0.028925  1.812744
122876  1.060529  1.629004  1.341069  1.361635  1.513426 -0.311533  1.647820
122877  1.166640  1.851086  1.458855  1.399505  1.735546 -0.652340  0.822864
122878  1.113639  1.851086  1.458855  1.739785  1.735546  0.028925  1.482897
122879  1.007528  1.740102  1.498197  2.080143  1.624543 -0.481762  1.317635
```

Fig. 13.1 Example of EEG data after normalizing

```
             AF1       AF2       AF7       AF8       AFZ        C1        C2  \
0       0.139511  0.141527  0.049631  0.122560  0.130401  0.036962 -0.094708
1       0.176874  0.178793  0.115233  0.183778  0.179729  0.046173  0.128080
2       0.193236  0.206926  0.212065  0.282409  0.207910 -0.081608  0.025890
3       0.180755  0.171021  0.257883  0.292920  0.183673 -0.081266 -0.114341
4       0.153321  0.142188  0.268237  0.201465  0.143310 -0.146373  0.096287
...          ...       ...       ...       ...       ...       ...       ...
122875 -0.014999 -0.047746  0.010908 -0.039341 -0.027740  0.011601 -0.013881
122876 -0.026541 -0.060060 -0.033519 -0.040269 -0.028394  0.011875 -0.025374
122877  0.007928 -0.030153  0.000000 -0.020353 -0.006862  0.013491 -0.028827
122878  0.074871  0.034942  0.106460  0.018588  0.072636  0.014146 -0.043527
122879  0.128568  0.095384  0.188027  0.070740  0.126733  0.011756 -0.036174
```

Fig. 13.2 Example of EEG data after standardizing

Normalization (preprocessing.normalize(x)) ensures that feature values have a uniform scale, preventing any one feature from dominating the model. Standardization (preprocessing.scale(x)) transforms the data so that it has zero mean and unit variance, making it more suitable for algorithms that usually assume distributed inputs, such as Support Vector Machine (SVM) and neural networks (Fig. 13.2).

```
# Standardization rescales the data so that each feature has:
#  - Mean = 0
#  - Standard deviation = 1
standardized_x = preprocessing.scale(x)
# Convert the normalized NumPy array back into a Pandas DataFrame
standardized_x = pd.DataFrame(standardized_x, columns=column_names)
print (standardized_x)
```

Properly processed EEG data enhances model stability, accelerates convergence speed, and improves classification accuracy in detecting patterns.

For the output data, Y, we do not need to perform this step since we have a binary classification, and it is already in the range of 0 and 1. However, suppose we aim to predict a quantitative assessment and have a corresponding dataset. In that case, this process must also be conducted in accordance with the algorithm designed for the input data X.

13.2 Hot Coding

In this dataset, we exclude subjects, their counts, and ordinal numbers as input data for the model. Our goal is to design a universal system capable of identifying patterns across various subject types. However, it is essential to address the use of the one-hot encoding technique, which represents categorical variables as binary vectors.

To illustrate, let's consider subject numbers. Using raw numerical values as input for a machine learning model can lead to ambiguity. The model may interpret these numbers as continuous, treating Subject 2 as twice the magnitude of Subject 1, even though they are categorical. This misinterpretation could negatively impact the model's performance. Using the following script, we can implement one-hot encoding. This can be achieved in Python with the NumPy library, which converts numeric or symbolic values for subjects into a format familiar to machine learning algorithms.

```
import numpy as np
# Define a custom encoding function that performs one-hot encoding
# on a categorical value (an integer between 1 and num_categories).
def custom_encode(value, num_categories=7):
# Ensure the input value is within the valid range (1 to num_categories).
    if value < 1 or value > num_categories:
        raise ValueError(f"Value must be between 1 and {num_categories}")
# Initialize a zero vector of length num_categories.
    encoding = [0] * num_categories
# Set the position corresponding to the given value to 1
# Subtract 1 since Python uses 0-based indexing
    encoding[value - 1] = 1
    return encoding
original_data = [1, 2, 3, 4, 5, 6, 7]  # Example number of subjects
# Apply the custom one-hot encoding function to each value in the dataset.
encoded_data = [custom_encode(value) for value in original_data]

# Show side-by-side: original value and its encoded vector.
for original, encoded in zip(original_data, encoded_data):
    print(f"{original} -> {encoded}")
```

```
Encoded data:
1 -> [1, 0, 0, 0, 0, 0, 0]
2 -> [0, 1, 0, 0, 0, 0, 0]
3 -> [0, 0, 1, 0, 0, 0, 0]
4 -> [0, 0, 0, 1, 0, 0, 0]
5 -> [0, 0, 0, 0, 1, 0, 0]
6 -> [0, 0, 0, 0, 0, 1, 0]
7 -> [0, 0, 0, 0, 0, 0, 1]
```

Fig. 13.3 Example of EEG data subject after one hot encoding

As a result, seven categorical subjects can be represented using the array shown in Fig. 13.3.

Hot coding can be used not only for output data but also for input data such as gender, age, and other factors.

13.3 Take Power for ML

In practice, because raw microvolt EEG values are more challenging to interpret and explain, as they represent a complex mixture of brain signals and noise in a time series, researchers prefer to use power in a given frequency range, which has the following positive aspects:

- **Captures physiologically relevant information**: Alcohol changes power in certain EEG frequency ranges (e.g. alpha), making power in these ranges a more direct and meaningful indicator of alcohol consumption than raw EEG voltages.
- **Simplifies time-dependent signals**: Raw microvolt EEG data is a time series with high variability over time, making it difficult for ML models to extract patterns consistently. Power in rhythm is a summary statistic (representing the total energy or strength within a frequency range), providing a stable and compact representation of EEG activity over time.
- **Noise reduction**: Raw EEG signals often contain noise from sources such as muscle movement, environmental artifacts, or electrode issues. Power calculation focuses solely on the energy within a given frequency range (8–13 Hz), automatically filtering out noise from irrelevant frequencies, thereby enhancing the signal-to-noise ratio.
- **Dimensionality reduction**: Raw EEG is a multi-dimensional signal with many channels, each producing hundreds of microvolt data points per second. For example, A 10-s signal from 64 channels sampled at 250 Hz produces 160,000 data points. Alpha power calculation reduces this to a single value per channel for a given time window, significantly reducing the dimensionality while preserving key information. Low dimensionality improves the training speed and generalization of ML models.

- **Better model generalization**: ML models trained on raw EEG voltages often suffer from overfitting due to the high variability and complexity of time series data. Power in a given frequency band (and other rhythms) is more robust to individual differences and recording conditions, allowing the model to generalize better across participants and datasets [3, 4].

In EEG (electroencephalography), the detection of alcohol consumption or its effects typically involves analyzing specific frequency bands in the brain's electrical activity. In theory, we know these frequency bands have the following features:

- **Delta (0.5–4 Hz)**: Often associated with deep sleep. Alcohol consumption can increase delta activity, especially in the frontal regions of the brain.
- **Theta (4–8 Hz)**: Linked to drowsiness and relaxation. Alcohol use is known to elevate theta activity, indicating sedation or cognitive slowing.
- **Alpha (8–13 Hz)**: Associated with relaxation and idling states of the brain. Alcohol can increase alpha power, particularly in posterior regions, reflecting reduced cortical activation.
- **Beta (13–30 Hz)**: Related to active thinking and concentration. Alcohol often leads to an increase in beta power, particularly in the frontal areas, due to its stimulating effects in particular phases.
- **Gamma (30–100 Hz)**: Linked to higher-level cognitive functions. Alcohol consumption may reduce gamma activity, impairing cognitive processing and attention [5, 6].

Theory suggests that increased theta and delta activity may indicate alcohol-induced sedation [7, 8]. Increased beta activity is often seen in people under the influence of alcohol. Changes in alpha activity are also common and can vary depending on the amount of alcohol consumed. Detection typically focuses on changes in the theta, alpha, and beta ranges, as these are the most sensitive to the effects of alcohol [7, 8]. Advanced machine learning models are often used to analyze these EEG patterns for accurate detection. Well, let's examine how well the theory aligns with practice.

The following script can be used to visualize the distribution of alpha EEG power on a human head model.

```
import mne
eeg_data_alco = alpha_power_df[:240] # eeg_data_alco.iloc[:61442] # Uses
integer-based indexing
print (eeg_data_alco)
 # Selects all rows from index 61442 onward
# Define your channel names (ensure they match the montage)
channel_names = ['AF1', 'AF2', 'AF7', 'AF8', 'AFz', 'C1', 'C2', 'C3', 'C4', 'C5', 'C6',
'CP1', 'CP2', 'CP3', 'CP4', 'CP5', 'CP6', 'CPz', 'Cz', 'F1', 'F2', 'F3', 'F4', 'F5', 'F6',
'F7', 'F8', 'FC1', 'FC2', 'FC3', 'FC4', 'FC5', 'FC6', 'FCz', 'Fp1', 'Fp2', 'Fpz', 'FT7',
'FT8', 'Fz', 'O1', 'O2', 'Oz', 'P1', 'P2', 'P3', 'P4', 'P5', 'P6', 'P7', 'P8', 'PO1', 'PO2',
'PO7', 'PO8', 'POz', 'Pz', 'T7', 'T8', 'TP7', 'TP8', 'T3', 'T4', 'T5']
# Create a montage (standard electrode positions)`
montage = mne.channels.make_standard_montage('standard_1020') #biosemi64
# Filter channel names to only those present in the montage
valid_channel_names = [ch for ch in channel_names if ch in montage.ch_names]
invalid_channel_names = [ch for ch in channel_names if ch not in
montage.ch_names]

# Create random values for demonstration (replace with your actual data)
#values = np.random.rand(len(valid_channel_names))
eeg_data_alco = np.array(eeg_data_alco)
reshaped_array = eeg_data_alco.reshape(64, -1).mean(axis=1)
# These are the values to plot as a scalp topomap
#  Get the 2D positions (X, Y) for each valid EEG channel from the montage.
values = np.array(reshaped_array)
# Extract positions for valid channels
positions = montage.get_positions()['ch_pos']
pos = np.array([positions[ch][:2] for ch in valid_channel_names])
# Plot the topomap (heatmap on the head)
fig, ax = plt.subplots()
im, cn = mne.viz.plot_topomap(values, pos=pos, axes=ax, show=False,
cmap='RdBu_r', contours=6)
plt.title("EEG Heatmap")
# Add colorbar
cbar = plt.colorbar(im, ax=ax)
cbar.set_label('Activity')
plt.show()
```

As a result, we have the following power distribution for the Alpha, Beta, and Gamma ranges, Fig. 13.4.

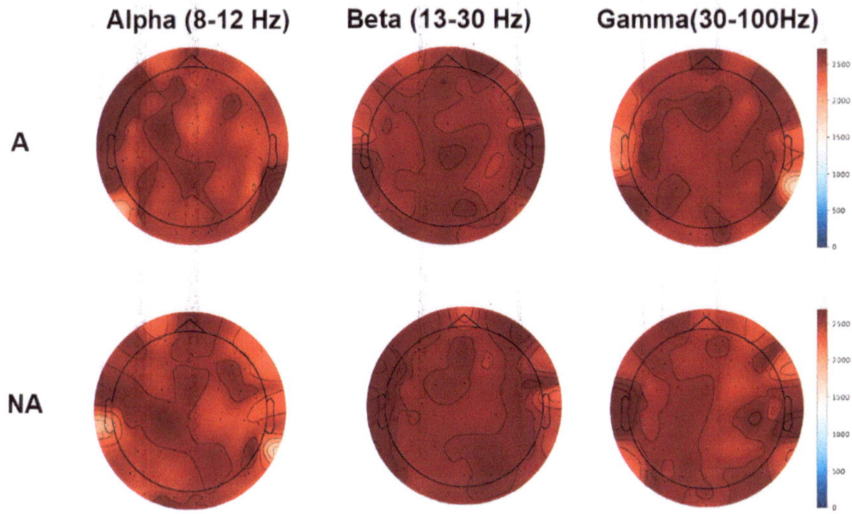

Fig. 13.4 Visualization of alpha-EEG power distribution on a human head model. First row—A for alcoholic and Second for Non-alcoholic control group

Visually, we can come to the following conclusion:

- **Alpha Band (8–12 Hz)**

Non-Alcoholic: The activity in the Alpha band appears relatively uniform, with moderate intensities spread across the scalp.

Alcoholic: The Alpha band for alcoholics shows more localized areas of high intensity, indicating increased alpha power in specific regions.

- **Beta Band (13–30 Hz)**

Non-Alcoholic: The heatmap reveals moderate Beta activity across the scalp, with no strong hotspots.

Alcoholic: A noticeable increase in Beta power can be seen in alcoholics, particularly in certain focal regions.

- **Gamma Band (30–100 Hz)**

Non-Alcoholic: Gamma power is moderately distributed with no significant intensities, reflecting typical activity levels in this high-frequency band.

Alcoholic: Alcoholics display stronger and more focused Gamma activity, suggesting an elevated power in this range.

Across all bands (Alpha, Beta, and Gamma), alcoholics demonstrate heightened activity compared to non-alcoholics. This is especially prominent in the Beta and Gamma bands, which are often associated with cortical excitability and hyperactivity. The elevated power in the Beta and Gamma bands in alcoholics could be indicative of neurological adaptations due to chronic alcohol use, potentially reflecting disrupted inhibitory control or heightened neural excitability. The Alpha power concentration in alcoholics might indicate alterations in baseline resting-state activity.

We use a window length of 256 samples to calculate power in the alpha band, which is a standard practice. This corresponds to computing the power in a specific frequency range every 1 s. An example data set for the Alpha power is shown in Fig. 13.5.

We provided a detailed introduction on EEG frequency bands, primarily to emphasize the importance of working with frequency-domain features. Most scientific studies tend to focus on these frequency ranges for analysis. However, it's important to remember that in some cases, using raw EEG data can be equally valuable. Raw EEG preserves richer temporal and waveform information, which may capture more subtle neural dynamics that frequency-based methods could overlook.

13.4 Logistic Regression

We begin by exploring machine learning using the Logistic regression algorithm, which we will examine in more detail by defining a structure that will enable us to work with other algorithms in the following chapters.

Logistic regression is an interpretable machine learning algorithm that can be effectively used for EEG classification tasks. EEG data, often high-dimensional and noisy, require proper preprocessing and feature engineering before being fed to a classifier [9, 10]. Logistic regression works well when combined with feature selection or dimensionality reduction techniques such as principal component analysis (PCA) to capture the most relevant patterns in brain signals. Despite its simplicity, it can produce competitive results, especially in binary classification tasks such as mental state detection, motor imagery, or seizure detection. When combined with techniques such as regularization (L1 or L2 penalties) and hyperparameter tuning, logistic regression can achieve robust and generalizable performance while maintaining interpretability [11, 12].

Graphically, this method is illustrated in Fig. 13.6. The algorithm learns the relationship between these EEG features and the class labels (alcohol vs. non-alcoholic). It then calculates the probability for each input window, outputting a value between 0 and 1. Based on a threshold (usually 0.5), it assigns a final label. This approach is especially effective when the features show a clear statistical separation between the two classes.

Logistic regression, like all the next algorithms, consists of 4 steps.

- First, we need to prepare the data, and then split the data, part of which will be used to train the model, and the other part of which will be used for testing. This is done in one line via the train_test_split method from scikit-learn. In this case, we specify the percentage ratio between the data test_size and set the random state to a particular value (e.g. 42), ensuring that the split will always be the same each time the code is run.

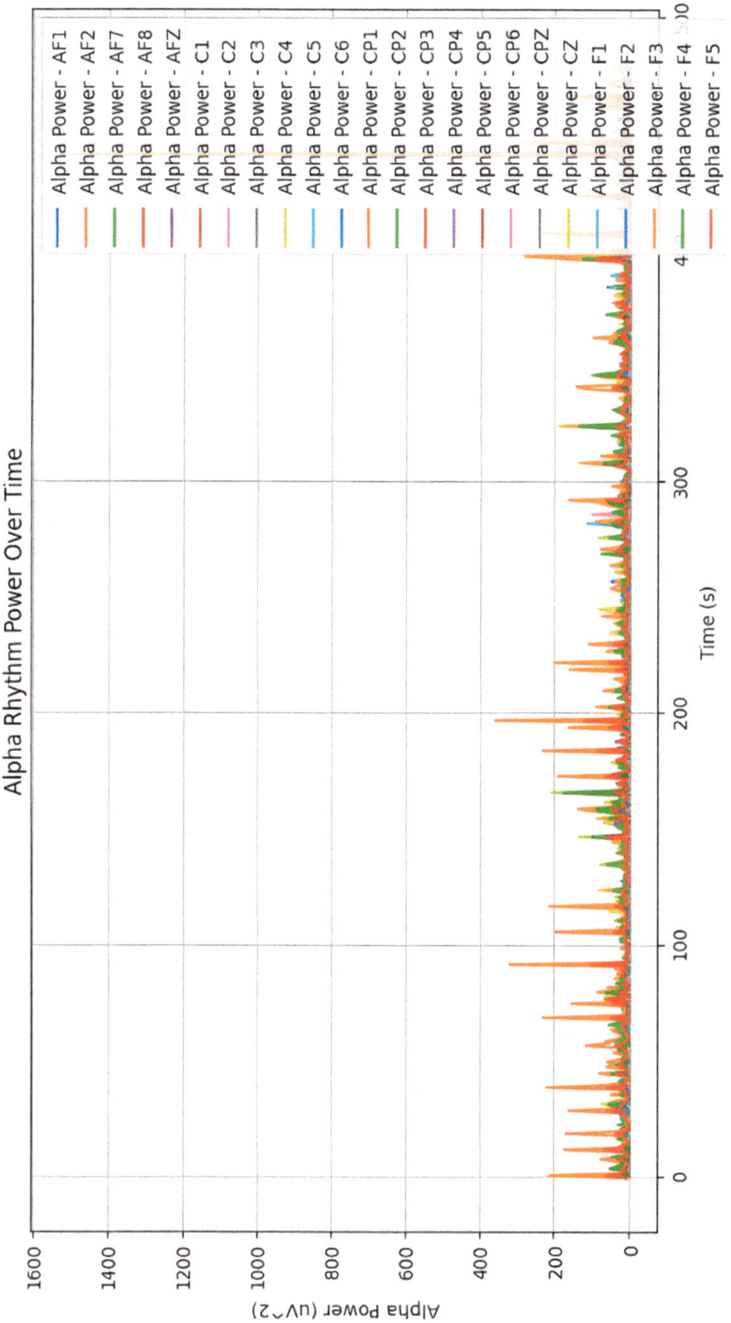

Fig. 13.5 Dataset converted to power for Alpha rhythm

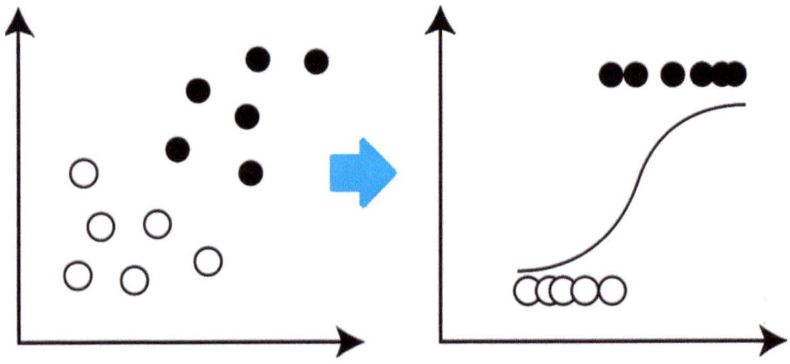

Fig. 13.6 Example of using Logistic regression for EEG classification, black color is alcohol, and white color is not alcohol. **a** data before, **b** data after logistic regression

```
X_train, X_test, y_train, y_test = train_test_split(x, y, test_size=0.2, random_state=42
```

- Next, need to assign a model and train it using the model.fit method. This method trains a logistic regression model by learning the relationship between the features (x_train) and the target labels (y_train) in the training dataset." It adjusts the key parameters of the model (weights and biases) to minimize the error or feature cost, which allows for effective prediction of the target variable.

```
model = LogisticRegression()
model.fit(x_train, y_train)
```

- The predict() method is used to make class predictions based on the trained model. It takes the test data (x_test) as input and outputs the predicted class labels for each data point in the test set.

```
predicted = model.predict(x_test)
```

- Evaluate the model using the accuracy_score() function from sklearn.metrics, which measures the accuracy of a classification model, which is the proportion of labels correctly predicted out of the total number of predictions. It compares the true labels (y_test) to the predicted labels (predicted) to assess the model's performance.

```
print(accuracy_score(y_test, predicted))
```

A simple implementation is possible in just a few lines for raw EEG data.

```
from sklearn import metrics
from sklearn.metrics import accuracy_score
from sklearn.linear_model import LogisticRegression
model = LogisticRegression()
x_train, x_test, y_train, y_test = train_test_split(normalized_x, y, test_size=0.7,
random_state=42)
model.fit(x_train, y_train)
expected = y_test
predicted = model.predict(x_test)
print(accuracy_score(y_test, predicted))
```

This may sound simple, but in fact, we have presented a standard implementation of linear regression. In practice, however, tuning a model requires many parameters, and it can be challenging to determine which parameters are necessary intuitively. These parameters, known as hyperparameters, can fortunately be optimized using automated tools.

13.5 Hyperparameters

In Scikit-learn, hyperparameters are settings or configurations used to control the behavior of a machine learning model or training process. They are not learned from the data but are set before training begins. Hyperparameters influence how a model learns and can significantly affect its performance.

Examples of hyperparameters include: Train-test split ratio Learning rate in optimization algorithms, choice of optimization algorithm (e.g., gradient descent, stochastic gradient descent, or Adam optimizer), choice of activation function in a neural network layer (e.g., Sigmoid, ReLU, Tanh), choice of cost or loss function the model will use number of hidden layers in a neural network, number of activation units in each layer, the drop-out rate in neural networks, number of iterations (epochs) in training a neural network number of clusters in a clustering task, kernel or filter size in convolutional layers.

13.5.1 Grid Search and Random Search

As mentioned earlier, selecting the right parameter is not always intuitive, so there are two methods for finding it: Grid Search and Random Search. Grid search in scikit-learn is an exhaustive search method used to tune the hyperparameters of machine learning models. It is implemented using the GridSearchCV class, which systematically tries multiple combinations of parameter settings, performing cross-validation as it proceeds to determine which setting yields the best performance. The method creates a grid of all possible combinations of parameters specified in the parameter grid, trains a model on each combination, and evaluates it using cross-validation. This process helps find the optimal set of hyperparameters that gives the best model performance based on the specified evaluation metric. Although grid search is thorough, it can be computationally expensive, especially for large parameter spaces, since it evaluates every possible combination of parameters. In grid_search, we set parameters for how the search is performed, as shown below:

```
grid_search = GridSearchCV(
    estimator=model,           # The model you want to optimize (e.g., SVM,
RandomForest, etc.)
    param_grid=param_grid,  # Dictionary with hyperparameters and values to try (e.g.,
{'C': [0.1, 1, 10]})
    cv=5,                      # 5-fold cross-validation: splits the data into 5 parts, trains
on 4, tests on 1 (for 5 times)
    scoring='accuracy',        # Metric used to evaluate model performance (can be 'f1',
'roc_auc', etc.)
    n_jobs=-1                  # Use all available CPU cores to speed up the search
process
)
```

The alternative to this method is a randomized search. This class can be used in much the same way as the GridSearchCV class. Still, instead of trying every possible combination, it evaluates a set number of random combinations, choosing a random value for each hyperparameter at each iteration. This approach has two main advantages: If you let the randomized search run for, say, 1000 iterations, this approach will explore 1000 different values for each hyperparameter (instead of just a few values per hyperparameter with the grid search approach). You have more control over the computational budget you want to allocate to the hyperparameter search by simply setting the number of iterations. The parameters for random_search are set and defined in a similar manner.

```
random_search = RandomizedSearchCV(
    model,                      # The base model you want to optimize
    param_distributions=param_distributions,  # Dictionary of hyperparameters
and their distributions
    n_iter=100,                 # Number of different combinations
    cv=5,                       # 5-fold cross-validation to evaluate model
    scoring='accuracy',         # Use accuracy as the scoring metric
    n_jobs=-1,                  # Use all available CPU cores
random_state=42,                # Seed for reproducibility of results
    verbose=1                   # Print progress messages during search
)
```

Realization of Logistic regression with grid search:

```
from sklearn.model_selection import GridSearchCV, train_test_split
from sklearn.linear_model import LogisticRegression
from sklearn.metrics import accuracy_score
# Define the parameter grid for Logistic Regression
param_grid = {
    'C': [0.001, 0.01, 0.1, 1, 10, 100],  # Regularization strength
    'penalty': ['l1', 'l2'],              # Regularization type
    'solver': ['liblinear', 'saga']       # Optimization algorithms
}
# Create the base model
model = LogisticRegression(random_state=42)  # The model to tune
# Create the grid search object
grid_search = GridSearchCV(
    estimator=model,             # The model to tune
    param_grid=param_grid,       # Dictionary with parameters names and lists of
values to try
    cv=5,                        # 5-fold cross-validation
    scoring='accuracy',          # Use accuracy as the evaluation metric
    n_jobs=-1                    # Use all available CPU cores for parallel
processing
)
# Split the data
x_train, x_test, y_train, y_test = train_test_split(normalized_x, y, test_size=0.7,
```

```
random_state=42)
# Perform the grid search
grid_search.fit(x_train, y_train)
# Print the best parameters and best score
print("Best Parameters:", grid_search.best_params_)
print("Best Cross-Validation Score:", grid_search.best_score_)
# Use the best model to make predictions
best_model = grid_search.best_estimator_
predicted = best_model.predict(x_test)
# Print the accuracy score
print("Accuracy Score:", accuracy_score(y_test, predicted))
```

We received the next optimal hyperparameters for model: {'C': 1, 'penalty': 'l1', 'solver': 'liblinear'}. Let's consider in detail what it means:

- **C = 1**

This is the inverse of regularization strength. A value of 1 is a moderate setting, meaning the model strikes a balance between underfitting and overfitting.

- Lower values (e.g., 0.01) enforce stronger regularization (simpler models).
- Higher values (e.g., 100) reduce regularization (more flexible models).

- **penalty = 'l1'**

L1 regularization (also called Lasso) forces some coefficients to be exactly zero. This helps with:

- Feature selection (ignores irrelevant variables).
- Producing sparse models.

- **solver = 'liblinear'**

This solver is appropriate for small datasets and supports both L1 and L2 penalties. It uses a coordinate descent algorithm that is well-suited for L1 regularization.

With these hyperparameters, we received the following result:

Best Cross-Validation Score: 0.6341. This means that during the fivefold cross-validation, the model correctly classified the samples ~ 63.41% of the time on average in the training data. This score reflects the model's generalization performance before seeing the test set.

Accuracy Score: 0.6371. This is the final evaluation metric on the unseen test set, meaning your model correctly predicted the label in ~ 63.71% of test cases. This is slightly better than the cross-validation score, suggesting the model generalizes decently well.

Realization of Logistic regression with Random search:

```
# Split the data
x_train, x_test, y_train, y_test = train_test_split(normalized_x, y, test_size=0.7,
random_state=42)

""" Define the parameter
'C' is the inverse of the regularization strength in logistic regression.
 Sampling C from a log-uniform distribution between 1e-5 and 100
 Allows exploration of a wide and realistic range of regularization values

'penalty' specifies the norm used in the penalization ('l1' for LASSO, 'l2' These
regularization options help prevent overfitting by creating simpler models.

'solver' denotes the optimization algorithm.
 'liblinear' works with small datasets and both l1/l2 penalties; 'saga' is scalable for
large datasets and also supports both.
 'max_iter' controls the maximum number of iterations taken by the solver to
converge.
 Varying this provides flexibility for convergence, especially for high-dimensional
or difficult problems.
."""

param_distributions = {
   'C': loguniform(1e-5, 100),
   'penalty': ['l1', 'l2'],
   'solver': ['liblinear', 'saga'],
   'max_iter': [100, 200, 300, 400, 500]
}
# Create a logistic regression model
model = LogisticRegression()
# Set up RandomizedSearchCV
random_search = RandomizedSearchCV(
   model,                              # The model to optimize
   param_distributions=param_distributions, # Parameter distributions to sample
from
   n_iter=100,                        # Number of parameter settings sampled
   cv=5,                              # 5-fold cross-validation
   scoring='accuracy',                # Evaluation metric is accuracy
   n_jobs=-1,                         # Use all available CPU cores
```

```
        random_state=42,          # For reproducibility
        verbose=1                 # Print progress messages
    )
    # Perform random search
    random_search.fit(x_train, y_train)
    # Get the best model
    best_model = random_search.best_estimator_
    # Make predictions on the test set
    predicted = best_model.predict(x_test)
    # Calculate and print the accuracy
    accuracy = accuracy_score(y_test, predicted)
    print(f"Best parameters: {random_search.best_params_}")
    print(f"Best cross-validation score: {random_search.best_score_:.4f}")
    print(f"Test accuracy: {accuracy:.4f}")
```

We received the next optimal hyperparameters for the model:

- Fitting 5 folds for each of 100 candidates, totalling 500 fits
- Best parameters: {'C': 0.9536602242620411, 'max_iter': 300, 'penalty': 'l1', 'solver': 'liblinear'}
- Best cross-validation score: 0.6341

And the next result:
Best Cross-Validation Score: 0.6342.

Accuracy Score: 0.6372.

By accelerating the model tuning process, we obtained similar hyperparameters and accuracy within the regularization range. In this case, Random Search proved to be effective.

Next, following the approach described in Chap. 15.2 Take Power for ML, we will extract and calculate power across different frequency bands. We'll apply the same algorithm as previously described, but instead of using raw EEG data, we will use power features computed over 1-s windows (256 samples). The results are presented in Table 13.1 for Delta, Theta, Alpha, and Beta ranges.

The best result was obtained for frequency components in the Gamma band (> 30 Hz), which yielded a test accuracy of 93.15%. This suggests that higher-frequency EEG activity may contain more discriminative features for differentiating between alcoholic and non-alcoholic brain patterns when using logistic regression.

Table 13.1 Alcoholism and not Alcoholism detection with logistic regression for power in different frequency ranges

Frequently range, Hz	Delta (0.5–4)	Theta (4–7)	Alpha (8–12)	Beta (13–30)	Gamma (> 30)
Test accuracy, %	0.7649	0.7024	0.7262	0.8690	0.9315

Interestingly, the Beta band (13–30 Hz) also performed well, achieving an accuracy of 86.90%, which indicates its relevance in tasks involving cognitive and sensorimotor processing that are often affected by alcohol use. In contrast, lower frequency bands such as Delta and Theta showed lower classification performance, potentially due to their stronger association with sleep and general background activity, which may be less distinctive in this classification task.

13.6 k-Nearest Neighbors (KNN)

The next most important is the algorithm, k-Nearest Neighbors (KNN), which is a simple yet powerful machine learning algorithm that can be effectively applied to EEG classification tasks [13, 14]. Due to its instance-based learning approach, KNN does not require a training phase; instead, it makes predictions based on the most similar data points in the feature space. This can be particularly useful for EEG data, where patterns may be subtle and highly individualized. However, due to the high dimensionality and noise in EEG signals, proper preprocessing and dimensionality reduction techniques such as Principal Component Analysis (PCA) are often necessary to improve performance and computational efficiency. KNN performs well in tasks like mental state classification, emotion detection, or motor imagery, especially when an appropriate distance metric and number of neighbors (k) are chosen. Although KNN may not scale well with large datasets, its simplicity, adaptability, and strong performance on smaller, well-preprocessed EEG datasets make it a valuable tool in neurotechnology research. The operating principle is visually shown in Fig. 13.7.

The implementation of the algorithm is shown below. The main difference is that we imported the necessary library for KNN from scikit-learn and specified this model in the script.

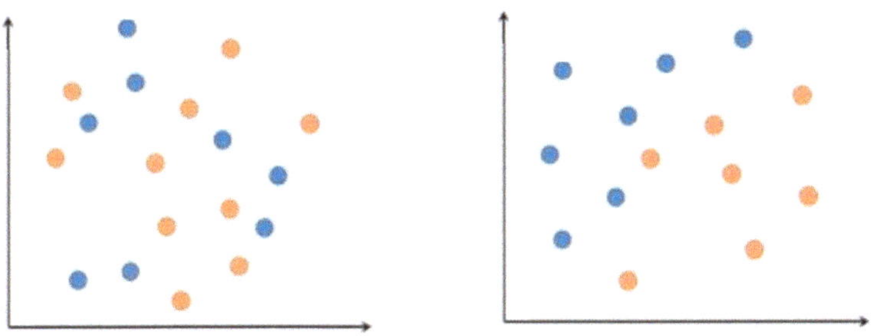

Fig. 13.7 An example of using k-Nearest Neighbors (KNN) for classification is that black is alcohol, and white is not alcohol. **a** data before, **b** data after, k-Nearest Neighbors (KNN)

```
from sklearn.neighbors import KNeighborsClassifier
model = KNeighborsClassifier()
```

Additionally, the hyperparameters are slightly different, and comments have been added throughout the script for clarity. The script implementation is given below with Grid Search, since the dataset we use is not very large.

```
model = KNeighborsClassifier()
# Define the parameter grid for K-Nearest Neighbors

"""
'n_neighbors' - Specifies the number of nearest neighbors to consider in the k-NN
algorithm.
Smaller values can capture more local structure, larger values smooth predictions.

weights - Determines how neighbors contribute to the prediction:
 'uniform' means every neighbor contributes equally.
'distance' means closer neighbors have a greater influence, weighted inversely by
their distance.

'metric' -
Defines the distance metric used to calculate neighbor proximity:
 'euclidean' is the straight-line (L2) distance.
 'manhattan' is the sum of absolute differences (L1 distance).
 'minkowski' is a generalization of Euclidean and Manhattan distances with a
parameter p.

"""
param_grid =
{
   'n_neighbors': [3, 5, 7, 9],                          # Number of neighbors
   'weights': ['uniform', 'distance'],                   # Weight function
   'metric': ['euclidean', 'manhattan', 'minkowski'] # Distance metric
}
model = KNeighborsClassifier()      # Create the base model
```

```
grid_search = GridSearchCV          # Create the grid search object
(
    estimator=model,                # The KNeighborsClassifier model to be tuned
    param_grid=param_grid,          # Hyperparameter search space
    cv=5,                           # 5-fold cross-validation
    scoring='accuracy',             #  Use accuracy as the performance metric
    n_jobs=-1                       # Use all available cores
)
x_train, x_test, y_train, y_test = train_test_split(normalized_x, y, test_size=0.7,
random_state=42)


# Perform the grid search
grid_search.fit(x_train, y_train)
print("Best Parameters:", grid_search.best_params_)
print("Best Cross-Validation Score:", grid_search.best_score_)
best_model = grid_search.best_estimator_
predicted = best_model.predict(x_test)
print("Accuracy Score:", accuracy_score(y_test, predicted))
```

We received the following optimal hyperparameters for the model:

Best Parameters: {**'metric': 'euclidean', 'n_neighbors': 3, 'weights': 'distance'**}.

And the next result:

Best Cross-Validation Score: 0.9

Accuracy Score: 0.91.

We now perform the same process, extracting and calculating power across different frequency bands, and show the results in Table 13.2.

The best result was obtained for frequency components in the Gamma band (> 30 Hz), where the test accuracy reached 88% using the k-Nearest Neighbors algorithm. This confirms that high-frequency EEG signals are rich in information critical for distinguishing between alcoholic and non-alcoholic subjects.

The Beta band (13–30 Hz) also provided relatively strong results with a 75% accuracy, further emphasizing the importance of higher-frequency activity in brainwave analysis related to alcohol use. On the other hand, Delta, Theta, and Alpha bands

Table 13.2 Alcoholism and not Alcoholism detection with k-Nearest Neighbors for power in different frequency ranges

Frequently range (Hz)	Delta (0.5–4)	Theta (4–7)	Alpha (8–12)	Beta (13–30)	Gamma (> 30)
Test accuracy %	0.601	0.61	0.61	0.75	0.88

yielded lower accuracy scores (around 60–61%), indicating limited discriminative power in these ranges for this specific classification task.

We achieved a test accuracy of 88%, showing that KNN, despite its simplicity, can be an effective model for EEG-based classification when combined with well-chosen frequency-domain features.

13.7 Support Vector Machines (SVM)

Support Vector Machine (SVM) is a robust and widely used machine learning algorithm that performs well in EEG classification tasks. SVM works by finding the optimal hyperplane that best separates data points from different classes in a high-dimensional feature space. This makes it particularly effective for EEG data, where the decision boundaries between mental states or neurological conditions may be complex and non-linear [13, 15].

To handle such complexities, SVM can use different kernel functions (e.g., linear, polynomial, or radial basis function) to transform the input features into a space where they become more easily separable. This flexibility makes SVM suitable for tasks such as detecting neurological disorders, distinguishing between cognitive states, or classifying motor imagery [15, 16].

Because EEG data is often noisy and high-dimensional, preprocessing techniques such as filtering, artifact removal, and dimensionality reduction (e.g., PCA) are essential to enhance the performance of SVM. While SVMs can be computationally intensive, especially with large datasets and complex kernels, they tend to generalize well and provide strong performance on well-preprocessed EEG signals. Their ability to model complex decision boundaries makes SVM a powerful choice in neurotechnology and brain-computer interface research [16, 17]. This method can be visually represented in Fig. 13.8.

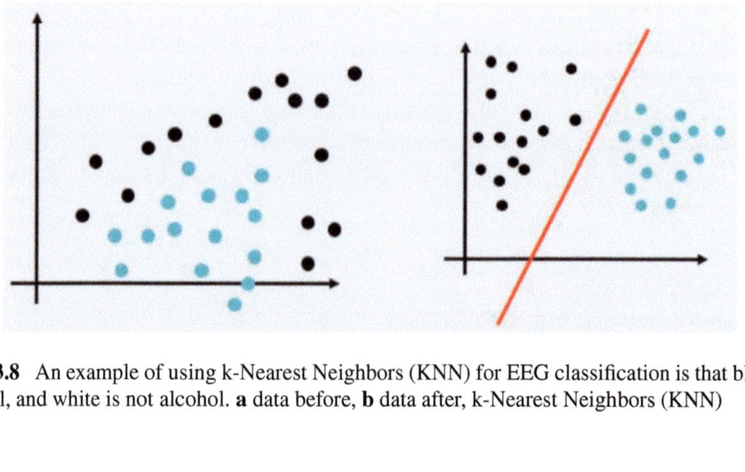

Fig. 13.8 An example of using k-Nearest Neighbors (KNN) for EEG classification is that black is alcohol, and white is not alcohol. **a** data before, **b** data after, k-Nearest Neighbors (KNN)

While SVMs can be computationally intensive, especially with non-linear kernels and large datasets, they often deliver good results and generalize well to unseen data, making them a valuable tool in EEG-based neurotechnology and brain-computer interface (BCI) research.

By the same logic, since we have already considered hyperparameters, we will now present the final code using the scikit-learn library.

```
"""
'n_neighbors' - Specifies the number of nearest neighbors t
"C" Regularization parameter for the SVM.
Controls the trade-off between maximizing the margin and minimizing
classification error.
Smaller values of C increase the margin but allow more misclassifications.

'kernel': -
Specifies the kernel type to be used in the algorithm.
'linear' for a linear decision boundary,
 'rbf' (radial basis function) for a non-linear boundary,
 'poly' for polynomial kernel, allowing more complex decision boundaries.

'gamma' -
Kernel coefficient for 'rbf', 'poly', and 'sigmoid' kernels.
'scale' (default) uses 1 / (n_features * X.var()),
'auto' uses 1 / n_features.
"""


param_grid =
{
   'C': [0.1, 1, 10, 100],  # Regularization parameter
   'kernel': ['linear', 'rbf', 'poly'],  # Kernel type
   'gamma': ['scale', 'auto']  # Kernel coefficient
}
# Create the base model
model = SVC(random_state=2)
# Create the grid search object
grid_search = GridSearchCV(
   estimator=model,             # The SVM model to be tuned
   param_grid=param_grid,  # Hyperparameter search space
   cv=5,                              # 5-fold cross-validation
   scoring='accuracy',          #  Use accuracy as the performance metric
   n_jobs=-1                       # Use all available cores
)
# Split the data
x_train, x_test, y_train, y_test = train_test_split(normalized_x, y, test_size=0.7,
```

```
random_state=2)
grid_search.fit(x_train, y_train)
print("Best Parameters:", grid_search.best_params_)
print("Best Cross-Validation Score:", grid_search.best_score_)
best_model = grid_search.best_estimator_
predicted = best_model.predict(x_test)
print("Accuracy Score:", accuracy_score(y_test, predicted))
```

Optimal hyperparameters for the model:

Best Parameters: {'C': 1, 'gamma': 'scale', 'kernel': 'poly'}.

Model result:

Best Cross-Validation Score: 0.99.

Accuracy Score: 0.91.

The same calculation power is calculated across different frequency bands, and the results are presented in Table 13.3.

The best classification performance using SVM was achieved in the Gamma band (> 30 Hz), with a test accuracy of 85%, highlighting the effectiveness of high-frequency EEG features in distinguishing alcoholic from non-alcoholic brain activity.

The Delta and Beta bands also demonstrated strong performance, with accuracies of 78% and 77% respectively, indicating that these bands may contain relevant neural markers linked to alcohol consumption.

In contrast, the Alpha band showed the lowest accuracy (55%), suggesting that SVM may struggle to extract meaningful patterns from lower-frequency features alone in this context.

Overall, SVM proved to be a powerful tool for EEG classification, particularly when applied to well-defined frequency power features, achieving an accuracy of up to 85% in this task.

While SVMs can be computationally intensive, especially with non-linear kernels and large datasets, they often deliver excellent results and generalize well to unseen data, making them a valuable tool in EEG-based neurotechnology and brain-computer interface (BCI) research.

Table 13.3 Alcoholism and not Alcoholism detection with support vector machines for power in different frequency ranges

Frequently range, Hz	Delta (0.5–4)	Theta (4–7)	Alpha (8–12)	Beta (13–30)	Gamma (> 30)
Test accuracy, %	0.78	0.672	0.55	0.77	0.85

13.8 Random Forests

Random Forests is a powerful ensemble machine learning algorithm that is well-suited for EEG classification tasks. It works by constructing multiple decision trees during training and combining their outputs to improve predictive accuracy and reduce overfitting. This ensemble approach makes Random Forests particularly robust when dealing with the noisy and high-dimensional nature of EEG data [18, 19].

In EEG analysis—such as emotion recognition, cognitive workload assessment, or seizure detection—Random Forests can handle a wide range of input features, including band power, statistical moments, or connectivity metrics. The algorithm naturally performs feature selection, identifying the most informative EEG features during training, which helps improve performance and interpretability [20].

Random Forests require minimal preprocessing compared to other algorithms and are relatively easy to tune. They are instrumental when working with moderate-sized datasets and when model interpretability (e.g., feature importance) is desired, as for detecting alcoholism. Despite their simplicity, Random Forests often achieve strong performance in EEG-based applications and are a popular choice in neuroinformatics and brain-computer interface research [21].

A random forest is a classification algorithm made up of many decision trees. It utilizes bagging and randomness in the features when building each tree to create an uncorrelated forest that is more accurate in its predictions than any single tree [21, 22] (Fig. 13.9).

The code implementation is given below:

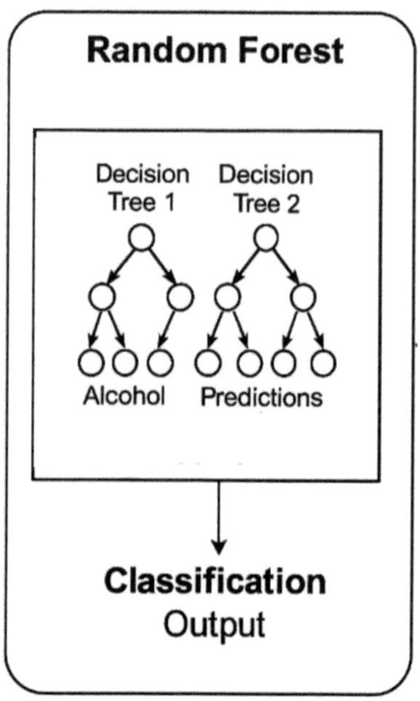

Fig. 13.9 An example of Random Forests

```
from sklearn.model_selection import GridSearchCV, train_test_split
from sklearn.ensemble import RandomForestClassifier
from sklearn.metrics import accuracy_score
# Define the parameter grid for Random Forest
param_grid = {
    'n_estimators': [50, 100, 200],       # Number of trees
    'max_depth': [None, 10, 20, 30],   # Max depth of the tree
    'min_samples_split': [2, 5, 10],      # Minimum number of samples to split an
internal node
    'min_samples_leaf': [1, 2, 4]        # Minimum number of samples required at a
leaf node
}
# Create the base model
model = RandomForestClassifier(random_state=42)
# Create the grid search object
grid_search = GridSearchCV(
    estimator=model,             #  The RandomForestClassifier model to be tuned
    param_grid=param_grid,  # Hyperparameter search space
    cv=5,                        # 5-fold cross-validation
    scoring='accuracy',          #  Use accuracy as the performance metric
    n_jobs=-1                    # Use all available cores
)
# Split the data
normalized_x_short = normalized_x.head(1000)
y_short = y.head(1000)
x_train, x_test, y_train, y_test = train_test_split(normalized_x_short, y_short,
test_size=0.7, random_state=42)
# Perform the grid search
grid_search.fit(x_train, y_train)
# Print the best parameters and best score
print("Best Parameters:", grid_search.best_params_)
print("Best Cross-Validation Score:", grid_search.best_score_)
# Use the best model to make predictions
best_model = grid_search.best_estimator_
predicted = best_model.predict(x_test)
# Print the accuracy score
print("Accuracy Score:", accuracy_score(y_test, predicted))
```

Optimal hyperparameters for the model:

Best Parameters: {'max_depth': None, 'min_samples_leaf': 1, 'min_samples_split': 5, 'n_estimators': 100}.

Table 13.4 Alcoholism and not Alcoholism detection with Random Forests for power in different frequency ranges

Frequently range, Hz	Delta (0.5–4)	Theta (4–7)	Alpha (8–12)	Beta (13–30)	Gamma (>30)
Test accuracy, %	0.6875	0.625	0.58	0.79	0.875

Model result:

Best Cross-Validation Score: 0.98.

Accuracy Score: 0.98.

The results of power measurements in the frequency connection are given in Table 13.4.

The best result for Random Forests was achieved in the Gamma band (> 30 Hz), reaching a test accuracy of 87.5%, which reinforces the importance of high-frequency EEG features in identifying alcohol-related patterns in brain activity.

The Beta band (13–30 Hz) also performed well, with 79% accuracy, indicating it holds useful discriminatory information for this task.

Lower-frequency bands like Alpha, Theta, and Delta yielded comparatively lower accuracies, with Alpha performing the worst at 58%, suggesting that these bands may not contain strong enough signal features for Random Forests to classify effectively on their own.

Random Forests delivered competitive results, particularly when applied to Beta and Gamma power features, also making it a viable and interpretable model for EEG-based alcoholism detection.

13.9 Conclusion

In this chapter, we explored the application of several machine learning algorithms—Logistic Regression, k-Nearest Neighbors (KNN), Support Vector Machines (SVM), and Random Forests—for classifying alcoholic vs. non-alcoholic EEG signals using frequency band power features.

The main findings can be summarized as follows:

Across all models, the Gamma band (> 30 Hz) consistently yielded the highest classification accuracy, reaching up to 93.15% with Logistic Regression and 88% with KNN, indicating that high-frequency activity is a key biomarker for distinguishing between alcoholic and non-alcoholic brain patterns.

The Beta band (13–30 Hz) also showed strong performance, particularly with Random Forests (79%) and SVM (77%), underscoring its importance in the context of cognitive and motor-related EEG activity affected by alcohol.

Lower-frequency bands, such as Alpha, Theta, and Delta, were less effective overall, although they still contributed moderately to classification, depending on the model.

In this study, we used straightforward features—absolute power values in each frequency band. However, it is worth noting that more sophisticated features, such as power ratios between different bands (e.g., Beta/Alpha, Theta/Delta), could further enhance model performance. These ratios can capture relative changes between brain activity patterns and may serve as even more sensitive indicators for detecting alcoholism.

Overall, this comparative analysis highlights that frequency band selection is as critical as the choice of machine learning model. For practical implementations, especially in real-time or low-cost brain-computer interface systems, utilizing power features from the Gamma and Beta bands, combined with models such as Logistic Regression or Random Forests, can provide reliable and efficient solutions.

References

1. Campos MSR, McCracken HS, Uribe-Quevedo A, Grant BL, Yielder PC, Murphy BA (2024) A machine learning approach to classifying EEG data collected with or without haptic feedback during a simulated drilling task. Brain Sci 14(9):894
2. Sanei S, Chambers JA (2013) EEG signal processing. Wiley
3. Rahul J, Sharma D, Sharma LD, Nanda U, Sarkar AK (2024) A systematic review of EEG based automated schizophrenia classification through machine learning and deep learning. Front Hum Neurosci 18:1347082
4. Watts D, Pulice RF, Reilly J, Brunoni AR, Kapczinski F, Passos IC (2022) Predicting treatment response using EEG in major depressive disorder: a machine-learning meta-analysis. Transl Psychiatry 12(1):332
5. Newson JJ, Thiagarajan TC (2019) EEG frequency bands in psychiatric disorders: a review of resting state studies. Front Hum Neurosci 12:521
6. Saby JN, Marshall PJ (2012) The utility of EEG band power analysis in the study of infancy and early childhood. Dev Neuropsychol 37(3):253–273
7. Mumtaz W, Vuong PL, Xia L, Malik AS, Abd Rashid RB (2016) Automatic diagnosis of alcohol use disorder using EEG features. Knowl-Based Syst 105:48–59
8. Mumtaz W, Vuong PL, Xia L, Malik AS, Rashid RBA (2017) An EEG-based machine learning method to screen alcohol use disorder. Cogn Neurodyn 11:161–171
9. Subasi A, Ercelebi E (2005) Classification of EEG signals using neural network and logistic regression. Comput Methods Programs Biomed 78(2):87–99
10. Tomioka R, Aihara K, Müller K-R (2006) Logistic regression for single trial EEG classification. Adv Neural Inf Process Syst 19
11. Arora A, Lin J-J, Gasperian A, Maldjian J, Stein J, Kahana M, Lega B (2018) Comparison of logistic regression, support vector machines, and deep learning classifiers for predicting memory encoding success using human intracranial EEG recordings. J Neural Eng 15(6):066028
12. Guerrero MC, Parada JS, Espitia HE (2021) EEG signal analysis using classification techniques: logistic regression, artificial neural networks, support vector machines, and convolutional neural networks. Heliyon 7(6)
13. Mehmood RM, Lee HJ (2015) Emotion classification of EEG brain signal using SVM and KNN. In: 2015 IEEE international conference on multimedia and expo workshops (ICMEW): IEEE; pp 1–5
14. Hamidi AA, Robertson B, Ilow J (2023) A new approach for ECG artifact detection using fine-KNN classification and wavelet scattering features in vital health applications. Procedia Comput Sci 224:60–67

15. Guler I, Ubeyli ED (2007) Multiclass support vector machines for EEG-signals classification. IEEE Trans Inf Technol Biomed 11(2):117–126
16. Saccá V, Campolo M, Mirarchi D, Gambardella A, Veltri P, Morabito FC (2018) On the classification of EEG signal by using an SVM based algorithm. Multidiscip Approaches Neural Comput 271–278
17. Lee H, Choi S (2003) Pca+ hmm+ svm for EEG pattern classification. In: Seventh international symposium on signal processing and its applications, 2003 proceedings. IEEE, pp 541–544
18. Antoniou E, Bozios P, Christou V, Tzimourta KD, Kalafatakis KG, Tsipouras M et al (2021) EEG-based eye movement recognition using brain–computer interface and random forests. Sensors 21(7):2339
19. Chen W, Wang Y, Cao G, Chen G, Gu Q (2014) A random forest model based classification scheme for neonatal amplitude-integrated EEG. Biomed Eng Online 13:1–13
20. Rieg T, Frick J, Hitzler M, Buettner R (2019) High-performance detection of alcoholism by unfolding the amalgamated EEG spectra using the Random Forests method
21. Vijayakumar V, Case M, Shirinpour S, He B (2017) Quantifying and characterizing tonic thermal pain across subjects from EEG data using random forest models. IEEE Trans Biomed Eng 64(12):2988–2996
22. Fraiwan L, Lweesy K, Khasawneh N, Wenz H, Dickhaus H (2012) Automated sleep stage identification system based on time–frequency analysis of a single EEG channel and random forest classifier. Comput Methods Programs Biomed 108(1):10–19

Chapter 14
Case Studies and Applications

14.1 Brain-Computer Interfaces: Now and Future

In recent years, the development of brain-computer interfaces (BCIs) has progressed rapidly on both the hardware and software fronts. Today, BCIs are no longer limited to large headsets—some devices now take the form of earphones with embedded electrodes that measure brain signals through the ear canal.

However, despite these hardware innovations, progress in data processing has begun to slow. This is largely due to challenges in collecting high-quality, labeled EEG data. While advances in machine learning are helping to address this, particularly through improved signal interpretation, the bottleneck remains in data labeling and artifact removal [1].

Looking ahead, the future of EEG data platforms lies in the development of universal algorithms for artifact removal. These would enable existing BCI devices to be adapted for general use, improving their accuracy and expanding their application range—ultimately making them as commonplace and user-friendly as smartwatches [2].

I. Rakhmatulin and G. R. Naik, *EEG Signal Processing with Python*, Brain Informatics and Health, https://doi.org/10.1007/978-981-95-4177-5_14

Thanks to recent advances in AI, we can now not only process EEG data more effectively but also execute these computations directly on hardware devices. This shift toward Edge AI enables machine learning models to run on specialized chips such as RISC-V, allowing real-time analysis without relying on external servers [3].

To support the development of embedded AI, platforms such as TensorFlow Lite for Microcontrollers (TinyML) have emerged. TinyML provides a lightweight framework for deploying machine learning models on resource-constrained hardware. Similarly, STMicroelectronics has introduced the X-CUBE-AI toolkit, which enables the integration of neural networks on STM32 microcontrollers [4].

Today, even deep learning models such as EEGNet, designed for interpreting EEG signals (e.g., for motion visualization in BCI systems), can be optimized to run efficiently on ARM Cortex-M microcontrollers. This is achieved by minimizing the input data size—both in terms of time and spatial resolution—and reducing the analysis window, which cuts down memory and processing demands.

As embedded hardware becomes more accessible and EEG applications continue to expand, the development of efficient, real-time machine learning models for EEG signal processing on limited-resource platforms will become increasingly important.

14.2 Consumer Applications

Commercial BCI devices are increasingly being used to enhance wellness and lifestyle, particularly in areas such as stress reduction, meditation, and cognitive performance. These systems utilize EEG sensors to monitor brainwave activity by analyzing frequency patterns across Alpha, Beta, Theta, and Delta bands. From these readings, they infer mental states like relaxation, focus, or emotional arousal. Common applications include real-time feedback for mindfulness, attention training, and sleep enhancement. For example, meditation apps connected to BCI headsets can provide visual or auditory cues to support relaxation, while focus-enhancement tools monitor concentration and prompt users when their attention wanes. While accessible and widely adopted, it's important to recognize that these devices are not diagnostic tools; their insights are based on general EEG trends and are intended for self-guided wellness rather than clinical evaluation [5, 6].

At the heart of BCI technology is the ability to control external objects using brain activity. This relies on the user's ability to generate specific mental patterns—such as imagining movement, focusing attention, or performing mental arithmetic—that translate into distinct neural signals. BCI systems interpret these signals to issue commands to various devices, including robotic limbs, wheelchairs, computer cursors, and smart home systems. Two primary paradigms are employed: exogenous paradigms, which rely on responses to external stimuli, such as flashing lights, and endogenous paradigms, which are self-initiated and include techniques like motor imagery and mental counting. Both aim to produce recognizable neural signatures that can be mapped to control functions. Ongoing research continues to enhance the accuracy and usability of these systems, making them increasingly relevant for assistive and human augmentation technologies [7].

One of the most accessible forms of BCI control involves blink detection. Intentional eye blinks, captured through EEG signals or dedicated sensors, can be translated into simple commands to operate external devices. This method offers an intuitive and low-effort communication channel for individuals with mobility impairments and can be integrated into larger BCI systems to enhance functionality. Similarly, event-related potentials (ERPs), particularly the P300 wave, are commonly used in stimulus-based interfaces. When users focus on specific stimuli, the brain's automatic responses allow systems to detect intent and trigger appropriate actions, such as selecting options from a menu. ERP-based controls require minimal motor involvement and offer high reliability, especially for users with severe physical limitations [8, 9].

Another promising BCI technique is motor imagery, where users mentally simulate movements to control mechanical limbs or prosthetics. By interpreting EEG signals associated with imagined motions, BCI systems can translate these mental commands into real-world actions. This approach provides a natural and intuitive interface for individuals with paralysis or limb loss, as it leverages existing motor pathways in the brain. Advances in machine learning and EEG signal processing continue to improve the accuracy and responsiveness of MI-based systems, making them an increasingly viable option for restoring motor function and enhancing user autonomy [10, 11].

14.3 Gaming and Entertainment

EEG-based gaming is reshaping the traditional landscape of interactive entertainment by enabling players to control game elements using their cognitive and emotional states, rather than conventional input devices like controllers or keyboards. Real-time analysis of brainwave patterns—particularly in the alpha, beta, theta, and delta ranges—enables the system to interpret mental intent, attention levels, or emotional engagement. This allows players, for instance, to control a flying object by focusing their thoughts or activate a protective shield through relaxation [12, 13].

The growing availability of commercial EEG headsets such as the Emotiv Epoc and NeuroSky has made brain-controlled gaming more accessible to both developers and consumers. These devices typically use dry electrodes, wireless communication, and ergonomic designs that support extended use. As a result, EEG gaming has diversified into categories that challenge players to apply mental acuity, manage stress, or maintain focus to progress. Puzzle-based games, for example, might require a calm state to unlock clues or demand concentrated effort to navigate obstacles [14].

Neurofeedback games add an educational and therapeutic dimension by offering players real-time feedback on their mental state. This feedback loop helps improve cognitive control, focus, and emotional regulation while maintaining entertainment value. Beyond games, EEG applications have extended into interactive media, digital art, and live performance. Artists now utilize EEG to create dynamic soundscapes or visual installations that respond to their brain activity, allowing audiences to experience art that evolves in response to their emotional engagement. Experimental films have even been created where the storyline develops in response to the viewer's level of attention or mood, as measured by EEG signals [15, 16].

The integration of EEG with virtual reality (VR) and augmented reality (AR) is pushing the boundaries of immersive interaction even further. Traditionally reliant on visual, auditory, and physical feedback, VR/AR systems now gain an additional neurophysiological layer, enabling environments that adapt to the user's mental and emotional states. For instance, a VR horror game might escalate in intensity based on rising fear levels. At the same time, a meditation app in AR could adjust its guidance in response to the user's level of calmness or distraction. Similarly, educational content can be fine-tuned in real time if cognitive overload or inattentiveness is detected [17].

EEG also enables the recognition of emotional states such as arousal, anxiety, or boredom, leading to dynamic changes in virtual settings—like shifting lighting, sound, or storyline elements—to match or counter the user's emotional trajectory. This capacity for real-time responsiveness holds great promise for therapeutic and educational use. In neurorehabilitation, for example, stroke patients can practice mental movement in VR environments that respond to their intent and focus, offering motivation and functional training simultaneously.

Looking ahead, the connection of EEG with VR, AR, and AI is setting the stage for fully thought-driven interfaces. These systems could profoundly change how users interact with digital environments—not just sensing the virtual world around them, but actively shaping it through attention, emotion, and intention. This evolution heralds a new era in entertainment, mental health, learning, and accessibility, where the mind itself becomes the controller.

14.4 Smart Home Control Systems

EEG-based brain-computer interfaces (BCIs) are expanding well beyond entertainment and therapeutic domains, increasingly finding a role in smart home automation. By interpreting brainwave activity—particularly patterns related to concentration, emotional state, or cognitive intent—these systems allow users to control their environment through thought alone. This not only enhances convenience for everyday users but also offers transformative accessibility for individuals with physical disabilities or motor impairments.

In modern smart homes, appliances and systems such as lighting, climate control, security, and entertainment are interconnected via the Internet of Things (IoT). While traditionally operated through voice commands, mobile apps, or physical interfaces, EEG technology introduces an entirely new modality: direct neural control. Using consumer-grade EEG headsets, the system detects mental signals—such as focused attention, voluntary blinks, or imagined movement—and translates them in real-time into actionable commands that interface with household devices [18].

Smart home control systems offer a transformative pathway to enhance independence and quality of life for individuals with disabilities [19]. By integrating voice-activated assistants, smart lighting, automated door locks, climate control, and entertainment systems, these technologies allow users to manage their environment with unprecedented ease. For those with limited mobility, vision, or hearing impairments, the ability to control appliances, adjust settings, and monitor security through simple voice commands or accessible interfaces eliminates physical barriers. It reduces reliance on others, fostering a greater sense of autonomy and safety within their own homes [19, 20].

More advanced implementations also incorporate emotion-aware functionality. These systems can sense signs of stress, fatigue, or relaxation and automatically adjust the environment to support well-being. For instance, calming music might play in response to elevated stress levels, ambient lighting may shift to improve mood, or gentle reminders could prompt hydration or rest when mental fatigue is detected. By responding to both cognitive commands and emotional cues, EEG-driven smart environments represent a significant step toward intuitive, personalized, and accessible living spaces.

14.5 Large Language Models (LLM) and EEG

The integration of electroencephalography (EEG) with large language models (LLMs) such as GPT, BERT, and their derivatives is ushering in a new era in neurotechnology. This convergence enables real-time brainwave data to be paired with advanced natural language processing and contextual reasoning capabilities, opening novel possibilities across communication, healthcare, accessibility, cognitive evaluation, and adaptive human–computer interaction. LLMs—deep learning models trained on vast text corpora—can interpret, generate, and process human language with high sophistication. When combined with EEG input, these models become powerful mediators between brain activity and language, translating neural patterns into structured text or speech outputs.

The Foundation of Convergence

At its core, this convergence hinges on the unique strengths of both technologies:

- **EEG's Temporal Precision**: EEG, while non-invasive and less spatially precise than invasive methods, excels at capturing the rapid fluctuations of neural activity. EEG signals can capture neural signatures related to internal speech, word formulation, or mental planning. These brainwave patterns hold crucial information about internal speech, word formulation, cognitive states (e.g., attention, cognitive load, decision-making), and mental planning. Its high temporal resolution provides real-time data on brain function and dynamics, making it invaluable for direct brain-device communication [21].

- **LLMs' Linguistic Sophistication**: LLMs, trained on vast text datasets possess an extraordinary capacity for interpreting, generating, and processing human language with great sophistication. By leveraging the predictive and generative power of LLMs, even incomplete EEG data can be extrapolated into meaningful language, allowing users to issue commands, compose messages, or engage in dialogue without speaking or typing. This fusion enables applications such as hands-free communication tools where user intent is inferred from EEG and converted into action by the LLM. Their transformer-based architectures and self-attention mechanisms enable them to effectively process sequential data, capturing both local and global dependencies in language [22].

When combined, LLMs act as powerful mediators, translating the complex and often incomplete neural patterns detected by EEG into coherent and contextually relevant language. This "*brain-to-text*" or "*brain-to-speech*" capability is a major stride towards truly intuitive brain-computer interfaces (BCIs) [23].

Novel Possibilities and Applications

The integration of EEG and LLMs unlocks a spectrum of novel applications:

- **Hands-Free Communication and Accessibility**: For individuals with speech or motor impairments, this technology offers a revolutionary communication pathway. User intent, inferred from EEG signals related to internal speech or mental planning, can be converted into structured text or speech by an LLM, enabling it to compose messages, issue commands, or engage in dialogue without physical interaction [24].
- **Personalized Healthcare and Therapeutic Interventions**:
  - **Cognitive Monitoring and Adaptation**: The system can monitor a user's cognitive and emotional state in real-time. For instance, if EEG signals indicate stress or cognitive overload, a virtual assistant could offer calming feedback, or educational content could be dynamically adjusted (slowed down, reworded, or reinforced) to optimize learning [25].
  - **Enhanced Diagnostics and Treatment**: LLMs can assist in interpreting complex EEG data for diagnostic purposes, integrating clinical guidelines and extensive datasets to support diagnostic suggestions and treatment options. This can lead to more accurate and efficient medical documentation and decision-making, particularly in areas like epilepsy detection or sleep studies [26, 27].
  - **Mental Health Support**: Emotional and cognitive context can also be taken into account: for example, a virtual assistant might offer calming feedback if stress is detected, or educational content could be dynamically adapted—slowed down, reworded, or reinforced—when signs of cognitive overload appear. The ability to infer emotional states from EEG and respond contextually opens doors for highly personalized mental health support, where AI systems can adapt fluidly to the user's emotional and mental states, offering deeply intuitive experiences [28].

- **Adaptive Human Computer Interaction (HCI)**: Beyond communication, integration fosters truly adaptive HCI. Systems can understand and respond to users' cognitive load, attention levels, and even decision-making processes, leading to more efficient and less taxing interactions. This has implications for optimizing interfaces, adjusting task difficulty, or providing timely assistance in complex environments [25].
- **Cross-Modal Generation**: This advanced capability allows for the translation of brain activity into other modalities beyond text, such as images or 3D objects, offering richer interpretations of neural signals and expanding the possibilities for brain-driven creative or functional outputs [22].

Emerging Research and Advancements

Current research is rapidly pushing the boundaries of this field:

- **Foundation Models for EEG**: Inspired by the success of LLMs, researchers are developing "*Large Brainwave Models*" (LBMs) or "*EEG Foundation Models*" like NeuroLM. These models are pre-trained on vast amounts of EEG data, enabling them to learn general-purpose EEG representations that are transferable across multiple tasks. They aim to unify diverse EEG tasks within a single model through instruction tuning, much like LLMs do for language [21].
- **Neural Decoding with LLMs**: Studies are demonstrating the efficacy of instruction-tuned LLMs fine-tuned with EEG data for direct text generation from brain signals, even for complex tasks like multimodal description generation from visual stimuli [23].
- **Personalized LLMs (PLLMs)**: Efforts are underway to personalize LLMs using domain-specific EEG data to interpret human emotions and cognitive states in a more tailored manner, showcasing applicability in human–robot interaction and assistive technologies [29].

14.6 Privacy and Data Security Concerns

As EEG-based brain-machine interfaces (BMIs) increasingly integrate with advanced AI systems like LLMs, critical concerns emerge around privacy, data ownership, and digital ethics. Unlike traditional digital inputs, EEG signals capture direct information from brain activity, revealing not just surface-level behavior but also emotions, intentions, cognitive states, and even subconscious responses. When this neural data is processed or interpreted through LLMs capable of inference and decision-making, the risks become more complex and far-reaching [30].

EEG data is uniquely sensitive. It is intimate, exposing mental health indicators such as stress, fatigue, or depression; continuous, offering a real-time stream of emotional and cognitive patterns; and inherently difficult to anonymize, as brainwave signatures can serve as "neural fingerprints" tied to individuals. This level of insight introduces the potential for misuse—from psychological profiling and behavioral prediction to targeted manipulation—especially when coupled with LLMs that generate responses or actions based on subtle neural cues [29].

Security risks grow further if EEG and LLM-generated logs are stored in the cloud or on unsecured platforms. Unauthorized access could reveal mental health profiles, emotional responses, and unintended inferences made by the AI. These insights, often beyond what users consciously share, may be misused by third parties or lead to biased outputs without explicit consent. When employers or advertisers use EEG-LLM systems, the potential for surveillance, mood tracking, or performance monitoring raises urgent ethical questions.

Compounding this is a lack of transparency and clarity around data consent. Users often remain unaware of how their EEG data is used, what insights LLMs may generate, and who owns or has access to the resulting information. Ownership of raw brain data-derived neural signatures, or AI-generated inferences, is typically undefined. Third-party integrations—through APIs, cloud services, or pretrained models—introduce further vulnerabilities.

From a legal and ethical standpoint, current data protection regulations, such as the General Data Protection Regulation (GDPR) and the Health Insurance Portability and Accountability Act (HIPAA), often fall short in covering the full scope of brain-derived data. Emerging legal concepts such as cognitive liberty, freedom of thought, and neuro rights are gaining traction globally to address these gaps. Additionally, EEG-LLM systems trained on biased datasets may produce discriminatory or unfair outcomes, particularly in sensitive areas like healthcare, hiring, or education [31, 32].

To mitigate these risks, clear privacy frameworks must be established. Best practices include data minimization—collecting only what is essential; on-device processing to avoid transmitting sensitive information externally; encryption of EEG and AI-generated data; and transparent, informed consent that outlines what data is collected, how it's used, and who has access. Incorporating anonymization techniques and differential privacy further protects individuals, while giving users meaningful control over their data through audit tools, opt-in settings, and the ability to delete personal records.

Together, these safeguards are essential not only for legal compliance but also for building trust in a future where the interface between the brain and machine is as powerful as it is personal.

14.7 Conclusion

In conclusion, BCI, particularly those enhanced by LLMs and EEG, are poised to revolutionize how humans interact with technology and each other. The ongoing advancements in decoding neural signals and translating them into actionable commands or meaningful language underscore a future brimming with possibilities for enhanced communication, accessibility, and personalized experiences. Yet, the profound implications of accessing the most intimate aspects of human cognition necessitate a proactive and collaborative approach to address the inherent ethical challenges, especially concerning privacy and data security. By prioritizing user autonomy, transparency, and robust safeguards, the neurotechnology community can ensure that this powerful convergence serves to empower individuals and enrich human lives responsibly.

References

1. Gao X, Wang Y, Chen X, Gao S (2021) Interface, interaction, and intelligence in generalized brain–computer interfaces. Trends Cogn Sci 25(8):671–684
2. Caiado F, Ukolov A (2025) The history, current state and future possibilities of the non-invasive brain computer interfaces. Med Nov Technol Devices 25:100353
3. Webster P (2024) The future of brain–computer interfaces in medicine. Nat Med 30:1508–1509
4. Vilchis G, Baltazar R, Alanis A, Francisco-Mosiño J, Casillas-Araiza MA (2023) Designing a BCI platform. In: Agents and multi-agent systems: technologies and applications 2023: proceedings of 17th KES international conference, KES-AMSTA 2023. Springer Nature, p 251
5. Aldayel M, Ykhlef M, Al-Nafjan A (2021) Consumers' preference recognition based on brain–computer interfaces: advances, trends, and applications. Arab J Sci Eng 46(9):8983–8997
6. Vărbu K, Muhammad N, Muhammad Y (2022) Past, present, and future of EEG-based BCI applications. Sensors 22(9):3331
7. Mashrur FR, Rahman KM, Miya MTI, Vaidyanathan R, Anwar SF, Sarker F, Mamun KA (2022) BCI-based consumers' choice prediction from EEG signals: an intelligent Neuromarketing framework. Front Hum Neurosci 16:861270
8. Douibi K, Le Bars S, Lemontey A, Nag L, Balp R, Breda G (2021) Toward EEG-based BCI applications for industry 4.0: challenges and possible applications. Front Hum Neurosci 15:705064
9. Ishtiaque F, Mashrur FR, Miya MTI, Rahman KM, Vaidyanathan R, Anwar SF et al: BCI-based consumers' preference prediction using single channel commercial EEG device. In: 2022 25th International conference on computer and information technology (ICCIT). IEEE, pp 43–48
10. Saibene A, Caglioni M, Corchs S, Gasparini F (2023) EEG-based BCIs on motor imagery paradigm using wearable technologies: a systematic review. Sensors 23(5):2798
11. Zhang W, Tang X, Wang M (2024) Attention model of EEG signals based on reinforcement learning. Front Hum Neurosci 18:1442398
12. Patino J, Vega I, Becerra MA, Duque-Grisales E, Jimenez L (2025) Integration between serious games and EEG signals: a systematic review. Appl Sci 15(4):1946
13. Wang L, Ding X, Zhang W, Yang S (2021) Differences in EEG microstate induced by gaming: a comparison between the gaming disorder individual, recreational game users and healthy controls. IEEE Access. 9:32549–32558
14. Keutayeva A, Nwachukwu CJ, Alaran M, Otarbay Z, Abibullaev B (2025) Neurotechnology in gaming: a systematic review of visual evoked potential-based brain-computer interfaces. IEEE Access
15. Machado FS, Frizera A (2022) Assessing the mental state of attention using a neurofeedback system and serious game tool. Entertain Comput 43:100492
16. Susnoschi Luca I, Putri FD, Ding H, Vuckovič A (2021) Brain synchrony in competition and collaboration during multiuser neurofeedback-based gaming. Front Neuroergonomics 2:749009
17. Lu J, Sun Q, Ma W, Liu T, Yao D, Gong D (2024) The effect of virtual reality action games on attention functions: an EEG study. Curr Psychol 43(41):32336–32346

18. Drăgoi M-V, Nisipeanu I, Frimu A, Tălîngă A-M, Hadăr A, Dobrescu TG et al (2024) Real-time home automation system using BCI technology. Biomimetics 9(10):594
19. Arachchige MDJ, Nafea M (2025) Brainwave and head motion control of a smart home for disabled people. In: Signal processing strategies. Elsevier, pp 195–215
20. Kremenska A, Lekova A, Kremenski S, Dimitrov G (2025) Validating the openBCI nodes through EEG-based BCI application for smart home automation control. J Commun Softw Syst 21(3):250–261
21. Jiang W-B, Wang Y, Lu B-L, Li D (2024) NeuroLM: a universal multi-task foundation model for bridging the gap between language and EEG signals. arXiv preprint arXiv:2409.00101
22. Babu N, Mathew J, Vinod A (2025) Large language models for EEG: a comprehensive survey and taxonomy. arXiv preprint arXiv:2506.06353
23. Mishra A, Shukla S, Torres J, Gwizdka J, Roychowdhury S (2024) Thought2text: text generation from EEG signal using large language models (LLMS). arXiv preprint arXiv:2410.07507
24. Zhang Y, Orthmann B, Welle MC, Van Haastregt J, Kragic D (2025) LLM-driven augmented reality puppeteer: controller-free voice-commanded robot teleoperation. In: International conference on human-computer interaction. Springer, pp 97–112
25. Leung SC (2025) The cognitive impacts of large language model interactions on problem solving and decision making using EEG analysis. Front Comput Neurosci 19:1556483
26. Carchiolo V, Malgeri M (2025) Trends, challenges, and applications of large language models in healthcare: a bibliometric and scoping review. Futur Internet 17(2):76
27. McLaren JR, Yuan D, Beniczky S, Westover MB, Nascimento FA (2025) The future of EEG education in the era of artificial intelligence. Epilepsia
28. Chen H, Zeng W, Chen C, Cai L, Wang F, Shi Y et al (2025) EEG emotion copilot: optimizing lightweight LLMs for emotional EEG interpretation with assisted medical record generation. Neural Netw, 107848
29. Ghamati K, Banitalebi Dehkordi M, Zaraki A (2025) Towards AI-powered applications: the development of a personalised LLM for HRI and HCI. Sensors 25(7):2024
30. Abdmeziem MR, Ahmed NA (2025) Leveraging IoT and LLM for depression and anxiety disorders: a privacy preserving perspective. Secur Priv 8(4):e70061
31. Conduah AK, Ofoe S, Siaw-Marfo D (2025) Data privacy in healthcare: global challenges and solutions. Digit Health 11:20552076251343960
32. Subramanian H, Sengupta A, Xu Y (2024) Patient health record protection beyond the health insurance portability and accountability act: mixed methods study. J Med Internet Res 26:e59674

MIX
Papier aus verantwortungsvollen Quellen
Paper from responsible sources
FSC® C105338

If you have any concerns about our products,
you can contact us on
ProductSafety@springernature.com

In case Publisher is established outside the EU,
the EU authorized representative is:
Springer Nature Customer Service Center GmbH
Europaplatz 3, 69115 Heidelberg, Germany

Printed by Libri Plureos GmbH
in Hamburg, Germany